The Commons

The Commons

Drivers of Change and Opportunities for Africa

Edited by Stéphanie Leyronas, Benjamin Coriat, and Kako Nubukpo

A copublication of the Agence française de développement and the World Bank

ISBN (paper): 978-1-4648-1960-5
ISBN (electronic): 978-1-4648-1992-6
DOI: 10.1596/978-1-4648-1960-5

Translation of the report from French: Cadenza Academic Translations.

Translation of the foreword: Agence française de développement.

Cover image: © Apsatou Bagaya / Fondation Hirondelle. Used with the permission of Apsatou Bagaya / Fondation Hirondelle. Further permission required for reuse.

Cover design: Ricardo Echecopar / Beyond SAC; original design by Bill Pragluski, Critical Stages, LLC.

Library of Congress Control Number: 2023909081

Africa Development Forum Series

The **Africa Development Forum Series** was created in 2009 to focus on issues of significant relevance to Sub-Saharan Africa's social and economic development. Its aim is both to record the state of the art on a specific topic and to contribute to ongoing local, regional, and global policy debates. It is designed specifically to provide practitioners, scholars, and students with the most up-to-date research results while highlighting the promise, challenges, and opportunities that exist on the continent.

The series is sponsored by Agence française de développement and the World Bank. The manuscripts chosen for publication represent the highest quality in each institution and have been selected for their relevance to the development agenda. Working together with a shared sense of mission and interdisciplinary purpose, the two institutions are committed to a common search for new insights and new ways of analyzing the development realities of the Sub-Saharan Africa region.

Advisory Committee Members

Agence française de développement
Thomas Mélonio, Executive Director, Research and Knowledge Directorate
Hélène Djoufelkit, Director, Head of Economic Assessment and Public Policy Department
Sophie Chauvin, Head, Publications Division

World Bank
Albert G. Zeufack, Chief Economist, Africa Region
Cesar Calderon, Lead Economist, Africa Region
Chorching Goh, Lead Economist, Africa Region

Sub-Saharan Africa

Source: World Bank.

Titles in the Africa Development Forum Series

2023

Africa's Resource Future: Harnessing Natural Resources for Economic Transformation during the Low Carbon Transition (2023), James Cust, Albert Zeufack (eds.)

*L'Afrique en communs. Tensions, mutations, perspectives (2023), *The Commons: Drivers of Change and Opportunities for Africa* (2023), Stéphanie Leyronas, Benjamin Coriat, Kako Nubukpo (eds.)

2021

Social Contracts for Development: Bargaining, Contention, and Social Inclusion in Sub-Saharan Africa (2021), Mathieu Cloutier, Bernard Harborne, Deborah Isser, Indhira Santos, Michael Watts

*Industrialization in Sub-Saharan Africa: Seizing Opportunities in Global Value Chains (2021), *L'industrialisation en Afrique subsaharienne : saisir les opportunités offertes par les chaînes de valeur mondiales* (2022), Kaleb G. Abreha, Woubet Kassa, Emmanuel K. K. Lartey, Taye A. Mengistae, Solomon Owusu, Albert G. Zeufack

2020

*Les systèmes agroalimentaires en Afrique. Repenser le rôle des marches (2020), *Food Systems in Africa: Rethinking the Role of Markets* (2021), Gaelle Balineau, Arthur Bauer, Martin Kessler, Nicole Madariaga

*The Future of Work in Africa: Harnessing the Potential of Digital Technologies for All (2020), *L'avenir du travail en Afrique : exploiter le potentiel des technologies numériques pour un monde du travail plus inclusif* (2021), Jieun Choi, Mark A. Dutz, Zainab Usman (eds.)

2019

All Hands on Deck: Reducing Stunting through Multisectoral Efforts in Sub- Saharan Africa (2019), Emmanuel Skoufias, Katja Vinha, Ryoko Sato

*The Skills Balancing Act in Sub-Saharan Africa: Investing in Skills for Productivity, Inclusivity, and Adaptability (2019), *Le développement des compétences en Afrique subsaharienne, un exercice d'équilibre : Investir dans les compétences pour la productivité, l'inclusion et l'adaptabilité* (2020), Omar Arias, David K. Evans, Indhira Santos

Safety Nets in Africa: Effective Mechanisms to Reach the Poor and Most Vulnerable (2015), *Les filets sociaux en Afrique : méthodes efficaces pour cibler les populations pauvres et vulnérables en Afrique subsaharienne* (2015), Carlo del Ninno, Bradford Mills (eds.)

2014

Tourism in Africa: Harnessing Tourism for Growth and Improved Livelihoods (2014), Iain Christie, Eneida Fernandes, Hannah Messerli, Louise Twining-Ward

Youth Employment in Sub-Saharan Africa (2014), *L'emploi des jeunes en Afrique subsaharienne* (2014), Deon Filmer, Louise Fox

2013

Les marchés urbains du travail en Afrique subsaharienne (2013), *Urban Labor Markets in Sub-Saharan Africa* (2013), Philippe De Vreyer, François Roubaud (eds.)

Enterprising Women: Expanding Economic Opportunities in Africa (2013), Mary Hallward-Driemeier

Securing Africa's Land for Shared Prosperity: A Program to Scale Up Reforms and Investments (2013), Frank F. K. Byamugisha

The Political Economy of Decentralization in Sub-Saharan Africa: A New Implementation Model (2013), Bernard Dafflon, Thierry Madiès (eds.)

2012

Empowering Women: Legal Rights and Economic Opportunities in Africa (2012), Mary Hallward-Driemeier, Tazeen Hasan

Financing Africa's Cities: The Imperative of Local Investment (2012), *Financer les villes d'Afrique : l'enjeu de l'investissement local* (2012), Thierry Paulais

Structural Transformation and Rural Change Revisited: Challenges for Late Developing Countries in a Globalizing World (2012), *Transformations rurales et développement : les défis du changement structurel dans un monde globalisé* (2013), Bruno Losch, Sandrine Fréguin-Gresh, Eric Thomas White

Light Manufacturing in Africa: Targeted Policies to Enhance Private Investment and Create Jobs (2012), *L'Industrie légère en Afrique : politiques ciblées pour susciter l'investissement privé et créer des emplois* (2012), Hinh T. Dinh, Vincent Palmade, Vandana Chandra, Frances Cossar

Informal Sector in Francophone Africa: Firm Size, Productivity, and Institutions (2012), *Les entreprises informelles de l'Afrique de l'ouest francophone : taille, productivité et institutions* (2012), Nancy Benjamin, Ahmadou Aly Mbaye

2011

Contemporary Migration to South Africa: A Regional Development Issue (2011), Aurelia Segatti, Loren Landau (eds.)

Challenges for African Agriculture (2011), Jean-Claude Deveze (ed.)

L'Économie politique de la décentralisation dans quatre pays d'Afrique subsaharienne : Burkina Faso, Sénégal, Ghana et Kenya (2011), Bernard Dafflon, Thierry Madiès (eds.)

2010

Gender Disparities in Africa's Labor Market (2010), Jorge Saba Arbache, Alexandre Kolev, Ewa Filipiak (eds.)

*Africa's Infrastructure: A Time for Transformation (2010), *Infrastructures africaines, une transformation impérative* (2010), Vivien Foster, Cecilia Briceño-Garmendia (eds.)

Challenges for African Agriculture (2011), Jean-Claude Deveze (ed.)

*Available in French

All books in the Africa Development Forum series that were copublished by Agence francaise de developpement and the World Bank are available for free at https://openknowledge.worldbank.org/handle/10986/2150.

Contents

Boxes

Figure

Maps

Tables

Foreword

In a context of rampant inequalities, a massive deterioration of natural resources, a generalized loss of trust in public institutions, as well as frequent market failures, *The Commons* is one of those books that help you think outside of the box and that, frankly speaking, give you hope. Given the complexity of all the challenges we face, a new path must be taken. What insights could the commons provide as we redefine our course of action?

First and foremost, *The Commons* sheds light on the astounding range of our collective practices, both the ones that we have inherited and the ones that are being invented and reinvented every day across the African continent. The book bears witness to a diverse, dynamic, adaptable, resourceful, and innovative Africa. It tells the stories of citizens who take an active part in collective endeavors as a way to experiment with and experience the type of society they want to live in. Taking a firm stand in support of local actors, the book takes us on a journey through the diverse landscape of African commons and reveals the breadth of local knowledge that fuels them.

Although it is hard to intuitively gauge their precise extent, African commons testify to the ability of collectives to initiate ecological, economic, and social transitions at their level of action, beyond the state and the market. Actually, an important part of Sub-Saharan African natural resources and rural areas are commons-based managed. Some commons deliver services (water or energy supply, waste management) when public infrastructure is lacking. At the same time, social and democratic practices are experimented within shared spaces (fab labs, cultural spaces) in urban areas. In parallel, digital commons are sprouting, with a view to generalizing public access to peer-produced knowledge. While being careful not to idealize them, this book supports the idea that these innovations deserve better recognition as one of the contemporary forms of collective action. The many examples throughout the book are a source of inspiration, not only for Africa but also for the Global North.

In parallel, the present book invites us to leave behind outdated and narrow notions of the commons, which have been too often described as static practices bound by tradition. On the contrary, the goal of the book is to emphasize the relevance and constant evolution of the commons. In contexts characterized by webs of interdependence and systemic challenges, it is critical that we overcome our tendency to work in silos and rather look at the Sustainable Development Goals in cross-cutting ways. In that regard, as emphasized in the final chapter of the present work, the question of commons strongly resonates with professional practices and current concerns that take place within and between public development banks, organized within the *Finance in Common* movement since 2020. When development projects succeed in bringing together all stakeholders around modes of governance attuned to the specificities of local contexts, do they not, in a sense, implement new commons-based dynamics? Can we go so far as to say that those development projects may be seen as commons in and of themselves?

The Commons advocates strong messages on which it might not be possible to reach a consensus. From a philosophical standpoint, this work enacts a potent decentering. Rather than being synonymous with a "universal approach that implies a movement of inclusion into some pre-existing entity," the commons are to be understood as a form of "being-in-common," which "presupposes a relationship of co-belonging across multiple singularities," in the words of my friend, historian Achille Mbembe.

By operating the switch from commons to "commons-based approaches," this book takes a firm stand in favor of an operational perspective and aims to enlist all actors in the search for solutions that are collectively built and accepted by all. In our effort to carve out a new path through the commons, we must be ready to question our biases, our ways of thinking, and our most deeply rooted certainties as well as our tools and methods. In that regard, this book asks us to reflect on the ways in which commons can contribute, alongside public and private actors, to the preservation of general interest. It offers a renewed and updated framework to guide future actions.

This book does not present commons as the ultimate solution. Yet it unambiguously shows that commons must be reckoned with when we think about alternative ways to live together as a society. My warmest thanks go to all involved in creating this beautiful and inspiring work.

Rémy Rioux
Chief Executive Officer
Agence française de développement

Acknowledgments

Many people contributed to the creation of *The Commons*, be it through their research and operational experiences or by way of formal and informal discussions.

First, we would like to express our gratitude to Lola Mercier, without whom this book would certainly not have been possible. We thank Mathieu Boche for his many insights during the framing of the general purpose of the book. We are also grateful for Etienne Charrière's valuable support and Nicolas Hubert's suggestions throughout the editorial process.

In addition to the contributors whose names figure in this publication, we would also like to thank all those involved in the study of commons and social innovations whose work or experiences made this book possible: Jean-François Alesandrini, Nicole Alix, Martine Antona, Sigrid Aubert, Stéphane Baudé, Émeline Baudet, Michel Bauwens, Florent Bédécarrats, David Bollier, Sarah Botton, François Bousquet, Sébastien Broca, Aurore Chaigneau, Olivier De Schutter, Etienne Delay, Louisa Desbleds, François Enten, Etienne Espagne, Geneviève Fontaine, Maxime Forest, Marilou Gilbert, Gaël Giraud, Philippe Karpe, Jean-François Kibler, Philippe Lavigne Delville, Martin Lemenager, Lionel Maurel, Fabienne Orsi, Vatche Papazian, Hélène Périvier, Audrey Perraud, Olivier Petit, Judith Rochfeld, Irène Salenson, Pierre Salignon, Frédéric Sultan, Magali Toro, Sarah Vanuxem, and Corinne Vercher-Chaptal.

We would particularly like to thank those who kindly read the first drafts of the various chapters. In this respect, we would also like to thank Pierre-Arnaud Barthel, Carl Bernadac, Raphaël Besson, Julien Calas, Jérémie Daussin-Charpentier, Hélène Djoufelkit, Nadège Legroux, Jean-David Naudet, Serge Rabier, and Françoise Rivière for their comments and suggestions.

Numerous meetings, discussions, and debates with researchers, commons stakeholders, and political actors also influenced the contents of this book. In this respect, we would particularly like to thank Jean-Pierre Olivier de Sardan for his important and constructive contribution to this project.

We also thank the International Association for the Study of the Commons, La Coop des Communs (Commons Cooperative), the Comité technique "Foncier et développement" (Technical Committee on "Land Tenure and Development"), GRET, Remix the commons, and the P2P Foundation.

It has been possible to include this book in this collection only because committed individuals working within operations funded by the Agence française de développement (AFD) (French Development Agency) have demonstrated that, despite the constraints, it is possible for commons in Sub-Saharan Africa to receive institutional support and recognition. The following list is by no means exhaustive, but we would like to express our gratitude to Jean-François Almanza, Quentin Ballin, Alexandre Berthon-Dumurgier, Marie Bjornson-Langen, Perrine Bonvalet-Döring, Cassilde Brenière, Antoine Chèvre, Sarah Crochon, Jérémy Gasc, Gilles Kleitz, Marie Le Gac, Grégoire Léna, Frédéric Maurel, Jean Millerat, Gwenaël Prié, and Stéphanie Wattrelos Rutily.

We would also like to pay tribute to those that we have lost but whose work continues to inspire us in so many ways: Silke Helfrich, Etienne Le Roy, Dominique Rojat, and Olivier Weinstein.

Finally, we would like to thank the anonymous reviewers for their valuable comments and suggestions. In addition, the editors wish to thank the World Bank for its pioneering work conducted with Elinor Ostrom and for the present opportunity to shed new light on African commons.

About the Editors and Contributors

Editors

Benjamin Coriat is an economist and professor emeritus of economics at Université Sorbonne Paris Nord, France. He has worked extensively on issues surrounding the industrial economy, innovation, and intellectual property. For 20 years, he has concentrated on the study of commons and common goods. In this area, he has written and co-coordinated numerous publications, including *Le retour des communs* (2015); *Vers une République des biens communs* (2019); *La Pandémie, l'Anthropocène et le bien commun* (2020); and *Le bien commun, le climat et le marché* (2021). He also cofounded the French group Économistes atterrés (the Dismayed Economists). Between 2016 and 2020, he led a multidisciplinary research program on "commons-based entrepreneurship." Its work is available at encommuns.com.

Stéphanie Leyronas is a research fellow specializing in the commons at the Agence française de développement (AFD) (French Development Agency). Previously, she held operational roles within the agency, first as the drinking water and sanitation challenges project team leader and subsequently as deputy manager of the AFD unit working in the same area. Currently, her work focuses on observing the commons in the various fields where the AFD operates: land, natural resources management, health, access to water and energy, urban commons, digital commons, and the collaborative economy. In this respect, she has been conducting an internal expert network within the AFD since 2020. Her work has been published in a variety of formats (scientific publications, book chapters, policy briefs, policy papers, and international conference proceedings).

Kako Nubukpo is an economist and has been commissioner in charge of agriculture, water resources, and the environment of the Commission de l'Union économique et monétaire ouest-africaine (UEMOA) (Commission of the West

African Economic and Monetary Union) since 2021. He is a former dean of the Faculty of Economics and Management at the University of Lomé, Togo. He is director of the Observatoire de l'Afrique subsaharienne (Sub-Saharan Africa Observatory) at the Fondation Jean-Jaurès (Jean-Jaurès Foundation) in Paris and a researcher at the Centre de coopération internationale en recherche agronomique pour le développement (CIRAD) (French Agricultural Research Center for International Development). He is a member of the AFD's scientific committee and on the board of the Fondation pour l'agriculture et la ruralité dans le monde (Global Foundation for Agriculture and Rural Development). He is a former fellow of the Global Economic Governance Programme run by Oxford University (United Kingdom) and Princeton University (United States). He recently published *Une solution pour l'Afrique: Du néoprotectionnisme aux biens communs* (2022).

Contributors

Patrick d'Aquino is an expert in social geography and participatory mechanisms at the Centre de coopération internationale en recherche agronomique pour le développement (CIRAD) (French Agricultural Research Center for International Development) based in Montpellier, France. At the beginning of the 1990s, his work focused on drawing out local knowledge in Burkina Faso. He was one of the first to design a participatory geographic information system in 1998. At the end of the 1990s, he codesigned a new approach to participatory modeling (www.commod.org) combining scientific and local knowledge. At the start of the 2000s, he extrapolated the approach for participatory development of public policy mechanisms using participatory modeling tools or simulation games (www.terristories.com). A collection of training mechanisms and methodological tools was produced to enable this approach to be reproduced on a large scale. It is currently being implemented in several regions across the world, particularly in the Sahel and Southeast Asia.

Mathieu Boche is an agricultural and development economist. His doctoral dissertation focused on large-scale land acquisitions in Mozambique. He subsequently joined the AFD in 2017 as an expert on land and development issues in rural areas of Sub-Saharan Africa and countries in the Amazonian basin. He chaired the Comité technique "Foncier et développement" (CTFD) (Technical Committee on "Land Tenure and Development") supported by the AFD and the Ministère français de l'Europe et des affaires étrangères (French Ministry for Europe and Foreign Affairs) for eight years. He is currently working at the AFD's Dakar office. Notably, he contributed to the CTFD-coordinated report *Approche par les communs de la terre et des ressources qu'elle porte—Guide opérationnel* (2020).

Bérénice Bon is a geographer and research fellow at the Institut français de recherche pour le développement (IRD) (the French National Research Institute for Sustainable Development) within the Centre d'études en sciences sociales sur les mondes africains, américains et asiatiques (CESSMA) (Centre for Social Sciences Studies on the African, American and Asian worlds) located in Paris, France. Her research focuses on urbanization trends in Sub-Saharan Africa, principally sites located in Kenya. She is coordinating the METROLAND project (Commodifying land: Capital, inequalities, and conflicts in Sub-Saharan African metropolitan peripheries in Mali, Senegal, and Kenya), which is funded by the Agence nationale de la recherche (ANR) (French National Research Agency) from 2022 to 2025. She is also participating in the GlobalSmog project that is researching atmospheric air pollution regulation in large cities in Africa and South Asia.

Tanella Boni is an Ivorian philosopher, essayist, poet, and novelist. A professor of philosophy at Université Félix Houphouët-Boigny in Abidjan, she is also a member of the Academy of Sciences, Arts and Cultures of Africa and African Diasporas. Over the past 40 years, she has been working across disciplines on important issues of our times, including migrations, border crossings, nature conservation, social and family connections, the position of African women, and the place of Africa in the world. Her most recent books are *Habiter* (essay, Muséo editions Muséo, 2018); *Matins de couvre-feu*, Ahmadou Kourouma Price 2005 (reprint 2022, Nimba editions); *Sans parole ni poignée de main* (novel, Nimba editions, 2022); *Le poème n'est pas un objet perdu* (collection of poems, Vallesse editions, 2022); and *Insoutenable frontière* (collection of poems, Bruno Doucey editions, 2022).

Éric Denis is a geographer at the *Centre national de la recherche scientifique* (CNRS) (French National Centre for Scientific Research) and director of Géographie-cités (Geography-Cities), an interdisciplinary research laboratory attached to the CNRS, Paris 1 Panthéon–Sorbonne University, Université Paris Cité, and the École des hautes études en sciences sociales (EHESS) (School of Advanced Studies in the Social Sciences) in France. He conducts multidisciplinary work with anthropologists and legal experts on informality and negotiations and setup methods in cities in the Global South, particularly in the Arab Republic of Egypt and in India. He coordinated research on access to housing in cities in the Arab world and on subaltern urbanization in India. He also coordinated the program on urban commons for housing in the Global South with Claire Simonneau (AFD 2018–20 funding) and is currently finishing multisite research into urban land conversions in the Global South with Bérénice Bon and Claire Simonneau (CTFD funding).

Alix Françoise is a research fellow at the AFD. Her work focuses on territorial transitions and the challenges surrounding urbanization and the environment.

She previously held operational roles at the AFD as the urban development project team leader in Paris and at the Tunisia office. With a background in political science and geography, she contributes to work on issues surrounding cities and climate, as well as food supplies in cities.

Nicolas Hubert is a postdoctoral researcher at the "Chaire Raoul Dandurand" (Raoul Dandurand Chair) at the Université du Québec à Montréal (UQAM), Canada. He is also deputy editor-in-chief of *VertigO–La revue électronique en sciences de l'environnement*. He uses the perspective of political science to examine the challenges surrounding the environment, natural resources management, social and political movements, and state-building and peacebuilding in fragile states or societies that have experienced conflict. His current research focuses more particularly on conflicts connected to environmental damage and the development of the extractive industry, as well as the management of national parks in West Africa.

Mamoudou Gazibo is a professor of political science at the University of Montreal, Canada. He specializes in comparative politics and international cooperation. His research focuses particularly on state formation, democratization, and development in Sub-Saharan Africa, as well as China-Africa relations. In 2010, he chaired the drafting committee of Niger's Constitution. His many publications include *Repenser la légitimité de l'État africain à l'ère de la gouvernance partagée* (2017).

Jan Krewer is a French-German digital public policies consultant. He was deputy secretary general of the Conseil national du numérique (France's National Digital Council) and has taught at Sciences Po Paris, France. He has also worked in Sub-Saharan Africa (Benin, Côte d'Ivoire, Rwanda, and Senegal), where he was a strategic adviser for the Smart Africa Alliance. He participated in designing pilot projects to integrate digital commons to support development cooperation, including, for example, with the German Agency for International Cooperation (GIZ) and the Mozilla Foundation. He has also written several articles on this subject.

Isabelle Liotard is a lecturer and researcher in economics at Université Sorbonne Paris Nord, France. Her research focuses principally on innovation and digital technology. She has studied fab labs in Sub-Saharan Africa within the framework of the "commons-based entrepreneurship" research program. Her work on innovation and digital technology has been published on numerous occasions, including in particular an article that appeared in the magazine *Innovations* in 2020, "The Fablabs in the Heart of the City: The Specificities of Places in French-Speaking Africa."

Thomas Mboa is a researcher in residence at the Centre d'expertise international de Montréal en intelligence artificielle (International Centre of Expertise in Montreal on Artificial Intelligence), Canada. He is also a lecturer at the École supérieure des sciences et techniques de l'information et de la communication (Information and Communication Sciences and Technology Graduate School), Cameroon. He has a PhD in public communication. His research interests focus on the digitalization of knowledge, artificial intelligence, and open science. He is a member of internationally respected laboratories (MICA in Bordeaux and LabCMO in Montreal). He also founded Mboalab (www.mboalab.africa), a fab lab specializing in health. His many contributions to scientific publications and conferences can be found on the following website: https://orcid .org/0000-0001-9678-7765.

Thomas Mélonio is an economist whose work focuses on funding for education, higher education, student loans, and international migration. Between 2012 and 2017, he was the deputy adviser and subsequently adviser to the president of France on African affairs and then joined the AFD's partnerships department. Since 2018, he has been the Executive Director for Innovation, Strategy, and Research at the AFD.

Lola Mercier is studying social sciences and political sciences at the École normale supérieure de Lyon (ENS de Lyon) and the École des hautes études commerciales de Paris (HEC Paris), France. Her work at the AFD focuses on governance and commons in Sub-Saharan Africa.

Guiako Obin is originally from Côte d'Ivoire. After his degree in computer science, he began his professional career in the field of Geolocation. Wanting to commit to a more inclusive digital world and to be a major player in Africa, he created in 2014 with friends, mostly computer scientists, the BabyLab in the popular commune of Abobo in the city of Abidjan. He has also worked closely with international organizations such as the Next Einstein Forum of the African Institute of Science and Mathematics to foster technological innovation in Africa. In recognition of his outstanding contributions, he has been awarded a dozen prizes and distinctions, including the National Award of Excellence for the best youth digital initiative in Côte d'Ivoire.

David Obura (coauthor of background research paper 2) is a founding director of Coastal Oceans Research and Development–Indian Ocean (CORDIO) East Africa, an organization that supports the sustainability of coral reefs and marine systems in the western Indian Ocean. His initial research focused on the resilience of coral reefs, particularly to climate change, and now extends to policy processes related to biodiversity, reefs, climate, and sustainability.

He has been part of the Earth Commission since 2019 and is active in the Intergovernmental Science-Policy Platform on Biodiversity and Ecosystem Services (IPBES) and Convention on Biological Diversity (CBD) technical processes.

Jean-Pierre Olivier de Sardan (author of background research paper 1) is a researcher at the Laboratoire d'études et de recherche sur les dynamiques sociales et le développement local (Laboratory for Research into Social Dynamics and Local Development) and an associate professor at the Université Abdou Moumouni (Abdou Moumouni University), Niger. He is also director emeritus for research at the Centre national de la recherche scientifique (CNRS) (French National Centre for Scientific Research) and director of studies at the École des hautes études en sciences sociales (EHESS) (School of Advanced Studies in the Social Sciences), France. For 30 years, the main focus of his work has been the social anthropology of the state and public services in Africa. He has also examined issues surrounding health, governance, and development. His latest book, published in 2021 by Karthala, is *La revanche des contextes. Des mésaventures de l'ingénierie sociale en Afrique et au-delà.*

Sophie Salomon is deputy director of the AFD's economic assessment and public policy department. As such, she has contributed to the internal expert network of commons conducted by Stéphanie Leyronas. Previously, she held operational roles. In Paris, she acted as an adviser for initiatives looking to improve working methods and internal processes. In Southeast Asia, she was in charge of managing infrastructure and public policy development projects required for the ecological and climate transition. Before joining the AFD, she managed projects seeking to modernize economic and financial governance in Vietnam for the public interest group Assistance au développement des échanges en technologies économiques et financières (ADETEF) (Agency for Technical Economic and Financial Cooperation) and in Algeria for the European Commission.

Sidy Mohamed Seck is a geographer and social economist. He is a lecturer and researcher at Université Gaston Berger (Gaston Berger University) (Senegal) and West Africa regional coordinator of the Comité scientifique et technique eau agricole (COSTEA) (Scientific and Technical Committee on Agricultural Water). He is a member of the Groupe interdisciplinaire de recherche pour l'appui à la planification régionale et au développement local (Interdisciplinary Research Group Supporting Regional Planning and Local Development), the Leïdi laboratory (land and development trends), the Comité technique "Foncier et développement" (CTFD) (Technical Committee on "Land Tenure and Development"), and the French organization Améliorer la gouvernance de la terre, de l'eau et des ressources naturelles (AGTER) (Association to Contribute to Improve the Governance of Land, Water and Natural Resources). His research and expertise in the development of rural areas and institutional support for producer organizations and local communities date back 40 years. He has worked in Senegal and West Africa on a number of occasions to perform research and provide expertise and scientific advice on behalf of international organizations.

Claire Simonneau is a lecturer and researcher at Université Gustave Eiffel (Gustave Eiffel University) (France) within the Laboratoire techniques, territoires et sociétés (Techniques, Lands, and Societies Laboratory). Her research focuses on the production and management of cities in the Global South, particularly Benin and Senegal. She examines land trends, how they are regulated, and how they are contested. In partnership with the AFD and the CTFD, she recently coordinated two comparative research programs: land-based commons for housing in the Global South (with Éric Denis) and land use conversions in the Global South (with Éric Denis and Bérénice Bon).

Issa Sory is a lecturer and researcher in the geography department of Université Norbert Zongo (Norbert Zongo University), Burkina Faso. Within the Groupe de recherche sur les initiatives locales (Local Initiatives Research Group) at Université Joseph Ki-Zerbo (Joseph Ki-Zerbo University) (Burkina Faso), his research focuses on urban policies, development, the environment, and urban services in Burkina Faso. He recently published "Les effets des mesures barrières contre la Covid-19 sur les perceptions des acteurs de la filière des ordures ménagères à Ouagadougou (Burkina Faso)" (2021) and "Public Land Policies at an Impasse in Ouagadougou (Burkina Faso)" (2019).

Sébastien Treyer (coauthor of background research paper 2) has been executive director of the Institut du développement durable et des relations internationales (IDDRI) (Institute for Sustainable Development and International Relations), France, since January 2019. He also chairs the scientific and technical committee of the Fonds français pour l'environnement mondial (French Facility for Global Environment) and is a member of the Lead Faculty of the Earth System Governance network. He is a graduate of France's École Polytechnique and served as chief engineer for bridges, waters, and forests. He has a PhD in environment management and was head of forecasting at France's environment ministry. He has played an active role in improving communication between scientists and policy makers and in scientific programming with the European Commission, the ANR, and regional stakeholders.

Overview

Stéphanie Leyronas and Benjamin Coriat

Emptiness did not exist in Africa. Even the deserts were inhabited. There was always someone, or something, alive.
—Léonora Miano, novelist, 2005

What do I mean by "Africa"? In fact, there are several Africas, each with its own trajectory, diverse history and memories, and very different experiences of the political. Any discussion of Africa can only truly be valid if the concept of the continent as a homogeneous reality is deconstructed. Africa is not a geographical space, but rather a collection of diverse perspectives, cultures, and approaches to life.
—Aminata Diaw, philosopher, 2004

The Commons explores the many forms of development being championed by Africa's residents, users, and citizens. In addition to managing property and shared tangible and intangible resources collectively, they are experimenting with a concept of "commoning" founded on values such as community, engagement, reciprocity, and trust. In practice, their approach takes the form of land-based commons, housing cooperatives, hybrid cultural spaces or places for innovation, and collaborative digital platforms. The purpose of this book, where observation of historical and recent practices converges with new theories within commons scholarship, is not to promote commons themselves. Rather, it examines the tensions, drivers of change, and opportunities that surround commons dynamics in Africa.

The Commons also considers to what extent these forms of development might contribute to constructing and initiating a continentwide innovative political project that nonetheless respects Africa's diversity. At a time when Africa's stakeholders are facing increasingly complex social and environmental dilemmas, its purpose is not to say *what* should be done or *how* it should be done but rather to open up avenues for discussion.

The Commons provides decision-makers, financial backers, researchers, and civil society actors with an opportunity to reflect upon their own positions and their relationship with the processes of individualization and ownership, standardization and formalism, and utilitarianism and commodification. It is essential to examine these issues in order to consider the diversity of institutional arrangements proposed by commons. This recognition is necessary for "commoning" to thrive on complex social challenges for which responsibility currently lies within public authorities and market powers.

The aim of *The Commons* is to encourage discussions around this concept rather than to provide a definitive assessment of it. Although it does set out the various fields in which commons take place in Sub-Saharan Africa, many themes (e.g., challenges surrounding public services provision, gender, climate change adaptation, and biodiversity) remain unexamined or require further consideration and should be the subject of future work.

Narrative Thread

In her influential book *Governing the Commons: The Evolution of Institutions for Collective Action* (1990), Ostrom shows that many generally renewable resources can be managed locally by small but diverse communities that develop collective rules to avoid their destruction. She also maintains that, in many cases, managing in such a way these "common-pool resources" can prove to be more effective than regulation by a superior authority (usually the state) or individualization and privatization. She advances this argument at a time when the prevailing wisdom concurred with the notion of the "tragedy of the commons" proposed more than 20 years earlier by the American biologist Garrett Hardin. According to this theory, only the nationalization or privatization of natural resources can prevent overexploitation. The reasoning and analysis framework developed by Ostrom, and more widely by the Bloomington School, has fueled much research over several decades. Commons scholarship has developed significantly in a variety of fields, and in particular very recently around the notion of "commons-based entrepreneurship" (chapter 1).

Commons have been observed empirically in Sub-Saharan Africa in numerous areas, and their presence is far from marginal. On the subject of land and natural resource management, African commons constitute an extension of the traditional practices that communities deploy and adapt to modern conditions. Economic activities and market rationale are subordinated to social relationships and environmental interdependencies. Against a backdrop of legal pluralism and frequent competition between land regulation stakeholders, these commons can only be secured if usage rights are guaranteed, the rules are suitable and effective, and their institutional framework is clear (chapter 2). Land-based commons are

currently undergoing significant change. In a period of rapid and diffuse urbanization, a number of factors drive the transformation of relationships with land
(commodification, individualization, land and housing needs, land's role as a
financial asset). They also contribute to the dismantling of commons on the outskirts of urban conglomerations, including on the rural-urban fringe that some
stakeholders anticipate as the new urban frontline. At the same time, new commons are emerging to enable not only vulnerable populations but also the middle
classes to access housing in the absence of any social housing policies (chapter 3).

African cities are also witnessing the emergence of hybrid places located
within urban sites and managed collectively by groups with a social, economic,
and political goal. They might focus on welfare and the improvement of living
standards (shared gardens, playing fields, community centers) or access to art and
culture, science, innovation, and digital technology. These commons serve different purposes. Activities with an environmental and social purpose sit alongside
educational activities. They challenge the way in which cities are shaped at a time
when local communities struggle to find solutions to the issues facing cities and
urban areas more widely (chapter 4).

Digital technology plays a special role in many of these hybrid places. It is more
widely part of most development strategies in Sub-Saharan Africa. In this context,
digital commons represent a credible alternative to a form of digital entrepreneurship based on ownership where the goal is exponential growth. However, digital
commons do not necessarily place themselves as part of a countermovement.
Rather, they propose pragmatic individual and collective approaches, combining
commons-based and more traditional entrepreneurial perspectives (chapter 5).

In terms of regulation, the extent of the relationship that African public
stakeholders (states and their agencies or local communities) choose to forge
with commons varies. Four main categories emerge: opposition or even predation, indifference, facilitation and establishment, and contribution and partnership. The nature of the position taken by a state and the resources that it
intends to deploy vis-à-vis commons is eminently political. Ultimately, commons can encourage a reexamination of the very notion of the state in terms of
its relationship with individuals and society. Commons offer a vision of a new
approach where the state is closer to its people (chapter 6).

To achieve this, public stakeholders must commit to looking again at their
own practices. Funders must also confront their universalist configurations and
their "managerialist" processes. If commons are to be supported, positions must
be changed to enable a "commons-based approach" to act as an operational
framework. This strategy can be broken down into four main objectives: moving away from an assumption of institutional uniformity to the recognition of
the diversity of practices, shifting from top-down observation to an embedded
approach, changing a results-based culture into one supporting the process, and
switching from expert knowledge to pluralist knowledge (chapter 7).

These considerations around African commons, both on the practices and on the values that they promote, open the door to further analysis of a number of issues, such as the provision of services of general interest. Sub-Saharan Africa's failing public services are in crisis. As a result, various forms of local governance (chiefdoms, religious institutions, sponsors, private stakeholders, local or international organizations) provide public goods to supplement the services delivered by municipal authorities or states and toward which the population still has high expectations. Some of the aforementioned bodies are highly dependent on external aid, therefore raising questions about the ability of commons to provide sustainable responses to absent or failing public services. The role of public stakeholders and their capacity for reform from within also deserve to be examined (background research paper 1).

Another area for consideration is biodiversity governance. Land-based commons can fulfill environmental functions in areas where loss of biodiversity is well established. Commons seem able to foster a unique position for Africa in terms of tackling the challenges surrounding biodiversity conservation and the methods required to achieve it using the "shared earth" polycentric approach. This strategy diverges from the dominant 30 × 30 discourse whereby 30 percent of the planet should be covered by a protected area by 2030 (background research paper 2).

Eight Key Messages

Why Do Commons in Sub-Saharan Africa Matter?

Message 1: In Sub-Saharan Africa, collective organizations take place to protect the common good.
Collective organizations produce, manage, and protect a variety of tangible and intangible resources. They sometimes spread out as "palliative solutions" when public intervention measures (central, provincial, decentralized, or local) have proved inadequate or are even absent. Consider, for example, urban commons used as hybrid cultural places or as places for innovation. These organizations may also focus on particular issues before they become part of the political agenda. For example, land-based commons seek to conserve biodiversity. Collective organizations sometimes also play a role in resisting individualization and commodification, something demonstrated by housing cooperatives.

These organizations are rooted in practices and experiences. Protection of the common good, understood as living in the world in a way that protects human and nonhuman communities and ecosystems, is part of their raison d'être. They are founded on people's right to exist. This right includes fundamental social rights (e.g., food, health, and education) but also the right to a social existence (i.e., to have a recognized and legitimate position and role in society).

This right to a social existence is expressed through a process of "commoning." Based on consultation, trust, and reciprocity, commons participants, particularly young people, develop diverse skills (problem solving and solution finding, creativity, cooperation, leadership, and entrepreneurship).

These collective organizations are not the only local responses deployed by African populations, but they are significant and deserve to be explored.

Message 2: The notion of "commons" can help explain and describe exactly what these organizations are and how they operate.

The concept of "commons" can help explain what these organizations are and give them visibility. Ostrom, the 2009 winner of the Nobel Memorial Prize in Economic Sciences, played a key role in the development of this notion. Today, the concept continues to evolve within academic circles in a variety of fields (e.g., knowledge commons, urban commons, digital commons, and cultural commons).

In this instance, the concept is not seen as a turnkey solution. Nor is it a question of idealizing these organizations in terms of their social inclusion capacities or, on the contrary, discrediting them in the name of modernity and economic efficiency. Rather, the notion is used as a frame of reference and an instrument of analysis for understanding the practices and organizations deployed in Sub-Saharan Africa via consideration of the various forms that commons can take in their different fields, as well as discussing and debating how societies should be made.

Message 3: Commons exist in their own space, beyond the market and the state, or public and private spheres.

Using peer learning and trial and error, these collective organizations generate their own operating rules to define positions for each participant, as well as the rights and duties associated with those positions. Their self-governing nature means that they can be deployed independently from the dominant state apparatus and can develop systems that stem from "consultative," experimental, and constructive democracy, including in environments where representative democracy is disputed.

These organizations can mobilize novel forms of entrepreneurship that we call "commons-based entrepreneurship." Its particularity is that it seeks satisfaction from the right to exist rather than profit and enrichment. Monetary and market exchanges may prove necessary, but they are not the aim in and of themselves. This form of entrepreneurship is also founded on consultative decision-making processes, rather than on the principles of authority and hierarchy. Finally, the right of ownership over shared resources is not private and exclusive. Instead, it is based on distributed rights, a concept tagged by Ostrom as "the bundle of rights."

In Europe, commons are sometimes presented as countermodels and alternatives to modern capitalism. However, those deployed in Sub-Saharan Africa do not really see themselves as part of a formal movement. Nonetheless, they do exist on the fringes of established systems. As such, African commons

experiment with and defend principles and values that foster examination of
how the economy, social institutions, and the state itself might be transformed.

What Are African Commons?

*Message 4: African commons are constantly evolving and respond to hybrid
dynamics.*
Commons in Sub-Saharan Africa are social constructs that continue to adapt
to the dynamic nature of environmental systems and to the evolution of human
societies. In some areas, such as land or natural resources, they can be an
extension of so-called traditional or customary commons. However, they can
also stem from recent creations.

Commons in Sub-Saharan Africa bring together different types of
communities and stakeholders. Some are partly structured around communities
that have some form of membership criteria such as the tribe, family lineage,
or the clan. They often involve a variety of socioeconomic stakeholders (young
workers, women, those working in cooperatives, or micro-entrepreneurs)
and work with administrative communities and stakeholders (e.g., villages
or local communities). In this instance, the "community" is therefore defined
on the basis of very specific social relationships, and it can therefore be very
heterogeneous. Communities can also become intertwined with one another
(e.g., through digital commons), as can the resources (e.g., land-based
commons). Similarly, hybridization is evidenced through the creation of
different standards where traditional rules for organizing local societies are
combined with some of the rules and operating standards defined within the
legal framework in which they work.

Commons are able to continue to evolve and tackle uncertain conditions
and increasingly complex social and environmental dilemmas thanks to the
institutional plasticity created by such hybridization.

*Message 5: African commons are subject to internal tensions and face external
threats, making them vulnerable.*
Commons are subject to internal tensions. The interests of individuals, or
the groups that they form, do not necessarily converge. The commons-based
perspective therefore presupposes consultation and a search for compromise.
Tensions can arise from different power relationships within the community,
inequalities, mechanisms for allocating authority, forms of exclusion and
discrimination (be they gender-based, social, political, or ethnic), and the
individual strategies of commons stakeholders.

Commons are also facing a number of changes to their environment. These
are transforming the social and political systems within which they evolve and
therefore modifying the conditions under which they operate. Such changes
might prove to be opportunities for commons or, on the contrary, might
endanger their very existence. The roots of these changes are many and varied:

individualization and commodification, uniformization of standards by public authorities, demographic dynamics (fertility and migration), and market or court-authorized appropriation by private owners or states, for example, of resources and spaces previously intended for collective use.

How to Take Action?

Message 6: Commons face dilemmas in terms of their sustainability, their scope, their economic model, and their political impact.
Our observation of commons in Sub-Saharan Africa has revealed some dilemmas, but the potential solutions are not black or white. On the contrary, our purpose is to suggest avenues for discussion and debates around these challenges and the way in which public authorities could or should provide support.

The first dilemma concerns the sustainability of commons. Are African commons ephemeral and temporary "creations" by residents, users, and citizens who have been abandoned by the authorities but who await the arrival of a more protective state? Or are they structuring, enduring solutions? Are the individuals involved in African commons investing in the long-term possibility of promoting innovative forms of citizen engagement? Or are their actions provisional with a view to reintegrating the dominant system characterized by exclusive ownership and entrepreneurship in its traditional capitalist forms?

The second dilemma concerns the scope of commons action. Should African commons remain niche innovative spaces whose strength lies in the specificity and contextualization of their work? Or are they destined to occupy wider social fields through the promotion of the values on which their work is based such as community, commitment, reciprocity, and trust? Should commons seek to influence and occupy positions in society more widely, or should they concentrate on providing local strategies?

The third dilemma is the economic model on which the work of commons is based. Should African commons be left alone to devise the institutional arrangements that enable them to develop autonomous economic models (e.g., combining market transactions and participant membership fees)? Or should it be considered that they provide products and services with a particular and recognized social or environmental function that must be developed and protected by public stakeholders immediately?

The fourth dilemma concerns the ambitions envisioned from the relationship between commons and the public authorities. Should African commons remain on the fringes of the state for fear of being altered, corrupted, instrumentalized, or captured, subjected to attempts to harmonize, fix, and standardize them? Or should they formulate their expectations vis-à-vis the public authorities, both to secure their existence and to contribute to promoting their expansion and development? Might public institutions limit their consideration of commons to policy intermediaries? Or should they commit to a partnership-based relationship with a view to strengthening their own legitimacy and ensuring that the population truly has the right to exist?

The fifth dilemma concerns the political impact of commons. Are African commons destined to remain "safety valves" within the dominant economic model, "places of refuge" for those excluded from the heart of that model? Or can they become part of a new polycentric system? Should commons be incorporated into market principles, or should an alternative political project be constructed on the basis of new purposes and shared values?

Message 7: The commons-based approach represents an operational framework for public stakeholders seeking to establish a close, supportive relationship with commons.

Public stakeholders (states and their agencies, as well as local governments depending on the extent of decentralization) already have a wide variety of instruments at their disposal for recognizing the diverse institutional arrangements proposed by commons and providing polycentric support for collective action. A relationship based on a partnership between commons and the public authorities requires the latter to adopt positions, perspectives, methods, and tools that do not enter in conflict with the expectations and needs of commons. The focus of these positions, perspectives, methods, and tools must be to involve collectives in addressing any specific problems that they may raise and in formulating political projects to resolve them. The public authorities must adopt a nonprescriptive, pragmatic, and contextualized approach, something that we call the "commons-based approach."

Message 8: Commons can inspire an innovative political project for Sub-Saharan Africa.

Our hope is that this book will open up avenues for additional opportunities. Sub-Saharan Africa has embarked on a period of significant economic, demographic, democratic, and environmental transition. This is a pivotal moment in which the climate and environmental crises heighten the continent's vulnerability. We believe that commons, as both a critical and constructive approach, can contribute to forging new perspectives for the African continent. In his latest essay, *Une solution pour l'Afrique* ("A Solution for Africa"), Kako Nubukpo, a Togolese economist, calls for the launch of a major singular political project. It should begin with the exploration of commons diversity, reflecting the variety of the "several Africas."

References

Diaw, A. 2004. "Nouveaux Contours de l'Espace Public en Afrique." *Diogène* 26 (2): 37–46. https://doi.org/10.3917/dio.206.0037.

Miano, L. 2005. *Dark Heart of the Night.* Lincoln, NE: Bison Books.

Abbreviations

AFD	Agence française de développement
BHS	Banque de l'Habitat du Sénégal
CAHF	Centre for Affordable Housing Finance
CLT	Community Land Trust
CPRs	common-pool resources
DNDi	Drugs for Neglected Diseases Initiative
FAO	Food and Agriculture Organization
FSH	Fédération sénégalaise des habitants
GDP	gross domestic product
GIZ	German Agency for International Cooperation
HIV	human immunodeficiency virus
IASC	International Association for the Study of the Commons
ICTs	information and communication technologies
IOM	International Organization for Migration
IoT	Internet of Things
NGOs	nongovernmental organizations
OECD	Organisation for Economic Co-operation and Development
OIF	Organisation internationale de la francophonie
PNCL	Programme national de construction de logements
POAS	Plan d'occupation et d'affectation des sols
SAED	Société d'aménagement et d'exploitation des terres du Delta du Fleuve Sénégal
SEZs	special economic zones
SMCs	school management committees
SSE	social solidarity economy
UNESCO	United Nations Educational, Scientific, and Cultural Organization
VHZs	village hunting zones

Chapter 1

Theoretical Framework, Methodology, and Structure of the Book

Benjamin Coriat and Stéphanie Leyronas

Introduction

The purpose of this chapter is to set out the theoretical framework for this book and to introduce its methodology and organization. We do so in three stages.

In the first section, we reexamine the concept of commons itself. In particular, we look at Ostrom's foundational work (Ostrom 1990) on the empirical observation of situations involving the management of renewable resources and their modes of appropriation, which led to the conceptualization of common-pool resources (CPRs). We then briefly mention two other major areas of her work (Antona and Bousquet 2017): the introduction of the theme of "polycentricity" with her husband Vincent Ostrom, which provides a decentralized and diversified vision of decision-making centers and modes of coordination, and the proposal of frameworks as tools for training and the coordinated analysis of field studies.

We then show that for at least two decades now, the principle of commons has been expanding. It is now being applied to increasingly varied domains (e.g., natural resources, habitat, culture, innovation, digital, services). Examples of this expansion include an autonomous organization based on an irrigated field to ensure the self-sufficiency of a group of relatives in a village; an association for urban concessions on shared habitats; the implementation of fab labs, which seek to provide digital education services; and tool sharing among a community of residents. We discuss how, unexpectedly, the internet and the Web 2.0 revolution have brought new life to this notion. In fact, entering into a social system that is abundant in nonrival goods (i.e., the information provided by the internet) has made it possible for communities to feed themselves with resources that cost very little and without damaging the ecosystems from which the resources are taken.

This section is not intended as an exhaustive review of the available literature on commons. The aim is to highlight those points that are most useful for understanding the objectives of the book. The subsequent chapters provide additional theoretical insights related to the specific themes addressed.

The second section proposes an extension of the notion of commons to that of "commons-based entrepreneurship." This designates a new and original form of entrepreneurship that is distinct not only from classic capitalist entrepreneurship but also from its various derivative forms such as cooperatives, social enterprises, and mutual health insurance. This section pays particular attention to the economic models that underpin commons. Commons take many different forms and are based on a variety of economic approaches, which can be divided into three major groups: full-market models, nonmarket models, and hybrid models. These underlying models of commons-based entrepreneurship are characterized by three main features: shared and inclusive (rather than exclusive) ownership, cooperative decision-making (rather than recourse to the principles of hierarchy and authority), and an objective of satisfying people's needs while respecting ecological balance (instead of merely making profit).

The third and final section outlines the methodology of the book. Emphasizing empirical analyses in different fields and locations in Sub-Saharan Africa, the range of disciplines employed has been extended to include socioanthropology, anthropology of law, political science, history, geography, urban planning, philosophy, and literature. Indeed, it is through this multidisciplinary approach that the book seeks to understand the dynamics of commons in African territories and how they are inserted into complex social and political ecosystems. This book seeks to be empirical as well as theoretical and political, and the methodology that has been adopted is based on the interplay between field analyses and theoretical conceptualizations at the frontiers of knowledge on commons. Finally, this section presents the general organization of the book.

The Concept of Commons: Origins and Scope

In order to grasp the concept of commons, it is prudent to look back to the origin of the term *commons*, which means turning to England in the Middle Ages. At that time, rural areas were marked by the existence of "lands of commons." Inhabitants of villages who were located on this unenclosed land or its immediate surroundings had the rights to use or take resources from it (e.g., fish in rivers and lakes, game in forests, fruit from fruit trees, pastures, the right to glean). These rights, which were customary and regulated by usage, disappeared between the sixteenth and nineteenth centuries because of the enclosure movement,[1] both private and parliamentary, which established the primacy of private property in its exclusive form (Neeson 1996; Thompson 1993).

The evolution of land tenure in the United Kingdom took place against the backdrop of the consolidation of the parliamentary monarchy in England, colonial expansion, and rapid industrialization—key features of modernity as it emerged in the nineteenth century. This led to a reconfiguration of commons in Europe, which was accompanied by changes in sociopolitical structures and power relations. It also saw the gradual construction of the liberal market-economy democracies, which are referred to as "the modern Western world" in the remainder of the book (Barkawi and Laffey 2006; Larner and Walters 2004; Teschke 2003; Walters 2012).

The Pioneering Work of Ostrom

Commons initially reappeared as a concept in the 1960s (box 1.1), but it gained momentum starting with the Annapolis conference (1983) organized by the National Research Council of the United States. This conference launched the revival of the theory of the commons (Coriat 2013). Based on field surveys in the tropics and subtropics, it hypothesized that these regions were being subject to enclosure movements at that time. These were similar to those experienced in Europe in the previous century, encouraged by structural adjustment policies. Subsequent empirical investigations showed that the destruction of commons results in rural exodus, overpopulation in cities, and various disruptions to people's lifestyles.

Ostrom, charged with drawing conclusions from the lessons of Annapolis, proposed a characterization of the concept of "commons" on these bases, to which she later added a series of refinements. She characterizes commons using three shared attributes (Ostrom 1990):[2]

- The existence of a shared resource, whether it already exists (e.g., a lake, a forest, or a pasture) or is created (e.g., irrigation systems or drinking water supply). This precondition presupposes a form of sharing and therefore of ownership that is different from the exclusive form that has become dominant today.

- Rights and obligations over this resource, distributed to individuals or groups, which Ostrom would later codify under the concept of a "bundle of rights" (Ostrom and Schlager 1992). These rights and obligations are essentially usage and extraction rights associated with the shared resource.

- A form of governance[3] that allows these rights and obligations to be respected and provides for the long-term preservation of the resource and the ecosystem to which it belongs.

BOX 1.1

The Emergence of the Concept of "Commons"—A Historical Perspective

In the 1960s, American environmentalist theories denounced the degradation of natural resources and the problems of congestion, pollution, and overcrowding. In 1968, this gave rise to the still widely held theory of the "tragedy of the commons"[a] (Hardin 1968). This theory is based on the idea that society is shaped by interactions between people who are motivated solely by individual strategies to maximize their self-interest. Therefore, what Hardin refers to as "commons" is necessarily doomed to degradation. These reflections support the idea of the exclusive ownership of land that classic liberal political economy has promoted since the eighteenth century.

The beginning of the 1970s saw this paradigm called into question. The Sahel experienced exceptional droughts that created episodes of mass famine and major intracontinental migratory movements. The US Agency for International Development, which invested massively in the region, explained the Sahelian crisis as resulting from the traditional values of the nomadic groups who were expanding their herds on arid land, combined with strong population growth spurred on by Western development aid. This Malthusian catastrophe would become the dominant explanatory model for the Sahelian crisis over the course of the decade (Locher 2016). The work of development anthropologists, however, has pointed to other causal factors, including an extreme climatic phase and government-led campaigns of sedentarization and forced displacement. These reflections have been accompanied by the emergence of a new paradigm, that of community management, which promotes the idea of relying on vernacular systems for the regulation of natural resources. In 1985, the US National Academy of Sciences organized the Panel on Common Property Resource Management, which sought to propose a new analytical framework based on the paradigm of commons (Bromley 2008).

a. See the contextualization of Hardin's proposal in Ingold (2008).

Ostrom favors a conception of institutions centered on the notion of rules, understood as "shared understandings by actors about *enforced* prescriptions concerning what actions (or outcomes) are *required, prohibited,* or *permitted*" (Ostrom and Basurto 2011, 319). For Ostrom, rules construct social structures by defining positions, along with the rights and obligations attached to those positions (Weinstein 2013). In a seminal article written in 1992, Ostrom and Schlager distinguish between three levels (Ostrom and Schlager 1992). The operational level concerns the rules that directly influence users' daily decisions: it includes the right to physical access to the area and withdrawal rights for each user. The collective choice level concerns the rules for elaborating principles and policies for managing the common resource: it includes the right to management (defining the level and conditions of withdrawals) and the right to exclusion (access, loss, or transferability of individual rights). The constitutional level concerns the rules that define how the resource is governed, such as who is entitled to it: it includes the right to alienate (authorizing the sale or lease of either of the two previous rights). Ostrom and Schlager define four types of actors according to the rights they hold: the owner (who holds all five rights), the proprietor (to whom the lease has been granted and who therefore holds all rights except the right to alienation), the claimant (who holds the right to manage the resource as well as the right to harvest and access it), and, finally, authorized users (who only hold the right to access and withdrawal).

Without going into detail here, we contend that the three attributes with which Ostrom characterizes commons render Hardin's (1968) proposal of the "tragedy of the commons" invalid. Ostrom's (1990) own critique of Hardin draws attention to the confusion between, on the one hand, ungoverned resources subject to the tragedy of open access and, on the other hand, commons whose governance arrangements protect resources from predation (box 1.2).

Ostrom, Gardner, and Walker (1994, 7) specify that the concept of "commons" is encountered in all situations where resources are characterized by both "high subtractability" (elements of the overall resource can be taken away unit by unit, such as fish from a lake) and "difficult exclusion" (it is difficult for individuals or groups to oppose the taking of these resources). Based on Samuelson's (1954) categories, which she modifies and redefines, she then proposes the typology of goods shown in table 1.1.

BOX 1.2

Alienation Rights—A Right Like Any Other?

The right to alienate property (i.e., the right to transfer it to a third party, usually in return for payment) is at the heart of the long-standing confrontation between the theorists of the legal realist school and the advocates of exclusive ownership. For the latter, even in situations of shared use rights, the right to alienate must be seen as the central attribute of ownership: as soon as this right is established and persists, the other attributes (various shared use rights) play only a secondary role (Orsi 2013). In contexts where different rights coexist, the question is whether the right to alienate always implies the loss of usage rights previously associated with the property that is involved in the transaction to a third party. If this is the case, the resource in question can be considered subject to "strong" ownership, where the "exclusive" character has not been undermined by the existence of shared use rights. If the transfer to a third party does not cancel the "easements" constituted by the shared use rights, the right to alienate does not then take precedence over the other rights and constitutes an attribute like any other of the general bundle of rights. We shall see that this distinction is central to the characterization of land-based commons (chapter 2) as well as commons of housing in urban areas (chapter 3).

Table 1.1 **Ostrom's Typology of Goods**

	Easy exclusion	Difficult exclusion
High subtractability	Private goods	Common-pool resources
Low subtractability	Club goods	Public goods

Source: Ostrom, Gardner, and Walker 1994, 7.

Goods defined as CPRs[4] are, according to Ostrom, those for which the constitution of institutions allowing their management and administration in the form of commons is most appropriate. Ostrom and Basurto (2011) analyze the institutional dynamics that a CPR may undergo during the gradual shift from a norm-regulated system (practical norms, informal norms)[5] to a more complex arrangement structured by a hierarchical set of rules (Weinstein 2013) in response to a collective action problem (Moritz 2016).

Ostrom's research program on commons has therefore made it possible to identify "action situations" (often called "arenas")[6] where the dilemmas linked to CPRs can be resolved through forms of cooperation and self-organization. Ostrom therefore spent many years developing a tool, the so-called Institutional Analysis and Development framework, for organizing the work of researchers, making it possible to compare the different analyses of socioecological systems (Ostrom 2009) and to direct activity toward more sustainable modes of governance according to the situation being studied (Ostrom 2007b).

In this way, through her work on commons and beyond, Ostrom is a theorist of institutions. She has constructed an institutionalist theory based on taking diversity and complexity into account as major dimensions of institutions (Weinstein 2013). She is a defender of the vision that the market and the state are not the only possible means by which economic relationships and organization can take place and that, in the face of collective action problems, the concerned parties can develop arrangements leading to the best results by themselves, instead of seeking recourse to a public intervention (Antona and Bousquet 2017; Chanteau and Labrousse 2013). From her earliest works and throughout the whole of her career, she has defended the idea of the efficiency of systems based on principles of polycentricity (i.e., on the interplay between different decision-making "arenas" in which the three levels of rules can be deliberated). She reaffirmed this vision in the speech she gave upon receiving the Sveriges Riksbank Prize in Economic Sciences in 2009.

Conditions for the Robustness of Commons

Commons, as Ostrom has identified and studied them from the outset of her work, have three attributes:

- For the most part, they refer to land-based commons: pastures, forests, lakes, rivers, and herds of free-ranging animals.

- They are generally small and possess well-defined boundaries.
- They are managed by communities of inhabitants or residents who, to varying degrees, depend on commons and maintain it, in the sense that they ensure that the ecosystem, despite the withdrawals that are made, is not altered or damaged. In some cases (e.g., shared irrigation systems), the community that manages commons may also decide to improve and enrich them.

Ostrom has extensively examined the conditions for the robustness of commons in the face of internal crises linked to the exacerbation of conflicts of interest between participants and external events that lead to imbalances in the functioning of commons. This reflection led to the definition of eight principles ("design principles," box 1.3) (Ostrom 1990, 90–102).

These eight principles, to which Ostrom would later add eight threats (Ostrom 1999), demonstrate conditions that are favorable or unfavorable to the long-term sustainability of the dynamics involved in common property. Based on observations of many different situations, they highlight the institutional regularities in commons systems that have been upheld over time. They indicate the factors that explain the greater or lesser robustness[7] of commons. They are not prescriptive, as Ostrom often reminds us. Nor do they necessarily define commons, which is made up of processes that are continually being reinvented.

The reflections on commons have given rise to a rich literature that goes beyond the usual economics frameworks, taking legal, social, and political issues into account. Agrawal (2003), for example, has listed some 30 criteria that have been identified as essential in the literature on commons (notably in Baland and Platteau 2007; Ostrom 1990; Wade 1988).

The Close Links between Commons, the Preservation of Ecosystems, Social Issues, and the Welfare of Future Generations

From the start, the concept of commons has had a close relationship with ecology, the preservation of ecosystems, and therefore the issue of public welfare. Even when commons only concern a restricted community around a limited and well-defined resource, their constitution intends to guarantee the management of the resource so that its reproduction is protected in the long term.

Ostrom's work goes beyond the question of sustainable resource management from an ecological point of view. Her questions are concerned more broadly with the search for effective solutions to situations that she refers to as "social dilemmas,"[8] which mix and match environmental, economic, social, and democratic issues at multiple levels.

BOX 1.3

The Eight Design Principles

Here we will provide a brief summary of the *eight design principles* Ostrom defined, organizing them according to the role that these rules play.[a]

Principles concerning the scope of validity of rules and their suitability for the local conditions:

1. Clear definition of the purpose of the community and its members. This is a prerequisite, without which no one knows what is being managed and by whom.
2. Consistency between the rules for the common resource and the nature of that resource. The rules for management and provision must be clear and appropriate to the nature of the shared resource.

Principles for the governance of commons:

3. Collective ways of organizing decision-making that allow most of the appropriators[b] to participate in the decision-making process.
4. Effective management (of the resource) by managers who themselves are appropriators or held accountable to them.
5. A graduated scale of sanctions for those (among the appropriators) who violate community rules.
6. Inexpensive and easily implemented conflict resolution mechanisms.

Principles for prioritizing and combining rules:

7. Self-organization of the community according to rules that have been accepted and recognized by higher authorities.
8. In the case of larger common-pool resources, multilevel organization of ownership, procurement, monitoring, enforcement, conflict resolution, and governance activities.

Three strong ideas emerge from these principles: First, commons include a dimension of self-organization that must involve the largest possible number of participants. Second, commons must be thought of as places where conflicts of interest exist, whether real or virtual, and must be organized as such. According to Ostrom, the purpose of sanctions is primarily to remind people of their obligation to conform to the rules, hence their initial low severity, adapted to the perceived intention of the transgressor to abide by the rules again. Finally, commons maintain relations with other established forms, including public authorities. The robustness of commons depends on the adherence of members to the rules that govern them and that cannot be imposed by an external authority. However, these rules must not ignore the rule of law—the laws and regulations that lie above them in the hierarchy.

a. See the "Design Principles" entry in Cornu, Orsi, and Rochfeld (2021).
b. For the distinction between "users" and "appropriators," see Colin, Lavigne Delville, and Léonard (2022).

This intrinsic connection between commons, the preservation of ecosystems, social concerns, and protecting the interests of future generations is a crucial point. It is taking this into account that makes it possible to distinguish commons from other forms of associationalism (or "communitarianism") organized with a view to the immediate appropriation of a good and its predation for the benefit of a few. Subsequent theorists of the concept of commons have therefore worked to characterize commons as goods that are managed and administered in such a way as to protect the interests of not only current users but also future generations. This is the definition given by, among others, the Italian jurist Rodotà, who had been entrusted with the mission of convening a senatorial commission to redefine and clarify the notion of "property" in the Italian civil code (Lucarelli 2013; Rodotà 2016).

Decision-Making Methods Based on Processes of Deliberation

The constitution of a commons is synonymous with the institution of a decision-making process based on deliberative principles. Such decision-making processes are necessary in order to change the rules as required or to decide on sanctions against those who violate all or some of their rights and obligations. It is not a relationship of authority as in most organizations (Simon 1951). Ostrom thus argues that these principles of deliberation must include the "voice" of those with the least guaranteed rights, such as the appropriators. It is a demonstration of the "wisdom of crowds" principle (Surowiecki 2004), according to which the resolution of a problem can be achieved more effectively through collective deliberation than by an individual who may or may not be involved (Dupont and Jourdain 2022).

The use of the voice principle, which necessarily must be plural, appears to be both integral to commons and a precondition for their cohesion and durability. Here, Ostrom is introducing a distinctive feature, among others (Weinstein 2013), from the new institutional economics (Williamson 2000) with which some of her work has been compared. Hirschman's (1972) work on voice can be usefully mobilized to help understand the issues at stake in the governance of commons. In his 1972 book, Hirschman defends the idea that democratic and political mechanisms are more effective regulators than the market and competition, including in organizations and companies in charge of producing goods. He introduces the notion of voice, which, according to him, has two advantages: first, it gives the organization time to undertake the necessary reforms, and second, it can help to determine the nature of the actions that should be undertaken to enable the company to regain the trust of its employees and customers. In the wake of Hirschman's intuitions, organizing opportunities to speak up is the preferred means of coordination in the governance structures of the majority of commons,[9] which, by their very nature, accommodate interests that are not always immediately aligned.

Beyond deliberation, some commons introduce a new form of contributory democracy that recognizes contribution as a criterion for participating in decision-making. The traditional boundaries between those who provide (a resource, service, or knowledge) and those who receive are modified. This is particularly the case with new types of commons, which we will see later, and with the resources offered by peer-to-peer sharing as a type of knowledge production that breaks with traditional forms of organization based on specialized individuals (Bauwens 2015).

Deliberation is at the heart of the social practices of what the Anglo-American literature refers to as "commoning." Commons manage systems of resources, material and immaterial, but also the social relations, internal and external, of the community (Aubert and Botta 2022). "Commoning" refers to acts of mutual support, conflict, negotiation, communication, and experimentation (Bollier and Helfrich 2015). It is a precondition for the emergence of commons (Fontaine 2019). It is an iterative process based on trial and error as well as individual and collective learning (Antona and Bousquet 2017).

Work on Commons across Different Fields
Since the seminal work of Ostrom and the researchers of the Bloomington School[10] at Indiana University, the academic literature on commons has undergone numerous developments in various fields. Many different approaches (empirical, theoretical, and normative) have been adopted, mobilizing various disciplines (economics, sociology, history, law, philosophy). The recently published *Dictionnaire des biens communs* (*Dictionary of Communal Goods*) considers the multiple registers that commons are a part of today through mapping out the concepts used in each discipline (Cornu, Orsi, and Rochfeld 2021). The work brings together a corpus of definitions and analyses relating to concepts and their multiple interpretations according to the disciplines, as well as to concrete commons-based practices.

For Ostrom, no typology can adequately describe the diversity of possible situations in which commons emerge. Several attempts at characterization and categorization have nevertheless been proposed. One example is Bollier, who distinguishes between six categories of commons: subsistence commons, indigenous commons, social and civic commons, economic enterprises embedded in commons, commons under legal guarantee, and digital commons (Bollier 2014). Another distinction, proposed by Coriat, is based on the nature of the resource. The "tangible commons" is organized around rival and exhaustible resources, the concern for preservation of which is at the root of collective action. The "informational commons," made up of nonrival resources (information and knowledge), is constructed more to ensure the extension and enrichment of commons: such is the case, for example, of Wikipedia and OpenStreetMap, which are universally accessible and designed to be continually improved (Coriat 2015). In his cartography of the new commons, Hess also suggests using the nature of the resource as a basis and distinguishes seven "sectors": the "cultural commons," the "neighborhood commons," the "knowledge commons," the "social commons," the "infrastructure commons," the "market commons," and the "global commons" (Hess 2008). A large body of work continues to conceptualize emerging forms of commons as possible prototypes by bringing together theoretical analyses and disparate empirical instances.[11]

The proposed classifications, presented here in a nonexhaustive manner, bear witness to the diversity and multiplicity of forms of commons in contemporary contexts. These categories are not intended to be rigid and are always open to improvement. For example, the dichotomy between material and immaterial commons begins to lose relevance when many material commons have an immaterial dimension and vice versa (Buchs et al. 2019). More generally, Bollier reminds us that "classification schemes tend to impose an overly tidy, regularized and intellectual understanding of commoning, which . . . is ultimately experiential and historically situated" (Bollier 2014, 128).

In this book, therefore, we do not propose a single, fixed categorization of commons. However, we do intend to deal with issues proper to specific fields in different chapters, on the premise that each type of commons generally mixes and combines several of these issues. Thus, fab labs share machines (material commons) but also experiences (knowledge commons) while contributing to multiple online resources and communities based around free software (digital commons).

Commons as New Forms of Entrepreneurship

Hybrid Economic Models
Three major economic models underlie these new entrepreneurial forms.[12] They can be applied in different ways and intersect in numerous hybrid forms.

A full-market model
The full-market model applies to situations involving shared resources (e.g., irrigated fields, pastures, or fisheries) where participants in the common pool value the units of resource taken from the common pool on the market as they see fit, as a result of the rights they have been allocated (box 1.4).

A nonmarket model
In its general form, this model is based on the gift and the countergift (Mauss 2007). It is most appropriate in cases where access to the resource can be universal, allowing for fundraising from large numbers of people and potential donors: Wikipedia, Framasoft, and OpenStreetMap provide examples of this. These organizations conduct public fundraising "campaigns," in return for which they make their products—usually software and specialized information processing tools—available to the public.

BOX 1.4

Examples of Commons in Sub-Saharan Africa Operating on the Full-Market Model

The Solidarity Lending Mechanism in Sub-Saharan Africa

Some financial services, such as solidarity lending, have proven successful in several Sub-Saharan African countries (Traoré, Bocoum, and Tamini 2020). Solidarity-based lending involves a group of individuals who organize themselves to act as guarantors for each other to obtain financing in national currency from a financial institution. The amount requested (between 80,000 and 150,000 euros in Burkina Faso, for example) depends on the needs of the members of the group (agricultural inputs, equipment, income-generating activities). The guarantee can be up to 25 percent of this amount, and interest rates vary between 10 percent and 18 percent (FAO 2012). The organization takes care of credit distribution and repayment to the financial institution. Repayment rates in West Africa are estimated to be between 95 percent and 100 percent (FAO 2012). This system helps to maintain trust between members of the organization and with financial institutions.

Commons-Based Entrepreneurship in the Senegal River Valley

In the precolonial period, land and resource management in Senegal was carried out according to collective, family, and kinship criteria, which were grounded in practices specific to each community. After independence and the colonial government's unsuccessful attempts to impose registration and individual property systems, the political authorities opted for a concept based on the common appropriation of land at the national level, on the one hand, and the recognition of the right to use it for all members of the community, on the other. While some communities continue to apply local land tenure practices, others facilitate individual land acquisitions to the detriment of certain rural activities and communities. To promote a better application of these principles and sustainable land governance, several tools and approaches have been tested since the end of the 1990s in certain areas of the country (see chapter 2). They made it possible to develop economic entrepreneurship based on jointly managed resources by acting at three levels of security: the transfer of social and land security tools; the establishment of a local financing line, as well as the transfer of capacities to manage it, for the realization of infrastructure that is essential for the development of economic activity; and the organization and development of local actors' capacities for better insertion in the most profitable sectors locally. This system initially provided the basis for a major part of Senegal's rice production before being extended to agrosilvopastoral resources in nonirrigated areas over the past decade.

This form of appeal for a donation or subsidy by a third-party contributor can also be envisaged for commons targeting specialized communities, such as tontines (box 1.5). In this case, the financing allows free access, or access at very low cost, to the products and services provided. This model refers to solidarity practices that act as a social springboard to enable a group to pool the assets it has and to share the constraints. More generally, these models allow entities (associations, nongovernmental organizations, foundations) to fundraise through the public or through intentional donors (e.g., international foundations, states, and local authorities) and to offer access—often free of charge—to open and shared resources such as health care, for example.

BOX 1.5

Examples of Commons in Sub-Saharan Africa Operating on the Nonmarket Model

Tontines in Sub-Saharan Africa

African tontines are a form of mutual protection and solidarity that are established through a relationship of debt (Lelart 1990). They are based on the voluntary decision of individuals to regularly pool a certain amount of their disposable income. There is then a reciprocal debt and an advance from certain members to others. The sum collected is allocated to the participants in turn, who spend it as they wish (for consumption, on particular events, as working capital for an activity, or for a new income-generating activity). Their modalities are variable and evolving (Servet 1996). This rotating savings system, which is widely practiced on the continent, is now available in the form of digital applications in some countries.

DNDi—A Foundation for Access to Medicines in Sub-Saharan Africa

In November 2018, the European Medicines Agency issued its approval for the registration of fexinidazole, a new drug to combat sleeping sickness (or human African trypanosomiasis). Fexinidazole, which is available only as a tablet, is the result of a partnership between the Drugs for Neglected Diseases Initiative (DNDi), Sanofi, and experts from endemic countries. Since its inception, the DNDi's funding policy has been based on the following principles: at least 50 percent of the budget must come from the public funding system, and no single donor can contribute more than 25 percent of all donations. To ensure independence from donors, the DNDi seeks a variety of funding sources—cash contributions, in-kind contributions, grants, sponsorships, and bequests or any other ethical funding source. The DNDi refuses direct grants from the pharmaceutical industry, not only to preserve its independence but also to prioritize in-kind contributions from pharmaceutical companies such as access to chemical libraries or product registration (Abecassis et al. 2019).

We can also mention certain forms of association, on a smaller scale, that are based on the direct and unpaid labor of families or communities that maintain a shared resource (e.g., a field, a well, a water table) in common. The management of this resource then mainly takes place "outside the market" for the personal use of participants in commons. Free labor and shared products follow jointly established rules and are forms of production and exchange based on gifts and countergifts. It should be noted, however, that in many situations, these forms of cooperation can include relations of domination, which is not without similarities to the problems of the domestic and "free" labor of women in the household (Federici 2020). The exercise of voice to end these distortions is then a condition for the sustainability of the common.

A hybrid model
The hybrid model brings together different approaches that combine market transactions (subscriptions and prices designed as monetary compensation for certain services) and services that are voluntary, free, shared, or exchanged (box 1.6).

This model differs from the full-market model. Market transactions are not the only source of income for commons or even necessarily the primary source. It is also different from the classic capitalist market model: market activity is not aimed at profit making and the accumulation of gains but at feeding the needs of the communities involved in the production of the common resource.

In certain cases, forms of contribution in kind or in monetary form confer rights of access to the shared resource: the sum of these contributions may constitute the main income of the common resource. These contributions may even make it possible to produce a resource that does not yet exist in the common pool, such as by drilling a well or building a community school.

In other cases, in addition to membership fees or general shareholding when the social capital of the enterprise allows for it, a certain amount of free labor allows costs to be lowered and members to have easier access to jointly managed resources. Market transactions are essential for the entity under consideration to function, but this also includes free labor for the organization to operate, as in the case of the hybrid (social, cultural, or innovation) sites described in chapter 4.

Characterizing Commons-Based Entrepreneurship
These archetypal models are deployed through distinctive forms of entrepreneurship, which we call "commons-based entrepreneurship," and have the characteristic feature of responding to a collective action problem by

BOX 1.6

Examples of Commons in Sub-Saharan Africa Operating on the Hybrid Model

School Management Committees

The literature review carried out by Dupain in 2021 for the United Nations Educational, Scientific, and Cultural Organization (UNESCO) has shown that the literature ascribes a major role to parents in financing education and in decision-making in schools (Dupain 2021). It highlights the paradigm shift enabled by the development of school management committees (SMCs) in Sub-Saharan Africa and the partnership between professionals, who may be in the minority, and parents in three main areas: the mobilization of additional resources and voluntary work to support school projects; the strategic governance and oversight of the school, particularly monitoring the school's projects; and the management and administrative and financial control of the school. The difficulties with these structures are the subject of an extensive literature, particularly on the actual levels of stakeholder participation, on the democratic processes at work, on the degrees of control and support from institutional actors (decentralized services of the central state and local authorities), and finally on the linkages with parent-teacher associations, through which parents' contributions have historically been channeled. Nevertheless, a significant part of the SMCs' activities is devoted to mobilizing additional resources, mainly from families, in the form of money or volunteer labor through the development of school projects and action plans and budgets. Parents also often take financial responsibility for the school's needs in terms of maintenance, upkeep, and the construction of classrooms and sanitation facilities.

Business Models for Third Places: The Example of GreenLab in Nigeria

The GreenLab was created in 2017 to provide Nigerians with the opportunity to learn by themselves how to solve their everyday problems (such as poor access to electricity, access to water, or access to digital education). The fab lab is an open and collaborative physical space that gives a community of nonspecialists access to digital machines of varying degrees of sophistication (assisted design and drawing software, laser cutting machines, digital milling machines, three-dimensional printers, vinyl cutting machines). The place thus allows the design and prototyping of objects and projects. To date, 20,000 students have been trained by the GreenLab community in eight Nigerian states. Like many third places (see chapter 4), the GreenLab's economic model is hybrid. It relies on the founder's personal finances, financial support from relatives and his parish, but also on income from the sale of technological parts via an e-commerce site.

mobilizing CPRs. These involve implementing organizational and institutional mechanisms for the design, production, and exchange of products and services that are necessary and useful for satisfying needs while respecting the general interest and the common good. Here it is understood that the organization of behaviors is geared toward ways of producing, inhabiting, and living in the world that guarantee the collective development of human communities and the ecosystems of which they are stakeholders and in which they act and are embedded.

Main distinguishing features
Commons-based entrepreneurship differs from entrepreneurship and enterprise in their classic capitalist forms in three key respects (box 1.7):

- **Exclusive ownership vs. bundle of rights.** Commons-based entrepreneurship is based on a bundle of rights that ensures access to and shared control over the tools, instruments, and resources that underpin the enterprise. This distinguishes it from classic entrepreneurship, including individual entrepreneurship. This bundle of rights undermines the exclusive nature of ownership, which is marginal and subordinate when it exists. This form of entrepreneurship presupposes actors engaged in collective actions with shared objectives. Often, regardless of who holds the title(s), the aim is to secure the usage rights of the individuals or communities concerned over productive resources (e.g., grazing land, rivers, ponds, digital data, resources, and technical equipment).[13]

- **Profit-seeking vs. satisfaction of basic needs.** The initiators and participants seek the satisfaction of their needs, or the needs of the people for whom the projects are intended, more than lucrativeness and acquiring wealth. It may be necessary to engage in monetary and market exchanges. In these instances, it is as an instrument put at the service of the achievement of the objectives that the community of participants in commons has set itself and does not constitute an end in itself. This distinction is fundamental in differentiating, for example, open-source software models and the productive models of the digital commons (Broca 2018; see chapter 5).

- **Principle of authority and hierarchy vs. organization of voice.** The internal relationships and coordination modes of commons are not based on hierarchy and the principle of authority but are instead organized around voice and the search for "horizontal" modes of coordination.

Multiple and hybrid institutional forms
These include a wide range of institutional and organizational forms that can be assembled into a variety of hybrids. They can be perfectly informal

BOX 1.7

Commons-Based Entrepreneurship and the Social Solidarity Economy—Conceptual Distinctions

The notion of "commons-based entrepreneurship" is closely related to the entrepreneurial activities of the social solidarity economy (SSE). A central feature shared by commons and SSE enterprises is the desire to marginalize the power of capital in the governance of the enterprise. Cooperatives within the SSE (which also includes mutual health insurance and associations) are pioneering and advanced in this respect. Innovations such as the one-person/one-vote principle or nonshareable funds are congruent with the philosophy and constitution of commons as we have defined them. In fact, many commons in France choose to adopt the status of Société coopérative d'intérêt collectif (collective interest cooperative), a status introduced in the 2014 Hamon Law on the SSE, when they seek to become formally established.

However, two differences should be noted (Coriat and Filippi 2022). First, cooperatives, like mutual health insurance, are based on salaried employment, that is, on a relationship of authority that is central to the employment contract (Simon 1951). In commons, on the other hand, the search for "horizontal" modes of coordination and the expression of the voice of each of the partners prevail as standard practices. Second, cooperatives, since their initial appearance in nineteenth-century France, have aimed to improve the working conditions and well-being of employees and, more generally, the standard of living and access to consumer goods. This is why many consumer cooperatives offer rebates (price reductions) to members of the cooperative. Commons, on the other hand, are created primarily out of a concern for the preservation of socioecological systems and, by extension, common goods.

Although the origins and initial objectives of SSE enterprises and commons are distinct, over time there have been some genuine connections between the two types of entities, as their practices and innovations feed off each other. There is frequent overlap between commons and SSE cooperatives, mutual health insurance, and associations, but it is not consistent because of the diversity of practices and models (values, aims) that each of them carries.

---

forms of cooperation, dictated by practical norms. More codified institutional forms such as associations, cooperatives, or social enterprises can be harnessed in these hybrid formations, which are frequently complex (box 1.8). In many cases, however, this type of entrepreneurship is based on simple associations of families or residents for the administration or production of a shared resource.

Forms of Commons-Based Entrepreneurship for the Right to Food

The right to food is one of the best established and most codified rights. Yet nearly 1 billion people, or one in nine, suffer from malnutrition. There are three main reasons for this. First, the highly concentrated and capital-intensive food markets are not geared toward meeting basic needs. Second, property rights in their exclusive form, like those deriving from the "free trade" enshrined in the free trade treaties, have a de facto primacy and a domineering effect on social rights. Finally, the subject of international law is not the individual (to whom the right to food is theoretically attributed) but the national state.

In this context, various nongovernmental organizations and associations, which often operate as joint ventures, have set themselves objectives in the fight against malnutrition, particularly in Sub-Saharan Africa. Misola, for example, is a French association that has registered a trademark for a food supplement deployed in West Africa to prevent malnutrition in young children under the age of five. The flour is made entirely from locally grown ingredients and is produced in the villages themselves. In this way, Misola helps to set up women's cooperatives in the villages that produce and sell food produced with local resources at very low prices. The Misola brand, registered by the association, is provided free of charge to any user who undertakes to respect strict specifications in the production process. Nutri'zaza is a social enterprise under Malagasy law committed to the fight against chronic malnutrition in Madagascar. Its social utility objectives are stated in its statutes (Coriat et al. 2019).

Objectives, Methodology, and Organization of the Book

Objectives and Position of the Study

Three complementary objectives

The study has three complementary objectives: an empirical objective, a conceptual objective, and a policy objective.

- The first objective is empirical and consists of observing practices and experiences of forms of commons and commons-based entrepreneurship in different contexts in Sub-Saharan Africa. The chapters examine three dimensions of commons at different levels of granularity: a technical dimension (objectives, conditions of emergence, resources mobilized, technical conditions of implementation), a socio-institutional dimension (definition of communities, decision-making systems, sharing and redistribution), and a territorial dimension (position and timeframe of the initiative, proximity links, and more extensive links with other types of organizations).

- The second objective is conceptual and consists in contributing to the theoretical reflections relating to the recent expansion of the concept of "commons" in various fields (urban commons, digital commons, service
commons) and to "commons-based entrepreneurship" by anchoring it in the
specific context in Africa.
- The third objective is normative and consists of examining the way in which
commons are integrated into public intervention in Sub-Saharan Africa and
the creation and implementation of public policies.

Our approach remains careful in several respects:

- The book compares an approach based on the interpretive model of commons with an understanding of the facts. It thus highlights, wherever legitimate and appropriate, situations where the concept provides a satisfactory
and novel account of empirical phenomena in Sub-Saharan Africa. It ana-
lyzes the opportunities that these forms of institutions represent in the face
of the continent's sustainable development challenges but also their limits,
the difficulties they encounter, and their weaknesses.
- The more conceptual approach aims at defining a clear boundary for the notions
of "commons" and "commons-based entrepreneurship" to avoid turning them
into a vague concept that is devoid of substance. The risk is all the greater when
we engage in a more normative approach. We adopt a realistic and pragmatic
stance here (Alix et al. 2018) and favor an approach based on a "triarchy" com-
prising the state, the market, and commons to achieve objectives deemed desirable, specifying the position and role to be played by each of these types of actors
as clearly as possible. This approach differs from more ideological perspectives
in which commons are considered a norm of political action and a way—in its
own right and exclusive of any other—of shaping society (Dardot and Laval
2014). In contrast, we argue that "commons" and "commons-based entrepreneurship" are, under these conditions, functional concepts to help conceive and
think about public action in Sub-Saharan African contexts. Because the potential
of these concepts remains largely unnoticed or underestimated, we felt it was
important and urgent to take an informed look at these initiatives.

A deliberately multidisciplinary approach

The multifaceted nature of the theme that is the subject of this book has natu-
rally led us to adopt a multidisciplinary approach and to compare different perspectives. This approach allows us to draw on the most recent work related to
the issues addressed in each of the chapters, such as environmental sciences for
chapter 2, urban studies for chapter 4, and the sociology of the digital for chapter 5. The choice of an Ivorian poet and philosopher for one of the afterwords to
this book aims to link the reflections proposed here in the economic and social
field to the wider space of imaginaries and representations that can be created
thanks to commons on the continent (box 1.9).

BOX 1.9

Commons in African Literature

African fiction allows us to see and experience commons. Since the 1950s, African novels have represented different modes of social, economic, political, and, in recent years, environmental breakdown, highlighting the inequalities and conflicts that fracture the continent. By inventing new ways of existing in society, or by reappropriating former modes of social, cultural, and political organization, African novels allow us to experience, through commons, connections within and between communities. All fiction is based on a "what if?" By formulating hypotheses about social and environmental bonds at the scale of novels, the latter offer us specific literary imaginaries and configurations (which rely on precise vocabularies and discursive strategies) that invite us to reflect on how we might embody these fictions in reality.

It would be a tall order to attempt to list the appearances of commons in African novels. Indeed, they are rarely present under that name but are more often encountered in the form of images and metaphors. A particularly significant example can be found in the work of the South African writer Zakes Mda. In *The Heart of Redness*, the population of a remote village is divided on whether to agree to the construction of a casino, which would create many jobs and bring in a financial windfall, at the expense of the environmental heritage of the hitherto unspoiled natural area in which the casino would be located. The solution to this debate is to create a cooperative run by women, based on the production and sale of handicrafts to local tourists. The economic structure of the cooperative allows the villagers to rally together and reach a consensus with the prospect of controlled wealth production, which would preserve the village's natural heritage.

In *L'Empire du mensonge* ("The Empire of Lies") by Senegalese author Aminata Sow Fall, commons is embodied in the yard, that essential space in the African rural landscape, located in the center of housing compounds, that represents a zone of strong social interaction for families as well as for their relatives. From the textual space provided by the plot to the yard as a concrete place of conviviality, it is thus literature itself that becomes a shared space, a privileged place for the construction of social bonds (Baudet 2020).

This multidisciplinary approach allows us to make use of the academic literature on fundamental issues for which the work of Ostrom and the Bloomington School has been criticized (Baron, Petit, and Romagny 2011):

- **Power relations between singular individuals acting within the framework of collective action.** Drawing on work in sociology and anthropology allows us to consider the interplay of actors in local arenas and policies, the dynamics of local authorities, and the relations between users and that between users and administrations (Olivier de Sardan 2021). In particular, work in the anthropology of law helps us to study and interpret existing legal systems, situations of legal pluralism, and bundles of rights (Le Roy 1978).

- **The nature and trajectory of states.** We engage with work in sociology, comparative politics, and history to look at the relationship between states and society (Gazibo and Thiriot 2009) and the different networks of actors who formulate a "public" problem, translate it into public policy, and implement these policies (Darbon et al. 2019). The use of development anthropology and sociological studies also allows us to take into account the fact that institutional trajectories in Sub-Saharan Africa are strongly marked by their colonial past, their diversity, and the dependence of their institutions on international aid (Colin, Lavigne-Delville, and Léonard 2022; Olivier de Sardan 2021; Valette et al. 2015). Finally, this perspective allows us to critically examine the development policies carried out in Sub-Saharan Africa by donors (Leyronas and Legroux 2019).

- **Interlocking scales and hybridity of rules.** Far from presenting a dogmatic vision of self-governance, we are interested in the hybrid nature of the modes of governance of commons. The literature in geography, political economy, governance studies, and the sociology of organizations allows us to refer to the hybridity of the levels of rules of the bundle of rights proposed in Ostrom's analysis (constitutional rules, rules of collective choice, operational rules).

Limitations of the work

This work is intended to be broad in scope. However, it is limited in several respects:

- Although the book assembles various disciplinary contributions, only a few chapters offer an interdisciplinary perspective and construct shared analytical frameworks both to describe the observed situations and to develop the concept from a theoretical point of view.

- Because the book favors entries by type of field (rural land, housing, urban, digital), a number of major cross-cutting themes such as inequality, gender, and poverty are not dealt with as such. However, these themes are present, in their cross-cutting nature, in certain chapters. Moreover, certain themes deserve additional research, particularly the ones related to the stakes of public service delivery, climate change adaptation, or biodiversity. Socioanthropological approaches would be particularly well suited to "document *implementation gaps*, unexpected effects, as well as discrepancies between official discourses data and actual practices" (Olivier de Sardan 2022).

- Because the book was conceived of as a tool for understanding the diversity of commons in Sub-Saharan Africa, the empirical chapters deal with a

variety of issues and analytical fields, each of which is the subject of extensive literature. Choices have been made by the authors to best serve the
topic at hand, but these choices may be frustrating for experts in the fields
covered.

- Similarly, the book does not go into much detail about the functioning of
the "communities" involved in the observed forms of commons.
Nevertheless, the authors do not have an idealized vision of the "communities" that are cited, and the reader will be able to find further details about
them (their emergence, homogeneity, trajectories, the politicization of
their resources) in the rich bibliography that served as a basis for the preparation of this book.

Our approach focuses on commons we have identified in Sub-Saharan
Africa and on the way in which these field experiments can constitute innovative forms of support for the development of commons-based entrepreneurship. The book offers an introduction to the ontologies and specific features
of Sub-Saharan African societies (see chapter 2 in particular). The conception
of commons adopted in this book differs from other approaches, which are
based on a relational ontology that rejects the opposition between humans
and nonhumans and the very concept of a "resource" as we have employed
it. Thus, approaches such as those that prevail through the qualifications of
Tsing's (2017) "latent commons," Papadopoulos's (2012) "eco-commons,"
Bresnihan's (2015) "more-than-human commons," or "undercommons"
(Harney and Moten 2013) have not been adopted here. Similarly, the work
conducted in legal sciences that focuses on modalities of the legal recognition
of nonhumans and nature as the subject of the law (Taylan 2018; Vanuxem
2018) is little addressed (see chapter 2).

Methodology of the Book
The methodology adopted is based on a reflexive approach with the aim of
integrating theory and observed practices (figure 1.1): our theoretical framework is informed by the observation of case studies, which continually enhances
this framework in turn. The wide range of case studies we have examined has
made it possible to build an argument establishing continuity between the different approaches and allowing us to consider the phenomenon in its entirety.
Without neglecting the contribution of theory, our approach therefore grants
priority to practices over concepts. It starts from real-life situations and ana-
lyzes the different forms of commons-based entrepreneurship that the social
organizations observed take part in and the ideas they generate in terms of new
resources and tools to ensure the social and ecological well-being of the communities concerned.

Figure 1.1 General Methodology of the Work

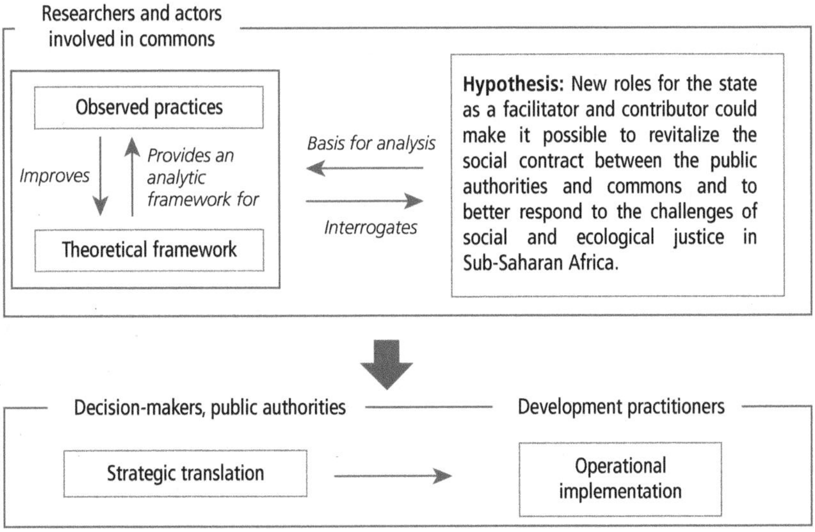

Researchers and actors involved in commons

Observed practices	**Hypothesis:** New roles for the state as a facilitator and contributor could make it possible to revitalize the social contract between the public authorities and commons and to better respond to the challenges of social and ecological justice in Sub-Saharan Africa.

Improves → ↑ *Provides an analytic framework for* ↓

Basis for analysis ←

Interrogates →

Theoretical framework

⬇

Decision-makers, public authorities ——————— Development practitioners

Strategic translation ——————→ Operational implementation

Source: Original figure for this publication.

Finally, these analyses lead to the hypothesis that new roles that the state can play (as a facilitator and partner), along with public institutions in general, could make it possible to profoundly revitalize the social contract between the public authorities and commons and thus better respond to the challenges of social justice and ecological transition in Sub-Saharan Africa.

By its broad thematic ambition and the strategic and political debate on the place of commons in the African societies of tomorrow, the proposed work differs from many existing studies on commons in the Global South, which mainly focus on case studies and often stop there.

General Organization of the Book

This book is the product of a collective endeavor and has resulted from several exchanges and collaborations, some of which are long-standing. It offers an overview of the forms of commons and commons-based entrepreneurship in Sub-Saharan Africa that is certainly not exhaustive. Nonetheless, it provides new and valuable material in many respects. Above all, it is a working tool for those (researchers, students, practitioners, specialists, public actors, politicians) who are looking for alternatives to the approaches promoted by the international community in Sub-Saharan Africa and often by African states themselves.

The book is structured into three main parts (table 1.2) that mark three different stages of the work:

- *An introductory and theoretical part* to situate and clarify the main issues within the book
- *A part presenting empirical analyses in different fields:* rural land tenure and natural resource management, urban land tenure and access to housing, urban spaces and access to education, and digital entrepreneurship and the internet commons
- *A more normative part,* dealing with the place of commons in African public policy, the arrangements between public actors and commons, and finally an action plan for international cooperation in support of new commons

In addition, background research papers (available on the World Bank's Open Knowledge Repository) open debates with authors not working in the field of commons. Their critical approaches and insights into the possible links between the commons research field and their respective work and academic fields introduce new perspectives for research. *Background research paper 1* (Olivier de Sardan 2022) focuses on the delivery of public services, and *background research paper 2* (Obura and Treyer 2022) examines international negotiation processes concerning biodiversity.

Each chapter of the book is based on original analyses by the authors and on a large body of academic and gray literature. Emphasis has been placed on the literature available in French, but numerous English-language references have also been used. The chapters include critical examinations of the issues, specific forms of analysis, case studies, and overviews of the various themes addressed.

Wherever possible, the chapters bring together researchers and practitioners of development or commons. This interdisciplinary spirit is a defining feature of the book and a major source of its relevance. This is reinforced by the substantial contribution African authors have made to the analyses presented here.

We have strived for editorial coherence while leaving the authors considerable room for maneuver. Each chapter has its own identity, in keeping with the authors' respective disciplinary approaches, and strikes a careful balance between empirical, theoretical, and normative objectives. Particular attention has been paid to the overall consistency of the epistemological positions of all the contributors to this book.

Table 1.2 **General Organization of the Book**

		Chapters	Authors
Part 1—Why this study	**Executive summary**	Overview	Stéphanie Leyronas Benjamin Coriat
	Chapter 1	Theoretical Framework, Methodology, and Structure of the Book	Benjamin Coriat Stéphanie Leyronas
Part 2—What we are talking about	**Chapter 2**	Land-Based Commons, the Basis for a Peaceful Form of Economic Development?	Mathieu Boche Patrick d'Aquino Nicolas Hubert Stéphanie Leyronas Sidy Mohamed Seck
	Chapter 3	Housing and the Future of Rural Land-Based Commons	Claire Simonneau Bérénice Bon Éric Denis Stéphanie Leyronas Issa Sory
	Chapter 4	Urban Commons: Reestablishing Social Ties in African Cities	Stéphanie Leyronas Alix Françoise Isabelle Liotard Lola Mercier Guiako Obin
	Chapter 5	Digital Commons and Entrepreneurship: Alternative or Complementary Approaches?	Jan Krewer Stéphanie Leyronas Thomas Mboa
Part 3—How to take action	**Chapter 6**	Commons, General Interest, and Public Policy: Issues for the State in Sub-Saharan Africa	Benjamin Coriat Mamoudou Gazibo Stéphanie Leyronas
	Chapter 7	Funders' Attitudes, Perceptions, and Actions: Taking Inspiration from the Commons-Based Approach	Stéphanie Leyronas Sophie Salomon
Afterwords	**Afterword 1**	The Commons: Choosing Solidarity and Looking Ahead	Tanella Boni
	Afterword 2	The African Commons at Global Crossroads	Thomas Mélonio Kako Nubukpo
Background	**Background research paper 1**	Delivering Public Interest Goods in Africa: Stopgap Measures, State Reforms and Commons	Jean-Pierre Olivier de Sardan
	Background research paper 2	A "Shared Earth" Approach to Put Biodiversity at the Heart of the Sustainable Development in Africa	David Obura Sébastien Treyer

Notes

1. Enclosures refer to the appropriation of resources or spaces intended for collective use by private owners or states. They can be commercial (e.g., land is confiscated for commercial purposes) or legal (e.g., the patenting of seeds).
2. For more details, see the "Commons" entry in Cornu, Orsi, and Rochfeld (2021).
3. We take the notion of governance in a descriptive sense—that is, as the result of a set of actions and decisions by heterogeneous actors and not as a normative ideal associated with transparency, ethics, and efficiency of public action (Pitseys 2010).
4. CPRs are to be distinguished from "common property regimes." In 2006, Hess and Ostrom wrote an article to clarify the frequent confusion between different terms, especially between *common property* and *open-access regimes*, *common-pool resources* and *common property regimes*, and *resource system* and *flow of resource units* (Hess and Ostrom 2006). They explain that the withdrawal, management, and ownership of common resources can take the form of a common property regime but that this is not mandatory. Conversely, not all common property regimes involve common resources.
5. Social norms (practical norms, informal norms) are, for Ostrom, attributes of communities and make it possible to overcome social dilemma situations that are specific to the management of common resources through their impact on behavior.
6. Ostrom (2007a) defines an "action arena" as a social space where participants interact, solve problems, and compete. Within this arena, an "action situation" is played out (i.e., a situation of interdependence between individuals whose potential actions jointly produce results).
7. The notion of "robustness," whose framework Ostrom would develop with John Anderies and Marco Janssen (Janssen, Anderies, and Ostrom 2007), refers to the maintenance of certain characteristics of the system when it is subjected to internal or external disturbances.
8. A social dilemma situation is defined as one in which the immediate self-interest of a particular individual and the interests of a larger social group come into direct conflict. In this situation, if all individuals attempt to maximize their own advantage at the expense of the group, at the end of the interaction, each member of the group has a much less favorable outcome than if the members of the group had adopted a cooperative strategy. For Ostrom, it is these situations that create the conditions par excellence for the emergence of commons.
9. In the case of the digital commons, a distinction must be made between the community of users, the community of contributors, and the community of administrators and funders (see chapter 5). While voice is the latter's mode of coordination, the former may use exit to mark their positions.
10. The Bloomington School, or "school of commons," is an interdisciplinary field of scholarly inquiry built around the Bloomington Workshop in Political Theory and Policy Analysis, the International Association for the Study of the Commons, and Ostrom (see the "Bloomington School" entry in Cornu, Orsi, and Rochfeld 2021). The *International Journal of Commons* is an outgrowth of this.
11. Examples include work on the "urban commons" (see, e.g., Borch and Kornberger 2015; Festa 2016; Foster 2011), the "cultural commons" (see, e.g., Hyde 2010;

Maurel and Lex 2018), the "knowledge commons" (see, e.g., Hess and Ostrom 2006; Madison, Frischmann, and Strandburg 2014), the "digital commons" (see, e.g., Aufrère et al. 2022; Benkler and Nissenbaum 2006; Broca 2013; Peugeot 2014), and the "social commons" (see in particular Defalvard 2017).

12. The groups of economic models presented here were identified and conceptualized through a research study entitled "Entreprendre en Communs" conducted from 2017 to 2021 by Benjamin Coriat. It was financed by Agence française de développement, Université Sorbonne Paris–Nord (Sorbonne University–Paris North), and the Crédit Coopératif bank. See http://encommuns.com/.

13. For example, "usi civici," as defined by the Italian Commercial Code, protect the rights of certain rural communities (regarding access to grasslands or watercourses, for example), regardless of who formally holds title to the area concerned (Marinelli 2018).

References

Abecassis, Philippe, Jean-François Alesandrini, Benjamin Coriat, Nathalie Coutinet, and Stéphanie Leyronas. 2019. "DNDi, a Distinctive Illustration of Commons in the Area of Public Health." AFD Research Papers Series 93. https://dndi.org/wp-content/uploads/2019/02/CommonsAreaPublicHealth_AFDResearchPaper_2019.pdf.

Agrawal, Arun. 2003. "Sustainable Governance of Common-Pool Resources: Context, Methods, and Politics." *Annual Review of Anthropology* 32: 243–62. https://doi.org/10.1146/annurev.anthro.32.061002.093112.

Alix, Nicole, Jean-Louis Bancel, Benjamin Coriat, and Frédéric Sultan. 2018. *Vers une république des biens communs?* Paris: Les Liens qui libèrent.

Antona, Martine, and François Bousquet, eds. 2017. *Une troisième voie entre l'État et le marché: Échanges avec Elinor Ostrom.* Versailles: Éditions Quæ.

Aubert, Sigrid, and Aurélie Botta. 2022. *Les communs: Un autre récit pour la coopération territoriale.* Versailles: Éditions Quæ.

Aufrère, Laura, Philippe Eynaud, Lionel Maurel, and Corinne Vercher-Chaptal. 2022. "Comment penser l'alternative au capitalisme de plateforme dans une logique de réencastrement polanyien?" *Revue française de socio-économie* 28 (1): 91–111. https://doi.org/10.3917/rfse.028.0091.

Baland, Jean-Marie, and Jean-Philippe Platteau. 2007. "Collective Action on the Commons: The Role of Inequality." In *Inequality, Cooperation, and Environmental Sustainability,* edited by Jean-Marie Baland, Pranab Bardhan, and Samuel Bowles, 10–35. Princeton, NJ: Princeton University Press.

Barkawi, Tarak, and Mark Laffey. 2006. "The Postcolonial Moment in Security Studies." *Review of International Studies* 32 (2): 329–52.

Baron, Catherine, Olivier Petit, and Bruno Romagny. 2011. "Le courant des 'common-pool resources': un bilan critique." In *Pouvoirs, sociétés et nature au sud de la Méditerranée,* edited by Tarik Dahou, Mohamed Elloumi, François Molle, Maher Gassab, and Bruno Romagny, 27–52. Paris: Karthala.

Baudet, Emeline. 2020. "Lire et écrire un monde délié: poétiques africaines d'une gouvernance écologique." PhD dissertation, Sorbonne Nouvelle University Paris 3.

Bauwens, Michel. 2015. *Sauver le monde: Vers une économie post-capitaliste avec le peer-to-peer.* Paris: Les Liens qui libèrent.

Benkler, Yochai, and Helen Nissenbaum. 2006. "Commons-based Peer Production and Virtue." *Journal of Political Philosophy* 14 (4): 394–419. https://doi.org/10.1111/j.1467-9760.2006.00235.x.

Bollier, David. 2014. *Think Like a Commoner: A Short Introduction to the Life of the Commons.* Gabriola, BC, Canada: New Society Publishers.

Bollier, David, and Silke Helfrich, eds. 2015. *Patterns of Commoning.* Amherst, MA: Levellers Press.

Borch, Christian, and Martin Kornberger, eds. 2015. *Urban Commons: Rethinking the City.* Abingdon: Routledge.

Bresnihan, Patrick. 2015. "The More-Than-Human Commons: From Commons to Commoning." In *Space, Power and the Commons,* edited by Samuel Kirwan, Leila Dawney, and Julian Brigstocke, 93–112. Abingdon: Routledge.

Broca, Sébastien. 2013. *Utopie du logiciel libre: Du bricolage informatique à la réinvention sociale.* Lorient: Le Passager clandestin.

Broca, Sébastien. 2018. "Du modèle du logiciel libre au modèle productif des communs. Les licences pair à pair contre le free software?" Working paper. https://hal.archives-ouvertes.fr/hal-03407580.

Bromley, Daniel W. 2008. "Formalising Property Relations in the Developing World: The Wrong Prescription for the Wrong Malady." *Land Use Policy* 26 (1): 20–7. https://doi.org/10.1016/j.landusepol.2008.02.003.

Buchs, Arnaud, Catherine Baron, Géraldine Froger, and Adrien Peneranda. 2019. "Dossier : communs (im)matériels. Conjuguer les dimensions matérielles et immatérielles des communs." *Développement durable et territoires* 10 (1). https://doi.org/10.4000/developpementdurable.17497.

Chanteau, Jean-Pierre, and Agnès Labrousse. 2013. "L'institutionnalisme méthodologique d'Elinor Ostrom: quelques enjeux et controverses." *Revue de la régulation. Capitalisme, institutions, pouvoirs* 14. https://doi.org/10.4000/regulation.10555.

Colin, Jean-Philippe, Philippe Lavigne Delville, and Éric Léonard. 2022. *Le foncier rural dans les pays du sud: Enjeux et clés d'analyse.* Montpellier: IRD Editions.

Coriat, Benjamin. 2013. "Le retour des communs." *Revue de la régulation. Capitalisme, institutions, pouvoirs* 14. https://doi.org/10.4000/regulation.10463.

Coriat, Benjamin, ed. 2015. *Le retour des communs. La crise de l'idéologie propriétaire.* Paris: Les Liens qui libèrent.

Coriat, Benjamin, and Maryline Filippi. 2022. "Commons and Cooperatives: Tensions, Complementarities, Convergences." *RECMA* 364 (2): 52–64. https://doi.org/10.3917/recma.364.0052.

Coriat, Benjamin, Nadège Legroux, Nicolas Le Guen, Stéphanie Leyronas, and Magali Toro. 2019. "Faire de l'alimentation un 'bien commun' : les enseignements tirés de trois expériences de lutte contre la malnutrition." In *Papiers de recherche,* 1–29. https://doi.org/10.3917/afd.leyro.2019.01.0001.

Cornu, Marie, Fabienne Orsi, and Judith Rochfeld, eds. 2021. *Dictionnaire des biens communs*. Paris: Presses Universitaires de France.

Darbon, Dominique, Rozenn Nakanabo Diallo, Olivier Provini, and Sina Schlimmer. 2019. "Un état de la littérature sur l'analyse des politiques publiques en Afrique." In *Papiers de recherche*, 1–36. Paris: Agence française de développement. https://doi .org/10.3917/afd.botto.2019.01.0001.

Dardot, Pierre, and Christian Laval. 2014. *Commun. Essai sur la révolution au XXIe siècle*. Paris: La Découverte.

Defalvard, Hervé. 2017. "Des communs sociaux à la société du commun." *RECMA* 345 (3): 42–56.

Dupain, Jonathan. 2021. "Gouvernement ouvert dans l'éducation : les comités de gestion scolaire en Afrique subsaharienne." Research project report. IIPE-UNESCO.

Dupont, Emmanuel, and Edouard Jourdain. 2022. *Les nouveaux biens communs ? Réinventer l'Etat et la propriété au XXIe siècle*. La Tour-d'Aigues: Editions de l'Aube.

FAO (Food and Agriculture Organization of the United Nations). 2012. "La situation mondiale de l'alimentation et de l'agriculture 2012 : investir dans l'agriculture pour un avenir Meilleur." Last modified 2012. https://www.fao.org/3/i2885f/i2885f.pdf.

Federici, Silvia. 2020. "Féminisme et politique des communs." In *Genre et économie solidaire, des croisements nécessaires*, edited by Isabelle Guérin, Isabelle Hillenkamp, and Christine Verschuur, 335–50. Geneva: Graduate Institute Publications.

Festa, Daniela. 2016. "Les communs urbains. L'invention du commun." *Tracés. Revue de sciences humaines* 16: 233–56. https://doi.org/10.4000/traces.6636.

Fontaine, Geneviève. 2019. "Les conditions d'émergence de communs porteurs de transformation sociale." In *Des émergences à la reconnaissance, trajectoires d'innovation*, edited by Juan-Luis Klein, Jacques L. Boucher, Annie Camus, Christine Champagne, and Yanick Noiseux, 39–48. Montréal: Presses de l'Université du Québec.

Foster, Sheila. 2011. "Collective Action and the Urban Commons." *Notre Dame Law Review* 87 (1): 57–134.

Gazibo, Mamoudou, and Céline Thiriot. 2009. *Le politique en Afrique: état des débats et pistes de recherche*. Paris: Karthala.

Hardin, Garrett. 1968. "The Tragedy of the Commons." *Science* 162 (3859): 1243–48.

Harney, Stefano, and Fred Moten. 2013. *The Undercommons: Fugitive Planning and Black Study*. Wivenhoe, U.K.: Minor Compositions.

Hess, Charlotte. 2008. "Mapping the New Commons." *SSRN Electronic Journal*. https:// doi.org/10.2139/ssrn.1356835.

Hess, Charlotte, and Elinor Ostrom, eds. 2006. *Understanding Knowledge as a Commons: From Theory to Practice*. Cambridge, MA: MIT Press.

Hirschman, Albert O. 1972. *Exit, Voice, and Loyalty: Responses to Decline in Firms, Organizations, and States*. Cambridge: Harvard University Press.

Hyde, Lewis. 2010. *Common as Air: Revolution, Art, and Ownership*. New York: Farrar, Straus and Giroux.

Ingold, Alice. 2008. "Les sociétés d'irrigation: bien commun et action collective." *Entreprises et histoire* 50 (1): 19–35.

Janssen, Marco A., John M. Anderies, and Elinor Ostrom. 2007. "Robustness of Social-Ecological Systems to Spatial and Temporal Variability." *Society and Natural Resources* 20: 307–22.

Larner, Wendy, and William Walters. 2004. "Globalization as Governmentality." *Alternatives* 29 (5): 495–514. https://doi.org/10.1177/030437540402900502.

Lelart, Michel. 1990. *La tontine, pratique informelle d'épargne et de crédit dans les pays en voie de développement.* Montrouge: John Libbey Eurotext.

Le Roy, Étienne. 1978. "Pour une anthropologie du droit." *Revue interdisciplinaire d'études juridiques* 1 (1): 71–100. https://doi.org/10.3917/riej.001.0071.

Leyronas, Stéphanie, and Nadège Legroux. 2019. *Commons: Towards a New Narrative on Development Policies and Practices?* AFD Research Papers, no. 2019-87, January. No. 41a69237-47b7-436a-940a-fa20ccd9676b. https://www.afd.fr/en/ressources/common s-towards-new-narrative-development-policies-and-practices.

Locher, Fabien. 2016. "Third World Pastures. The Historical Roots of the Commons Paradigm (1965–1990)." *Quaderni storici* 1: 303–33.

Lucarelli, Alberto. 2013. *La democrazia dei beni comuni.* Roma-Bari: Laterza Edizione.

Madison, Michael, Brett Frischmann, and Katherine Strandburg. 2014. *Governing Knowledge Commons.* Oxford: Oxford University Press.

Marinelli, Fabrizio. 2018. *Un'altra proprietà. Usi civici, assetti fondiari collettivi, beni comuni.* Pisa: Pacini Giuridica.

Maurel, Lionel, and S. I. Lex. 2018. "Réinvestir les communs culturels en tant que communs sociaux." Last modified July 28, 2018. https://scinfolex.com/2018/07/28/ reinvestir-les-communs-culturels-en-tant-que-communs-sociaux/.

Mauss, Marcel. 2007. "Essai sur le don. Forme et raison de l'échange dans les sociétés archaïques." *L'Année sociologique*: 30–186. First published 1925 by Presses Universitaires de France. https://www.jstor.org/stable/27883721.

Moritz, Mark. 2016. "Open Property Regimes." *International Journal of the Commons* 10 (2): 688–708. http://doi.org/10.18352/ijc.719.

Neeson, Jeanette M. 1996. *Commoners: Common Right, Enclosure and Social Change in England, 1700–1820.* Cambridge: Cambridge University Press.

Obura, David, and Sébastien Treyer. 2022. "A 'Shared Earth' Approach to Put Biodiversity at the Heart of the Sustainable Development in Africa." *AFD Research Papers* 265. Paris: AFD. https://www.afd.fr/en/ressources/shared-earth-approach-put -biodiversity-heart-sustainable-development-africa.

Olivier de Sardan, Jean-Pierre. 2021. *La revanche des contextes. Des mésaventures de l'ingénierie sociale en Afrique et au-delà.* Paris: Karthala.

Olivier de Sardan, Jean-Pierre. 2022. "La délivrance des biens d'intérêt général en Afrique. Pratiques palliatives, réformes de l'Etat et communs." Papiers de Recherche AFD 264. Paris: AFD. https://www.afd.fr/fr/ressources/la-delivrance-des-biens -dinteret-general-en-afrique-pratiques-palliatives-reformes-de-letat-et-communs.

Orsi, Fabienne. 2013. "Elinor Ostrom et les faisceaux de droits: l'ouverture d'un nouvel espace pour penser la propriété commune." Revue de la régulation. Capitalisme, institutions, pouvoirs 14. https://doi.org/10.4000/regulation.10471.

Ostrom, Elinor. 1990. *Governing Commons: The Evolution of Institutions for Collective Action*. Cambridge: Cambridge University Press.

Ostrom, Elinor. 1999. "Design Principles and Threats to Sustainable Organizations That Manage Commons." Working paper, Workshop in Political Theory and Policy Analysis, and the Center for the Study of Institutions, Population and Environmental Change, Indiana University, Bloomington, IN. https://hdl.handle.net/10535/5465.

Ostrom, Elinor. 2007a. "Challenges and Growth: The Development of the Interdisciplinary Field of Institutional Analysis." *Journal of Institutional Economics* 3 (3): 239–64. https://doi.org/10.1017/S1744137407000719.

Ostrom, Elinor. 2007b. "Institutional Rational Choice: An Assessment of the Institutional Analysis and Development Framework." In *Theories of the Policy Process*, edited by Paul Sabatier and Christopher M. Weible, 21–64. Boulder, CO: Westview Press.

Ostrom, Elinor. 2009. "A General Framework for Analyzing Sustainability of Social-Ecological Systems." *Science* 325 (5939): 419–22. https://doi.org/10.1126/science.1172133.

Ostrom, Elinor, and Xavier Basurto. 2011. "Crafting Analytical Tools to Study Institutional Change." *Journal of Institutional Economics* 7 (3): 317–43.

Ostrom, Elinor, Roy Gardner, and James Walker. 1994. *Rules, Games, and Common-Pool Resources*. Ann Arbor: University of Michigan Press.

Ostrom, Elinor, and Edella Schlager. 1992. "Property-Rights Regimes and Natural Resources: A Conceptual Analysis." *Land Economics* 68 (3): 249–62. https://doi.org/10.2307/3146375.

Papadopoulos, Dimitris. 2012. "Worlding Justice/Commoning Matter." *Occasion: Interdisciplinary Studies in the Humanities* 3. https://www.academia.edu/17678803/Worlding_justice_commoning_matter.

Peugeot, Valérie. 2014. "Les communs, une brèche politique à l'heure du numérique." In *Les débats du numérique*, edited by Maryse Carmes and Jean-Max Noyer, 77–98. Paris: Presses des Mines.

Pitseys, John. 2010. "Le concept de gouvernance." *Revue interdisciplinaire d'études juridiques* 65 (2): 207–28. https://doi.org/10.3917/riej.065.0207.

Rodotà, Stefano. 2016. "Vers les biens communs. Souveraineté et propriété au XXIe siècle." Translated by Guillaume Calafat. *Tracés. Revue de sciences humaines* 16: 211–32. https://doi.org/10.4000/traces.6632.

Samuelson, Paul A. 1954. "The Pure Theory of Public Expenditure." *Review of Economics and Statistics* 36 (4): 387–9. https://doi.org/10.2307/1925895.

Servet, Jean-Michel. 1996. "Risque, incertitude et financement de proximité en Afrique: une approche socioéconomique." *Revue tiers monde* 145: 41–57.

Simon, Herbert A. 1951. "A Formal Theory of the Employment Relationship." *Econometrica* 19 (3): 293–305.

Surowiecki, James. 2004. *The Wisdom of Crowds: Why the Many Are Smarter Than the Few and How Collective Wisdom Shapes Business, Economies, Societies, and Nations*. New York: Doubleday.

Taylan, Ferhat. 2018. *Concepts et rationalités. Héritages de l'épistémologie historique, de Meyerson à Foucault*. Paris: Éditions Matériologiques.

Teschke, Benno. 2003. *The Myth of 1648: Class, Geopolitics, and the Making of Modern International Relations*. London: Verso.

Thompson, Edward Palmer. 1993. *Customs in Common*. New York: New Press.

Traoré, Arahama, Ibrahima Bocoum, and Lota D. Tamini. 2020. "Services financiers: Quelles perspectives pour le déploiement d'innovations agricoles en Afrique?" *Économie rurale* 371: 77–94. https://doi.org/10.4000/economierurale.7549.

Tsing, Anna Lowenhaupt. 2017. *Le champignon de la fin du monde: Sur la possibilité de vivre dans les ruines du capitalisme*. Paris: La Découverte.

Valette, Héloïse, Catherine Baron, François Enten, Philippe Lavigne Delville, and Alicia Tsitsikalis. 2015. "Une action publique éclatée? Production et institutionnalisation de l'action publique dans les secteurs de l'eau potable et du foncier (APPI). Burkina Faso, Niger, Bénin." Gret.

Vanuxem, Sarah. 2018. *La propriété de la terre*. Marseille: Editions wildproject.

Wade, Robert. 1988. *Village Republics: Economic Conditions for Collective Action in South India*. Cambridge: Cambridge University Press.

Walters, William. 2012. *Governmentality: Critical Encounters*. Abingdon: Routledge.

Weinstein, Olivier. 2013. "Comment comprendre les 'communs': Elinor Ostrom, la propriété et la nouvelle économie institutionnelle." Revue de la régulation. Capitalisme, institutions, pouvoirs 14. https://doi.org/10.4000/regulation.10452.

Williamson, Oliver E. 2000. "The New Institutional Economics: Taking Stock, Looking Ahead." *Journal of Economic Literature* 38 (3): 595–613.

Chapter 2

Land-Based Commons: The Basis for a Peaceful Form of Economic Development?

Mathieu Boche, Patrick d'Aquino, Nicolas Hubert, Stéphanie Leyronas, and Sidy Mohamed Seck

Introduction

Many natural resources and rural spaces in Sub-Saharan Africa are shared and commons-based managed by one or more social groups. These land-based commons are established forms that adopt a practical perspective on land relations in accordance with use. In many situations, they define the local regulations for accessing land and natural resources.

Land-based commons respond to multiple challenges that go beyond the already complex issue of resource management. In certain situations, they curb threats to social stability by safeguarding access to resources and land for various categories of people in local populations, as well as mitigating threats to ecological balance by relying on flexible and extensive ways of making use of resources. Finally, they support formal and informal forms of entrepreneurship that prioritize cooperation and the maintenance of a certain redistribution of resources on the basis of principles and rules that have been inherited or developed by the community (Lange, Wodon, and Carey 2018; World Bank 2018, 2019).

However, African commons are facing numerous challenges, which are linked to demographic, social, and economic transformations, as well as to climate change. This trend is multiplying the number of actors involved, with mounting pressure to come up with practices that are better suited to specific situations. On the one hand, commons are being undermined by land policies that, since independence and despite some legislative advances, have massively favored a standardized approach to the question of land, one seeking to promote the exclusive ownership of land along with its commodification. On the other hand, they are being threatened by public policies that seek to extract natural resources as a driver of macroeconomic development.

In this chapter, we will examine how these forms of land-based commons can provide the basis for a type of economic development that preserves social stability and enables the sustainable use of natural resources. We will analyze this dynamic in three stages. In the first section, we will go through the issues related to preserving natural resources in Sub-Saharan Africa and provide an overview of the evolution of the normative regimes that define and regulate land-based commons. This section will make it possible to characterize these commons in terms of the resources they offer, the rights and arrangements on which they depend, and the social organizations that are responsible for their governance. In the second section, we will highlight and demonstrate how land-based commons are facing a series of transformations that are changing the social and political regimes that regulate their management and access. The aim of the third and final section is to provide a survey of the guarantees of security and support that these modes of managing and using natural resources require to support peaceful and sustainable economic development. In particular, it will analyze the ways to rethink the involvement of states and local authorities.

Construction and Representation of Land-Based Commons in Sub-Saharan Africa

Issues Relating to the Preservation of Commons-Based Managed Natural Resources

Despite its increasing urbanization, Africa remains a predominantly rural continent. The land available for agriculture is about 456 million hectares, nearly half of which consists of forests and protected areas (Chamberlin, Jayne, and Headey 2014). The labor market remains dominated by agriculture, which accounted for 53 percent of the workforce in 2019.[1] Land and natural resources are the economic base for millions of people living in rural areas; they impact upon issues of food security, peacekeeping, and economic growth (Lavigne Delville and Durand-Lasserve 2009).

For decades, African territories have been subject to extreme variations in the availability of natural resources, in both time and space (variability from one plot to the next or from one region to another within the same season, variability from one year to the next). This variability has been accentuated by the demographic growth observed on the continent and the reduction in surface area of arable land (Milleville and Serpantié 1994). Since the 1970s, Africa has also been one of the areas of the world that has been most severely affected by the consequences of climate change. Several studies highlight the impact that sulfur dioxide emissions from Asia, Europe, and the United States have had on the reduction of rainfall in the Sahel, which led to the major droughts of the 1970s and 1980s (Ackerley et al. 2011; Chang et al. 2011; Westervelt et al. 2017). According to the Food and Agriculture Organization (FAO),[2] the continent is thus losing almost 3 million hectares of forest each year, while desertification affects 45 percent of the land, and up to 65 percent of productive land is considered degraded.[3]

To adapt to this variability, African societies have developed collective organizations that rely on local, composite, and evolving rules (Berkes, Colding, and Folke 2000; Ellis and Swift 1988; Scoones 1994). The purpose of these rules is to regulate access to land and natural resources (box 2.1). Their resilience lies in the fact that they can be adapted in such a way that everyone has access to sufficient resources to support themselves, whatever the environmental conditions. This flexibility can be illustrated, for example, in the rules for organizing the occupation of space in the Sahel, where agricultural, pastoral, and fishing practices are closely interconnected in the same areas. In zones where agricultural uses are a priority, pastoralism can be practiced provided that the measures necessary to protect the resource for the former are taken by the latter (e.g., limiting the damage caused by herds in cultivated fields in zones where agriculture takes priority) and vice versa. Fishing practices serve as a complementary means of development depending on changes in the water level.

These organizations, which we refer to as "land-based commons," use and manage resources in many situations in Sub-Saharan Africa (Abernethy and Sally 2000; Beck and Nesmith 2001; Brockhaus, Djoudi, and Kambire 2012; Williams 1998). They operate through sophisticated practices, in multiscalar groupings from the nuclear family unit up to subregional coordination, such as for the purpose of transhumance (Armitage et al. 2009; Berkes 2002).

A Diversity of Land-Based Commons Situations

African land-based commons are often described as "customary," but this adjective, which yokes practices to tradition, ignores their social and political evolution (Mansion and Broutin 2013). In Sub-Saharan Africa, we find a real diversity of situations involving commons, from action situations known as "primo-commons," in which there is very little commodification, or where this at least occurs in forms that are distinct from market mechanisms, to "neo-commons," which do, in contrast, feature commodification (Le Roy 2016). This distinction is not stabilized and can lead to discussion, but it allows us to highlight the conflict of legitimacy that exists between repositories of traditional and customary rules and norms and the normative framework of the state.

Primo-commons are the domain of local communities that have developed a common-pool means of organizing access to land and natural resources for centuries (Barrière and Barrière 2018; Brossier, Jourde, and Cissé 2018; Juul 2001;

BOX 2.1

Collective Organizations to Adapt to Natural Resource Variability—The Example of Water and Grazing Resources in Kenya

In Aubert et al. (2019), Hess shows how access to water and pasture in the same territory can be organized in a variety of ways that can be continuously reconfigured according to the status of the resource in question. The Waso rangelands cover over 95 percent of the Kenyan county of Isiolo (about 20,000 square kilometers) and are part of a vast commons that stretch into the neighboring counties of Marsabit to the north, Wajir to the northeast, and Garissa to the east. In the county of Isiolo, management of the Waso rangelands is the responsibility of the Borana pastoralist group. In the course of history, other groups of herders have acquired seasonal or even multiyear access rights. Depending on the season and the resource's strategic importance, several systems of regulation and resource management are now being applied at different institutional levels:

- *Warra:* the household. The movements of the family and livestock are controlled by the head of the household.
- *Olla:* grouping of 30 to 100 *warra*. Each *olla* is headed by a chief who is responsible for community welfare. He decides, in consultation with certain heads of household, on the community's strategic mobility and its livestock.
- *Artha:* grouping of two to three *olla*. Each *artha* coordinates the use of the pastures during the dry and wet seasons.
- *Dedha:* a grazing area delimited and used by several *artha*. Each *dedha* is managed by a council of elders (*jarsa dheda*).
- *Mada:* a grazing area surrounding a water source (dam or well). Access to each *mada* is regulated by a clan (*aba ella*) that has priority rights of access to the water point. The use of wells and reservoirs is coordinated at the community level by a subgroup of the council of elders (*aba erega*), which decides on how water rotations are organized.

Strategic water sources are jointly managed by the *aba ella* and *aba erega*. The *aba ella* assign priority access rights to water, based on clan membership. If water and pasture are plentiful, secondary access rights are assigned by the *aba erega*. These secondary rights define not only who has access but also the order of priority. Access to the main water points during the dry season is strictly controlled by the council of elders (*jarsa dheda*) to avoid overuse.

Access to pastures is regulated by the *jarsa dedha*. The council allocates seasonal access rights to the land, taking into account different animals' needs (young animals, lactating females, and the rest of the herd) and the level of abundance of pasture. The council also defines reserve areas to accommodate herds during periods of drought. The council thus has authority over the seasonal movements of the entire community and over the dates of access to grazing reserves. It is also responsible for negotiating occasional access to its territory by neighboring pastoral communities.

Thébaud and Batterbury 2001). These include, for example, the management of Sahelian water sources and adjoining pastures by the lineages or fractions that founded them. Relationships within a predetermined social group (e.g., kinship, alliance, place of residence) set entitlement status and govern access to land and natural resources. Primo-commons refer exclusively to the rules, norms, and institutions of the traditional organization of societies.

These social and political constructions are often inherited from precolonial, long-standing traditions. They are based on ontologies, imaginaries, and representations of nature that are grounded in the sacredness of mother earth and its association with supernatural powers (Chene-Sanogo 2012). Recent interdisciplinary scholarly debates addressing the cultural approach to environmental systems emphasize the mutually constitutive relationships between human societies and the environment (Berkes, Folke, and Colding 2000; Cudworth and Hobden 2011; Fish, Church, and Winter 2016; Folke 2006; Masterson et al. 2017). These co-constitutive relationships are central mechanisms of many primo-commons in Sub-Saharan Africa and contribute to shaping the material and symbolic lifestyles, values, and practices attached to them. From this perspective, the environment and the various elements of nature do not refer solely to shared resources or spaces but to social constructs forming socioecosystems out of which commons are constructed (box 2.2).

First and foremost, primo-commons are shaped by representations of the world and sociopolitical structures that are unique to each society. They are structured according to the traditional rules, norms, and institutions of social groups. To understand them, it is essential to consider the different power relationships, inequalities, mechanisms of authority distribution, and processes of exclusion, whether they are gendered, social, political, or ethnic.

In a changing world, and as a result of the multiple challenges facing rural territories, fewer and fewer instances in Sub-Saharan Africa can be classified exclusively as primo-commons. Rural space brings increasingly heterogeneous actors into play (e.g., farmers, herders, miners, customary authorities, entrepreneurs, and urban elites), along with different modes of exploiting the environment[4] in relation to market mechanisms.[5] These actors do not share the same social norms and are engaged in intensifying competition (Hesse et al. 2013), yet it is from their interaction and their perceived interdependence that primo-commons are transformed and neo-commons emerge from them as an extension (box 2.3).

Thus, by their very nature, land-based neo-commons bring together different types of communities and actors: administrative communities and actors (e.g., villages or local governments), social communities (e.g., tribes, lineages, or clans), and socioeconomic actors (e.g., working youth or women). The "community" here is defined based on social relations as much as on membership and can therefore be very socially and economically

Interdependent Socioenvironmental Relationships—The Example of Primo-Commons in Burkina Faso

The numerous anthropological and sociological studies of the groups that make up contemporary Burkina Faso (Dassetto and Laurent 2006; Hagberg, Gomgnimbou, and Somé 1996; Héritier-Izard 1973; Izard 1986a, 1986b, 1990) show that their social and political structures incorporate substantial interpretive dimensions that influence the definition of cultural, social, and political structures while determining the terms of access to land, agricultural crops, and wildlife. Izard (1986a, 1986b, 1990), for example, describes the construction of social and political identities in Mossi kingdoms in Burkina Faso as being based around a trichotomy of power, autochthony, and ancestralism. Each of these elements proves decisive in the different ways in which the environment is interpreted and the associated access and management arrangements are made. Cultural power is connected to the immaterial dimension of the environment (or invisible world), with which it is necessary to interact to allow access to environmental services (Izard 1986b, 231). Some resources are designated as religious sites, such as sacred groves or marigots, access to which may be prohibited for agropastoral practices. Specific customs and practices associated with the intangible dimensions of the environment allow these religious sites to be maintained. In some Burkinabe communities, elders sow *néré* seeds, or seeds from other fruit trees, during their walks in the bush; in endogenous cultural representation, it is the "spirits" (or intermediaries with the invisible world) who sow the seeds (Hubert 2021a).

Primo- and Neo-Commons—The Case of Mohéli Park in Comoros

In the local history of commons, the island of Mohéli is regarded as a relay island between the Comoro Islands and Anjouan. All fishers, regardless of where they reside, are allowed access to the marine area. Conflicts related to accessing resources are dealt with by three Councils of Elders (recognized leaders) and the Ulema Council (the religious authority). In the context of the establishment of the national park, on the other hand, the management of natural resources is carried out by three institutions: the park leadership, its Management Council, and its Scientific Council. The confrontation between these two models gives rise to a composite system drawing on Muslim law, Comorian law, and custom. This arrangement makes it possible to secure ancestral rights to shared resources and to build on the achievements of the fishing rules already in place, while at the same time being part of a process of subsidiarity set up by the state. This example illustrates the emergence of neo-commons that reconcile the traditional dynamics of primo-commons based on fishing and the new natural resource regulation measures linked to the establishment of the Mohéli National Park in 2001 (Aubert et al. 2017).

heterogeneous (Aubert et al. 2017). Neo-commons involve the hybridization of different registers of norms: the traditional rules for organizing local communities and the norms defined by the legal framework of the state. Integration into the community can occur for several reasons. In the context of state-supported common property, individual membership in an association holding an exclusive right to the resource may be the origin of the group of right holders. The community can also result from the very processes of creating the resource (e.g., the construction of collective irrigation canals), in which case the investment of work time is the determining factor in membership of the collective. Finally, it can result from a territorial claim or an affirmation of identity—for example, the Collectif de défense des terres de Fanaye (Fanaye Land Defense Collective).[6]

Like primo-commons, neo-commons may feature certain anachronisms and elements of vertical decision-making. However, they usually develop horizontal mechanisms for deliberating the rules with varying degrees of success. They should not be perceived as static structures that are frozen in time. On the contrary, they are exposed to the dynamic character of environmental systems and to the ongoing development of human communities.

Finally, land-based commons are increasingly confronted with the interlock of multiple resources, both tangible and intangible (Aubert et al. 2017). For example, managing a commons based around a pasture zone requires paying attention to the production, processing, and marketing of products, as well as their interactions with other domains and resources (e.g., agricultural, forestry, and nontimber forest product chains).

Resources, Users, and Authorities: An Analysis of Commons through Modes of Access

Returning to the characterization of commons as presented in chapter 1, land-based commons in Sub-Saharan Africa present some unique features: territorialized resources, modes of access organized as "bundles of rights," and flexible governance mechanisms.

African commons develop practical approaches to land relations. There is not *one* resource but *many* resources, both tangible and intangible, whose access and use are governed by rules developed and implemented by collectives operating at different scales (Delay, Aubert, and Botta 2020). An ecosystem consists of different "ecological facets" in the sense of "spatial units for combining ecological and usage data" (Blanc-Pamard 1986, 19, cited in Colin, Lavigne Delville, and Léonard 2022; Papazian et al. 2016). Each ecological facet comprises a certain number of resources, potentially varying according to the season and used by a variety of people based on a set of access and exploitation rules. Cultivated spaces can therefore also be spaces for grazing (after the harvest), gathering (trees present in the field, for fruit, foliage, bark, wood), and hunting, for actors who may be different from the owner of the field. This results in an overlap of uses in the same space (Fache, Ancey, and Lavigne Delville 2022). Conversely, the same resource (e.g., forage resources) can be found in different ecological facets (e.g., lowlands, wooded areas, fallow lands, moors, permanent pastures, pastures on harvested fields). In each of these facets, the resource may be subject to specific ecological dynamics and to different rules of access and exploitation (e.g., free access on bushes and fallows, manure contracts with the field holder for crop residues). These different ecological facets are themselves integrated into collectively owned and organized territories.

Through the use of the "bundles of rights" principle, as discussed in chapter 1 (Epstein 2011; Penner 1995; Schlager and Ostrom 1992), African land-based commons recognize one or more functions of land and resources for the benefit of one or more persons (Le Roy, Karsenty, and Bertrand 2016). On the same piece of land, rights for the passage and grazing of animals, agricultural cultivation of the soil, hunting, and wood harvesting or gathering may coexist, each right being held over different spaces and resources and at different times by several individuals or groups (Mansion and Broutin 2013). The different components of a bundle of rights are embedded in given cultural and historical contexts and are often character- ized by oral and informal agreements. They may be managed by different individuals and regulated by different authorities (such as the state or local government) and transferred separately. The practice of tutelage illustrates, for example, the possibility for indigenous rights holders to transfer part of their rights (e.g., cultivation rights) to migrant families who arrived after the initial distribution of land. The counterpart can either be a share of the harvest or monetary (Chauveau 2008). It is therefore not the status of the land (communal, private, or state owned) that determines land relations in Sub-Saharan Africa but the rights that govern access to land and resources.

Finally, African land-based commons develop flexible governance arrangements[7] that draw, depending on the context and purpose of land tenure security, on different tenure regimes derived from custom, religion, law, gov- ernmental bodies, or elections (Papazian et al. 2016). The rules arising from the different registers are (or are not) made use of by participants in commons, depending on whether they are (or are not) seen as opening up new oppor- tunities in the management of commons. African land-based commons thus have to deal with the legal pluralism at work in African territories (Goldstein et al. 2015), which we will discuss in the next section, with an understanding of "juridicity" in order to "be emancipated from legal science" (Le Roy 2021).[8]

In the next section, we will discuss in greater detail how these different regimes that mutually constitute commons are adapting to different structural developments. These evolutions can be environmental and initiated by climate change or social, triggered by internal political reconfigurations in Sub-Saharan

African countries or by the multiscale integration generated by globalization, which puts the local in competition with the global. These changes can be self-sustaining and emerge locally from the very communities that make up commons, or they can be perceived as being imposed from above by exogenous actors. In each case, they can represent both threats and opportunities for the perpetuation of land-based commons.

Drivers of Change in African Land-Based Commons

Land-based commons are facing a series of changes that are transforming the social and political regimes that govern their management and access. These changes can be opportunities for commons, or they can jeopardize their very existence. They are associated with different phenomena, ranging from the process of modernization to the reconstruction of political regimes, as well as demographic and land pressure and urbanization processes. In this section, we emphasize four main drivers of change and risk for commons: the orientations of policies for formalizing land rights, competition between the uses of natural resources and conservation issues, the processes of individualization and commodification, and, finally, the processes of monopolization.

Commons-Based Managed Spaces and Resources: The Poor Relation of Land Policies

Colonization was the source of profound changes in land tenure systems in that it imposed a modern legal framework that was far removed from customary norms and oriented toward private property. The latter was then determined by the administration and based on the issuance of land titles and the establishment of a land registry (Chauveau 2018; Payne, Durand-Lasserve, and Rakodi 2009). The legitimacy of land-based primo-commons was contested, to the point that they were considered "vacant and ownerless" spaces (the principle of state ownership) and declared the eminent property of the state, which appropriated the natural resources (e.g., wood, minerals, land).

Following independence, a large part of the population occupied, lived on, and made use of land without having legally recognized rights to it. This situation went on for a long time. The colonial and postcolonial regimes gradually created a dualism in land management. This dualism manifests itself in several forms. The first is spatial dualism, because the legislative texts make a distinction between the way in which land can be managed and used by colonists, on the one hand, and indigenous populations, on the other. Second, it manifests itself in legal pluralism as a result of the superimposition of regimes in areas where the land tenure systems associated with primo-commons, based on use, have persisted alongside the so-called modern land tenure systems, based on ownership of the land base, after independence. In the same territory, different sources of legitimacy (customary, neo-customary, colonial, and neocolonial[9]) can thus overlap or clash, opening up the possibility for actors to circumvent local rules by mobilizing other norms and other authorities and vice versa.

This legal pluralism is coupled with a plurality of authorities (bodies issuing access rights and arbitration bodies): land chiefs, administrative village chiefs, territorial administration, technical services, and communally elected officials (Lavigne Delville 2012). In contexts of strong legal and institutional uncertainty, the limits of legitimacy of the different norms and the hierarchy of mandates between these different authorities are regularly called into question. As competition for resources increases with growing demographic pressure, the selective and competitive mobilization of one tenure regime or another and the appeal to various arbitration bodies lead to land use conflicts, land grabs, and social and even political tension (Chauveau 2018).

It was at the time of structural adjustment policies that the formalization of land rights in written form was promoted as a condition for economic development (Lavigne Delville and Mansion 2015). Spurred on by World Bank research on land programs in Thailand (Feder and Nishio 1998; Feder and Onchan 1987)[10] and the theories of De Soto and Diaz (2002), many land formalization programs have emerged in Sub-Saharan Africa with the objective of unifying rights through the promotion of individual private property. Land legislation has then often led to the weakening, or even delegitimization, of local land-based commons (Chauveau 2018).

This systematic registration approach aims to make an inventory of all plots of land and to formalize the rights that apply to them. These policies aim to group "informal" rights into one of the legal categories provided for by the law. This may result in the issuance of a land title resulting from the registration procedure or from certificates or attestations (Lavigne Delville 2018). However, these documents generally do not specify the content of the rights held by the various rights holders over a plot. They are therefore interpreted as evidence of exclusive private ownership. The systematic application of these policies most often amounts to a profound transformation of rural land rights and the exclusion of many rights holders. Those with rights of access to natural pastoral or forestry resources in areas under shared governance are generally the ones who are forgotten and lose out the most in these approaches.

Since the early 2000s, alternative hybrid approaches to land tenure security based on governance and securing social arrangements have emerged. The evolution of some of these approaches over the past 20 years, aimed at ending the principle of state ownership and recognizing different land tenure relationships, has in part allowed for the securing of land-based commons. These reforms, which represent a legal and sociopolitical revolution, remain insufficient and still have many shortcomings (Mansion and Broutin 2013).

Perceptions of Nature and Conservation Policies

In Sub-Saharan Africa, the colonization process not only profoundly shaped the relationship to land and its management but also attempted to impose a Western perception of the environment and sociocultural representations of nature. From the colonial perspective, Sub-Saharan Africa was seen as a primitive natural sanctuary to be exploited or protected, one devoid of any human presence (Hartmann 2014; Rodary 2011; Selby 2014; Selby and Hoffmann 2014; Verhoeven 2014). Under the aegis of colonial administrations, numerous natural protected areas (parks and reserves) were then created (box 2.4), relying on a conservative perception of the environment based on the control of territory and the exclusion of riparian communities (Duffy 2006; Hagberg, Gomgnimbou, and Somé 1996).

The establishment of nation-states inherited from the colonial period was a continuation of the objective of increasing control over natural resources (wood, minerals, land), which often led to local powers being undermined and the increased protection of parks and reserves. The deployment of water and forestry agents in West and East Africa in the twentieth century resulted in the claim to a "monopoly of nature protection" in the name of "public utility" and "raison d'Etat" (Bergeret 1994). While constituting a security force within those regions where natural protected areas are located, these water and forestry agents have often been met with reluctance by local populations and have even resulted in major local conflicts (Duffy 2006; Hagberg, Gomgnimbou, and Somé 1996; Hubert 2021b; Massé 2020; Poda 2001; Sachedina 2010). In South Africa, nature management and the creation of reserves and protected areas was also one of the centerpieces of the territorial engineering involved in colonial segregation and subsequently in apartheid (Giraut, Guyot, and Houssay-Holzschuch 2005). Later, the rise of climate change and biodiversity preservation issues on the international scene reinforced these dynamics (Obura and Treyer 2022), with environmental conservation spaces being considered crucial in the fight against climate change (Saradoum et al. 2022; Villette 2021).

These conservation areas were established by demarcating large areas originating from colonial hunting reserves. The riparian communities were then deprived of access to environmental services, including flora, traditional medicines, and fauna. Hunting activities, traditionally practiced for dietary subsistence, were criminalized and treated as poaching, unless hunting permits were obtained at prohibitive costs. These large conservation areas, such as the Transfrontier Conservation Area in Kavango-Zambezi, have favored

BOX 2.4

The Protected Natural Areas Model in Sub-Saharan Africa

The model of protected natural areas that are exclusively for conservation is proving to be increasingly controversial. These environmental protection areas, including reserves and national parks, represent a real asset for biodiversity conservation, especially in those regions that are most vulnerable to climate change (Turner et al. 2021). However, the imposition of a restrictive vision of conservation on fenced areas that do not allow any other use of previously shared resources has led to numerous local and national conflicts. The example of the Ngorongoro Conservation Area in Tanzania illustrates this tendency toward conflicts (Gagnon-Champigny 2020).

Faced with this observation, several local initiatives have emerged on the continent and are making it possible to generate a true entrepreneurial model combining the preservation of commons, the management of conflicts over use, and local economic development. This is notably the case of the alternative "Fortress Conservation" model in Tanzania (Blache 2020) or the village hunting zones (VHZs) in Burkina Faso. In southeast Burkina Faso, communities bordering the Pama Reserve, located within the socioeconomic integration zone of the Arli National Park, have formed a VHZ in order to develop their own tourism industry based around wildlife observation and small game hunting. This self-managed nature reserve makes it possible to increase the economic benefits of tourism and to distribute them more equitably among local communities. VHZs also play a role in protecting the environment and preserving land-based commons in areas marked by the expansion of agricultural activities. By integrating the socioeconomic fabric endogenous to environmental conservation and increasing the economic benefits associated with tourism, these self-constituted areas reinforce both riparian populations' appropriation of natural protected areas and the efficiency of their role in protecting biodiversity (Hubert 2021b, 8–10).

We can observe a similar dynamic with the conservancy model deployed in Namibia (Galvin, Beeton, and Luizza 2018). These conservancies are constructed on a communal basis but remain under the administration of regional conservation associations. They have both a conservation mission, involving managing conflicts of usage and local development through the sustainable use of natural resources, notably via tourism and hunting, but also including social objectives (notably through investments made in communities, e.g., in education and health services). The conservancies in Namibia benefit from many international donors but are seeking greater autonomy by attempting to diversify the funding sources available for their operations. This shift in the business model, however, risks generating a certain dependence on international finance, whose primary objectives may appear distant from the social benefits also offered by the conservancies. Similarly, although these conservancies are designed to be self-managing and to integrate traditional authorities, as well as to work closely with local populations, local decision-making bodies generally have no rights to the land and remain dependent on the decisions that national authorities may make on land management. This is one of the main limitations expressed by conservancy members.

These community-based conservation models thus face a range of challenges (Campbell and Shackleton 2001): clarifying the mandates of regulatory authorities, governance and collaboration with local governments, transparency of management bodies, funding for ongoing social engineering over time, and respect for legitimate land rights within land policies.

centralized governance and an economic model based on revenue from international tourism.

As an alternative to these major conservation programs and the establishment of public protected areas, a wave of programs supporting community-based natural resource management emerged in the 1990s. Faced with the failure of large national programs, community-based forms of natural resource management conservation have emerged, directly rooted in land management approaches and embracing the dynamics of decentralization in many countries across the continent (Bollig 2016; Rodary 2008).

The Process of Individualizing and Commodifying Commons-Based Managed Land and Resources

Demographic pressure, the rise of market forces, and the desire that younger members of society have for greater autonomy have led to the restructuring of domestic units. Larger family units, where they formerly existed, are tending to fragment in the direction of the household scale, which is asserting itself as an economic unit (Quesnel and Vimard 1996; Raynaut and Lavigne Delville 1997). These changes can coexist with the maintenance of land management at the level of extended family groups. However, they influence the rules of land transfer within the family group.

These processes of individualization can be coupled with the commodification of the land (Lavigne Delville et al. 2017). Depending on the rural society, this commodification may be part of a long-term process or more recent in nature (box 2.5). There are multiple drivers of this: insertion into commodity chains, emergency or distress sales (e.g., medical expenses, family events, weddings, and funerals), reconversion strategies, adjustments related to the fragmentation of inheritances, or offers from external actors. Administration rights and usage rights tend to be bundled together in these processes and become similar to property rights. The holders of land rights then act as de facto owners (Bon et al., forthcoming).

The individualization and commodification of rights do not necessarily go hand in hand (Colin and Bouquet 2022). There can be commodification (e.g., at the level of lineage segments) without complete individualization of rights (Diongue et al. 2021; Magnon 2013). Conversely, when faced with financial opportunities, younger members of society who normally do not have the right to sell, or even actors with no land rights, may engage in land transactions or question arrangements made by their elders.

The conditions under which agriculture is practiced, particularly natural parameters (climate and soil fertility) and the framework provided by public policies, also influence land tenure practices in rural areas (see chapter 3). Thus, the marginalization of agriculture or the lower profitability of production due to agricultural policies (cost of labor and inputs) and climatic unpredictability

BOX 2.5

The Emergence of Private Ownership and the Commodification of Family Land in Southern Benin

Simonneau (2015) recalls the relatively long-term processes of the emergence of individual ownership and the commodification of land in Benin. The traditional regime, as in other Sub-Saharan African countries, sees land as a sacred and inalienable resource. Its management on behalf of the community is conducted by a land chief, who is also a spiritual leader. The notion of individual ownership does not exist (Ouedraogo 2011). Several political, social, and economic developments nevertheless led to the emergence of individual ownership before the colonial period (Mondjannagni 1977; Pescay 1998).

An initial shift took place at the beginning of the seventeenth century with the creation of the great royalties, whose kings claimed land powers for themselves. The latter had their palaces built on domains that were initially ancestral or gave them to royal delegates for management, which constituted a first type of private appropriation of the land.

At the end of the seventeenth century, under demographic pressure, the king's authority weakened, as did the spiritual component of the bond between human beings and the land. Work gradually became the main basis of the right to land, and the previously inalienable and sacred character of the land became more flexible. In addition, ancestral lands were gradually being organized around more segmented categories (clan, ethnic group, lineage, family). The dispersion of clans and ethnic groups, migrations, and the assimilation of foreigners mean that only family properties remain.

Individual ownership emerged in the nineteenth century for three reasons: (a) royal delegates ended up taking over the land they were only previously responsible for managing and sometimes gave it to freed slaves; (b) after the abolition of slavery in 1848, the explosion of trade in palm oil products increased the economic importance of palm grove ownership; and (c) certain social groups emancipated themselves from customary land rules, such as freed slaves returning from Brazil with a strong attachment to the notion of land ownership acquired on the plantations.

Facilitated by these developments, the sale of land by customary owners became possible in the 1990s (Sotindjo 2010). Colonial legislation ("Coutumier du Dahomey" 1933) provided for the sale of family land. The commodification and individualization of rights increased in the 1990s under the influence of democratization, structural adjustment programs, and the collapse of the banking system (1988). Land ownership, even when semiformal, embodies aspirations for social ascension and has a central savings function in the household economy.

(violent weather events, hydric stress, and irregularity of rainfall) stimulates the sale of land, particularly for real estate development (Bon et al. forthcoming).

The emergence of urban middle classes in Africa with savings and investment capacity has reinforced the development of land markets in many rural areas of the continent. With the capacity to invest, but also with political influence or support, executives have acquired land in order to engage in agriculture or for real estate purposes. In Côte d'Ivoire, investments by urban executives are one of the major determinants of the development of the cocoa and rubber plantation economy (Ruf, Salvan, and Kouamé 2020). The development of land markets also occurs in conjunction with urban sprawl (Durand-Lasserve, Durand-Lasserve, and Selod 2015). In many cases, appropriations occur on spaces that are commons-based managed or used for different purposes.

Multiple Land-Grabbing Processes

Land-based commons are also exposed to land-grabbing processes (box 2.6). These land grabs are the result of internal dynamics as well as the attraction of national and international investors.[11] These large-scale land grabs have taken on many forms, most often involving the granting of land concessions by states to investors (Boche 2014). National laws allow the state to expropriate land valued by local populations in the name of public interest so that it can facilitate the arrival of investors seeking to develop agroindustrial plantations.

Special economic zones (SEZs) have also proliferated on the continent in recent years. In general, SEZs are intended to promote investment to foster industrial development. States invoke the concept of public utility in order to register the land in its name and transfer management to the administration. In Senegal, the law creating SEZs was adopted in January 2017. In the face of the stalled land reform process, concerns have been expressed that the establishment and operation of SEZs could facilitate a form of state reappropriation of land control over areas with "high economic potential." In Madagascar, successive laws and programs have established various forms of SEZs: free zones and free enterprises, industrial investment zones, and agricultural investment zones. The SEZ law led to public challenges in 2017 and reservations issued by the High Constitutional Court. A draft law on "special status land" was also created in 2020 to formalize the status of areas dedicated to investment but also protected areas or pastures. It too is controversial, as it provides that the lands concerned, including community lands, be titled in the name of the state and managed by the administration (Burnod et al. 2022).

This process has three major consequences. It alters the social and cultural roles that co-constitute land-based commons. It modifies the relationship of populations to the land, deconstructing the social structures that were previously associated with it. It intensifies the conversion of land uses (for industry, agribusiness, or real estate) in areas often already heavily used by local communities for their own food production (agriculture, livestock, gathering,

BOX 2.6

Commons Undermined over Mineral Resources

According to the report *Structural Transformation and Natural Resources* (AfDB et al. 2013), opening up access to natural resources to international economic actors is encouraged to stimulate the growth of a country's gross domestic product and to take advantage of the revenue from mining or other industries (Ashukem 2020; Delors 2019; Gyapong 2021; Oliveira, McKay, and Liu 2021) so as to initiate national development projects (Campbell 2009). Actors exploiting natural resources for industrial means are guaranteed priority access by modern land codes and land tenure regimes (Campbell 2009; Chouli 2014; Hubert 2018).

In most cases, mining codes rely on the modernization of land tenure regimes and codes to establish "financial compensation" for populations expropriated by mining development. This process can have positive spillover effects on local populations (Chuhan-Pole, Dabalen, and Land 2017). However, it assigns a monetary value to the land, which is calculated in terms of the economic value of the farmers' annual agricultural yields and transposed onto the individual property regime.

In Burkina Faso, this monetary value is directly associated with a sense of danger by communities in the sense that it tends to negatively modify living habits, intracommunity relationships, and the connection to the land. With the inflation generated locally by the establishment of industrial mining sites, people who have received financial compensation often find themselves quickly short of money. They are not used to managing their budget over several years, do not have access to infrastructure that allows them to store large sums of money over the long term, and no longer have agropastoral spaces or economic activities in which they could invest their capital. They are then exposed to theft, racketeering, and predation, which quickly places them in situations of great insecurity.

The mining companies also exploit the confusion generated by overlapping land tenure regimes, as described earlier. The Burkinabe mining code states that the subsoil is the property of the state and decides on the procedures for determining compensation in case of expropriation. In accordance with this code, compensation for mining companies is set in exchange for the transfer of exclusive ownership of the land and natural resources. They are determined according to a price per hectare set by the mining companies based on a fixed indemnity, calculated on the annual yield of agropastoral operations over a three-year period. The operators, on the other hand, sign an agreement for the transfer of their exploitation rights for a temporary period.

Thus, the most striking alteration brought about by the financial compensation of land expropriations in Sub-Saharan Africa is the monetary value conferred on land. It effectively establishes the private and individual character of property and deprives land tenure of its sociopolitical role in the environment (Hubert 2018, 2021a).

or fishing). The expropriated people then look for new land on which to practice their agricultural or pastoral activities, or else they decide to emigrate. Thus, in addition to accelerating the transformation of ecosystems, the privatization of spaces where common-pool resource management takes place leads to the transformation of the social, economic, and cultural fabric of land-based commons.

To conclude the first two sections of this chapter, observation of the dynamics under way in the field reveals the vitality and ingenuity of local actors in land-based commons. Building on traditions and experiences of land and resource pooling in situations of climatic and socioeconomic uncertainty, original and innovative forms of pooling are emerging and gradually being structured so as to respond to the multiple social, economic, and ecological challenges they face. However, the institutional and political frameworks in which these dynamics are emerging are not evolving at the same speed. They remain anchored in standardized frameworks, fixed and unsuited to current and rapid changes in the environmental and socioeconomic context. The forms of commons-based entrepreneurship that emerge from these social innovations therefore find themselves in an institutional context that does not allow for sufficient recognition, security, and support to ensure their sustainability.

Developing Commons-Based Entrepreneurship for Land and Natural Resources

Under certain conditions, land-based commons can lead to the monitored and measured development of agro-entrepreneurship. Developing commons-based economic entrepreneurship (see chapter 1) requires several levels of security that must be addressed in an integrated manner (box 2.7). The first is the establishment of land governance arrangements that take charge of the management of territories and allow the rules, agreements, and use of commonly managed resources to be established. Second, it is about securing the financial and economic conditions for the development of these economic activities. Finally, it is a matter of (re)thinking the commitment of the state.

Safeguarding Use Rather Than Ownership
Legal pluralism and the involvement of a number of different authorities result in significant land tenure insecurity for holders of land-based commons in Sub-Saharan Africa. This feeling of security of tenure is understood here as the ability to have confidence in the fact that the rights one holds over land and natural resources will not be challenged without reason and that, if they are, they will be confirmed by arbitration bodies considered legitimate. It is therefore required that land regulation institutions be effective, that their decisions be predictable, and that conflicts be arbitrated in favor of legitimate right holders.

Supporting the Development of Commons-Based Economic Entrepreneurship in the Senegal River Valley—An Integrated Approach

Support for the growth of commons-based economic entrepreneurship in the Senegal River Valley has been organized in a triple-pronged strategy, the systems and tools for which were progressively developed by a cluster of projects financed by the Agence française de développement (AFD) (French Development Agency) since 2012, which were then implemented throughout the territory by local actors. The strategy involves (a) the provision of social and land security tools; (b) the establishment of local development funds, managed by municipalities, for the realization of infrastructure essential to the development of economic entrepreneurship; and (c) the organization and development of local actors' capacity for greater integration into the most profitable local sectors. These tools have facilitated the emergence of numerous entrepreneurial initiatives in the region's agrosilvopastoral sectors.

The securing of the use of natural resources has been formalized in a communal document called the Plan d'occupation et d'affectation des sols (POAS), which is enshrined in Senegalese decentralization laws and policies (Bourgoin et al. 2020; d'Aquino et al. 2020; Papazian et al. 2016; Richebourg 2019). The POAS allows for the official recognition and safeguarding of common lands included in these plans. This recognition implies a legal recognition of local, common-pool governance of these resources. Commons have been secured through precise registration maps of secured rights in affected plots registered in a Land Information System at the communal level. In the case of commons-based managed spaces, the question of allocating land to collectives in a form that is not considered private appropriation (or "internal monopolization," as some villagers have pointed out) arises. Several legal formats are being experimented with, such as economic interest groups, users' associations, and the creation of communal zones.

The areas that are communally managed in the valley are generally located in the area outside the major riverbed. This is an area that suffers from a lack of basic infrastructure, particularly that which is necessary for economic development (cattle pens, meat markets, pastoral water points, dairies, collection centers for harvested products, pastoral and forestry facilities). Financial securitization has focused on financing public infrastructure in such a way that the management of funds is adapted to joint social organizations. A local financing line has been created, the Fonds d'Appui aux Investissements (Investment Support Fund), the management of which has been entrusted to local authorities. The infrastructure is installed on land allocated by the local authority, which is legally responsible for managing the land and then grants a mandate to an association of local users to manage the infrastructure. An effort has also been made to create pastoral units that assemble the users of an area surrounding a permanent water source (usually a borehole) for the more productive development of this area as a commons. Physical or

(continued next page)

Box 2.7 (continued)

organizational developments (pasture management) and technical support for productivity are implemented and can follow the same management mandate scheme as for infrastructure, in order to promote more productive resource management while making it possible to organize their use collectively. This formula thus allows this community to better ensure the preservation of local resources, the health of animals and ecosystems, the concerted management of natural and pastoral resources, and an increased income for the actors and the local community in an integrated way and under its own direction.

The process of ensuring economic security has focused on identifying high value-added sectors. The forms of support have been diverse, ranging from strengthening the organizational dynamics to enhancing the value of the entire value chain.

This integrated system initially provided the basis for a major part of Senegal's rice production, before being extended over the past 10 years to agrosilvopastoral resources in nonirrigated areas.

The way in which land tenure is secured has been the subject of controversy since the colonial period. There is tension between the objective of promoting access to legally recognized rights for efficient economic agents and the objective of protecting existing rights, particularly for those in the most vulnerable groups. Since the 1990s, most countries in Sub-Saharan Africa have implemented large-scale formalization policies for "customary" rights. These policies, referred to as "registration," "legalization," or "securing land rights through title," have had mixed results, and in Africa, only 5 to 20 percent of land is now reportedly registered, that is, recorded and entered in a land book or registry that is guaranteed to be maintained by the state (Mansion and Broutin 2013).

This property-based perspective, which is the predominant approach today, raises several questions:

- It equates the land base (the spatial surface) with the resources it contains (Delay, Aubert, and Botta 2020). Access to the resource is guaranteed by access to the space, which amounts to ignoring the possible interconnection of resources within the same space, the connectivity of these resources with other spaces, and the different users and forms of use at work discussed in the first section of the chapter. This approach obscures those practices of commons that stem from societies' historical adaptation to their environment and whose sense of land security depends more on social recognition than on legal recognition (Le Roy et al. 2019).

- In a context of legal pluralism, any new land policy is not imposed de facto but is added to existing modes of regulation so it can be reinterpreted and hybridized (Papazian et al. 2016).

- Colonial and then postcolonial authorities had already shown some reservations about systematic and authoritarian campaigns to securitize land and distribute it among peasantry, entrepreneurs, and international firms because of the risks of aggravating social and ethnic divides (Chauveau 2017).

- The idea that lack of access to full ownership is the main obstacle to investment has been challenged in numerous analyses (Binswanger, Deininger, and Feder 1993) that point to the price relationship between agricultural production and inputs, dysfunctions within the sectors, difficulties in accessing bank credit, and climatic risks. The expected benefits of formalization do not, therefore, take into account the need to act at a more global level of agricultural and economic policies in order to combat the precariousness of farmers in Africa (Bromley 2009).

The legal and social securitization of land-based commons presupposes that the formalization of rights is considered just one means among others and that it paves the way for a flexible approach to safeguarding rights. This requires a fine-grained understanding of "action situations" (see chapter 1) and adopting a pragmatic approach to land relations. Goulin et al. (2018) show, for example, that the development of family fish farming in certain communities in Côte d'Ivoire helps to meet national market demand while developing local entrepreneurship, strengthening the socioeconomic fabric, and making use of swampland or partially swamped locations that are less exposed to land pressure. This agro-entrepreneurship is developed through the acquisition of land from customary authorities, either by donation, counterparty, negotiation, or purchase for nonnative actors, or by inheritance for native actors. This development of entrepreneurship participates in the shift in regimes that jointly constitute commons as well as in the transformation of environmental uses and services. Goulin et al. (2018) conclude that the transformations brought about, when they remain within commons, have "made it possible for fish farmers, regardless of their mode of access, to enjoy the right to make use of the fish farming areas that had been ceded to them in an almost uninterrupted and continuous way. It should be concluded that these modes of access are all favorable to fish farming when the fish farmers are guaranteed permanent exploitation rights."

In concrete terms, the rights of access to and use of natural resources can be secured through the adoption of land use planning and land tenure security tools. The knowledge and sharing of information on ecological potential and users, as well as the mapping of uses and management rules, are essential prerequisites. Security is achieved through the mapping of priority zones, the formalization and dissemination of the access and management rules in force, and a permanent coordination mechanism to ensure that these provisions are respected.

Securing and Promoting the Conditions for the Emergence of Commons-Based Entrepreneurship

If we refer to the categories proposed in chapter 1, the economic models of land-based commons are most often market based, in the sense that participants in commons value the units of resource taken from commons in the market through the rights they have been allocated. But land-based commons are also based on hybrid models. Beyond the safeguarding of access and usage rights over natural resources, the development of commons-based entrepreneurship relies on four additional factors.

The first factor is the financing of collective infrastructure that makes it possible to create value from natural resources. This includes large-scale hydro-agricultural developments, pastoral water systems, storage, marketing and distribution infrastructures, and access roads, for example. This development requires prior negotiation with the rightful claimants and local actors as well as their free, prior, and informed agreement on the compensation for the damage caused, then their involvement in the creation of these collective resources, in the form of contributions in kind (e.g., free labor) or in cash (e.g., cofinancing of the acquisition of equipment or replenishment of a maintenance fund). The delegation of the management of the work must be accompanied, if necessary, by capacity building and be carried out in a proportionate manner based on commitment contracts signed between the beneficiaries, the state services, and the representatives from the local authorities.

The second factor is the organization of sustainable collective action. Understood as arising from the mobilization of a group of people who are aware of their common interest and their advantage in defending or advancing it (Froger and Méral 2002, 15), collective action can take the form of multiple institutional arrangements combining actors and instruments of public, market, and community regulation. The development of collective action in natural resource management is made difficult by a set of factors such as the identification of the relevant territorial scale, conflict between objectives that are at odds, and the difficulties of carrying out precise monitoring that allows for decision-making and is supported by an institution recognized as legitimate by all participants (Petit 2019). The mobilization of preexisting ecological and social solidarities and the recognition of the heritage value of the territory and of natural resources are powerful vectors for ensuring mobilization over time. Collective action will flourish on this fertile ground provided certain conditions for effectiveness are met (box 2.8).

The third factor that abets the emergence of commons-based entrepreneurship is the existence and accessibility of a technical and economic management support system to enable the establishment of a stable economic model. Entrepreneurs are too often left alone to develop their production and marketing

BOX 2.8

Conditions for the Effectiveness of Local Agreements Establishing Collective Action

The 2012 Negos-GRN research program Promouvoir une gestion locale concertée et effective des ressources naturelles et foncières (Promoting Concerted and Effective Local Management of Land and Natural Resources) identified a set of conditions for effective collective action:[a]

- Having a shared understanding of the problem and the key resource management issues in order to develop a collective, shared commitment.

- Co-constructing and negotiating clear, applicable, and adaptable rules for access, operation, and administration. The rules must be appropriate, make sense to the actors for whom they apply, and be simple and workable.

- Putting in place low-cost and inexpensive monitoring and sanctioning mechanisms.

- Considering local negotiation frameworks and representation issues (e.g., historical links between villages or elders' rights in speaking and decision-making).

- Identifying and working on substantive issues with common actors.

- Obtaining support from the state's technical services to allow a margin of flexibility between the legal framework and the application of local arrangements. The involvement of decentralized local authorities is crucial to lend a certain legitimacy to the operating agreements of commons and to ensure mediation with the state services.

- Mobilizing a set of actors recognized as legitimate to provide information or legal recognition. The perceived legitimacy of technical services to provide technical oversight and support is an important factor. Similarly, local governments and local communities are generally relevant for the legalization of agreements to form the group of common participants.

- Ensuring compliance with existing rules at the time of the first infractions. The credibility of the management system depends on it. A second litmus test occurs when the collective must adopt the rules it has set for itself.

a. The source for this information is policy briefs developed under the Negos-GRN program implemented by a consortium of actors led by the French nongovernmental organization GRET.

models. Advisory and management systems are often lacking because of low government investment in agricultural and rural training. On the continent, there are several systems financed and supported by producers' organizations and agricultural sectors (including management and rural economy centers in Senegal, local agricultural advice from the Malagasy professional agricultural organization Fifata, service delivery centers in Mali, and the program to consolidate and sustain agropastoral advice in Cameroon).

The fourth factor is the capacity for commercialization, which makes it possible both to secure the income of participants in commons and to provide the means for collective action. The economic model is necessarily dependent on the nature of the products and their destination. Economic sustainability requires the integration of the economic activities of commons into promising sectors, including the organization of production, collection, processing, and contracting with other actors in the sector. This also requires regulatory mechanisms such as hunting quotas or financial mechanisms such as taxation, which recognize the social and environmental value of the services provided by commons. The marketing of production and the certification of accounts by management and rural economy organizations allow participants in the common property grouped in associations, cooperatives, or economic groups to have access to rural credit.

Rethinking the State's Commitment

Safeguarding land-based commons, as well as the forms of entrepreneurship they encourage, depends on negotiated and institutionalized local management that allows for the strengthening of both collective and public action. With few exceptions, African land-based commons need the technical and political support of public, state, and decentralized actors in order to bolster their legitimacy. They also need to be able to mobilize these public actors to strengthen their capacity to act, particularly to have access to technical support and to ensure that their rights are respected. Proper coordination between these modes of regulation makes it possible to reduce uncertainty about the norms governing the exploitation of natural resources and about the authorities' capacity to ensure the effective implementation of the rules (Ndione and Lavigne Delville 2012).

The effectiveness of negotiated local management depends on many factors (box 2.9). Above all, it presupposes a reciprocal recognition of legitimacy but

---

BOX 2.9

Success Factors for Conservancies in Sub-Saharan Africa

According to Campbell and Shackleton (2001), the success of conservancies depends on eight factors: the genuine political will of governments to transfer decision-making authority to the local level across the entire bundle of rights; clarification of the mandates and relationships between the different actors; integration of natural resource management commissions into decentralized local governments; representativeness, accountability, and transparency of management bodies; continuous social engineering over time; recognition of the place of traditional authorities; support for the private sector to generate income based on the use of resources; and recognition of the added value created in order to determine the best organizational structure.

also of the interests and needs of each party. It calls into question both the commitment of the authorities and the position of the communities concerned (box 2.10).

On the side of the public authorities, negotiated local management requires the construction of real subsidiarity frameworks that make the coexistence of practices and decision-making at the appropriate scales coherent (Hesse 2011). This consists in coordinating the legitimate authorities at the different levels of rules as recalled in chapter 1 (operational level, collective level, and institutional level). Users remain in control, in space and in time, of the development of operational rules and of part of the collective rules (Delay, Aubert, and Botta 2020), which are therefore not based on externally imposed norms (see chapter 7). From this perspective, for example, a land or natural resource

---

BOX 2.10

The Principles of a Tripartite Agreement—The Example of the Senegal River Valley

The contractual form chosen to safeguard commons-based entrepreneurship in the valley is a tripartite agreement, one between users of natural resources, a local community, and a public technical partner. It takes up the fundamental principle of the traditional management of commons in the valley (Schmitz 1994) and incorporates the diversity of the parties involved into the agreement, each assuming its traditional role in the organization of society.

This type of contract defines the rights and duties of the three partners, each one bearing witness to the commitments of the other two. It provides legal and social security for the economic exploitation of the area, without private appropriation. This formula was implemented, starting in 2005, for the use of water in the context of hydro-agricultural developments: the contract, called the Charte du domaine irrigué (Irrigated Domain Charter), brought together the water user (irrigation farmer on a public hydro-agricultural development), the Société d'aménagement et d'exploitation des terres du Delta du Fleuve Sénégal (SAED) (Society for the Organization and Exploitation of the Senegal River Delta), and the local community, which was responsible for the land base. This tripartite contractual form has been extended to public infrastructure for investment, with the addition of a management mandate, as well as to the agrosilvopastoral development of a common space.

This type of contract makes it possible to empower and legally recognize the moral identity of a collective of users without transferring property rights. It also makes it possible to provide regulated access to users who are not members of the association or group of legal entities managing the infrastructure, the space, or the resource. However, the day-to-day benefit of these tools is still underutilized, and their inclusion in the long term constitutes a strategic challenge for SAED.

management law must remain a framework law to allow local actors to design, propose, and define operational and collective rules and processes for resource management (GELOSE Law in Madagascar, Land Law in Niger).

On the side of the communities involved in land-based commons, mobilizing the support of public authorities entails engaging with them and recognizing their interests, which can be manifold: "for local authorities, an interest in seeing their legitimacy reaffirmed; for elected officials, a political and symbolic interest in getting involved in a subject of interest to their fellow citizens; for technical services, interest in being able to present instances of sustainable management" (Lavigne Delville and Djiré 2012a, 1).

The modalities for implementing collaborative management have been the subject of an extensive literature (Bachir, Vogt, and Vogt 2007; Djiré 2003; Djiré and Dicko 2007; Faye, Haller, and Ribot 2018; Ostrom 1990; Petit 2019; Seegers 2005; Tall and Gueye 2003). It appears that in many situations, agreements benefit from being formalized by law. Legal recognition lends agreements between parties the power of local regulation that can be enforced against third parties and limits the possibility of their being challenged by the state. The involvement of commons, when the decentralization processes at work allow it, is often preferable to the technical services of the state, as commons are elected bodies that are normally closer to the concerns of citizens (Lavigne Delville and Djiré 2012b). However, legal formalization remains a first step, and it is over time, in the face of reality, that the effectiveness of such mechanisms is to be determined (box 2.10).

Conclusion

Land-based commons are rooted in the age-old experience of African societies when it comes to adapting to environmental and socioeconomic uncertainty while preserving access to resources, and thus survival, for the maximum number of users. Their nature and form evolve with each new context. Over the past few decades, hybrid neo-commons have emerged that combine pooled administration, individualized initiatives, and private investment. Many examples therefore show that a more peaceful form of entrepreneurship is being integrated into the evolution of commons, in innovative forms that ensure a social balance that can prevent tensions and conflicts from arising.

The sociopolitical nature of the regulation of land and natural resources is thus emphasized in this context and leads us to question the most appropriate forms of regulation and public policy, in a situation characterized by legal plurality and frequent competition between land regulation actors.

A strong guideline emerges from this chapter: given the nature of states in Sub-Saharan Africa, in many situations, only local populations have an interest in preserving natural resources over the long term. However, they can only do so to the extent that they retain the capacity to define and enforce their collective rules of operation within a clear institutional framework that is backed up by the state. It is not so much the legal status of the area in question that seems to be decisive but rather the guarantee of exploitation rights, the suitability and effectiveness of the rules, and the clarity of the institutional framework.

In this context, the challenge is to establish the foundations for collaborative management and development involving participants in land-based commons, public actors, and private investment. This type of collaborative management necessarily involves internal processes of negotiation between local actors and the state. It also implies rethinking public support policies to secure and boost the innovative entrepreneurial dynamics that emerge. A new intersectoral approach to public policy (land tenure, decentralization, investment support, structuring of value chains) must be developed, not in a standardized way, but in a way that is different for each cultural, social, institutional, and economic context. The best way to achieve this is to rely on a multiactor dialogue at the local level.

What emerges from these trends is a new role for the state, a profound paradigm shift that should be encouraged, where the challenge is not only to respond to contemporary environmental crises but also to build links and coordination between different authorities in a context where they are distinctively numerous. It is important to strengthen local authorities as a space where these links between the social realities of the territory and the national state system can be forged, thus participating in the construction of a new social pact between the state and its citizens, consistent with the processes of democratization and decentralization in the face of the loss of momentum of the modes of governance that have emerged since independence.

Notes

1. "Employment in agriculture (percentage of total employment) (modeled ILO estimate)—Sub-Saharan Africa," World Bank, accessed October 26, 2022, https://data .worldbank.org/indicator/SL.AGR.EMPL.ZS?locations=ZG.
2. United Nations, "La restauration des terres dégradées en Afrique progresse lentement et nécessite des efforts accrus (FAO)," September 29, 2021, https://news.un .org/fr/story/2021/09/1105052.
3. These figures presented by the FAO may be open to interpretation and dispute. Nevertheless, they remain representative of environmental degradation in Sub-Saharan Africa.
4. For example, the evolution of irrigation techniques toward pressurized systems with high investment costs per hectare means that the same rules of cohabitation between farmers and breeders can no longer be maintained.

5. For example, a land base managed by the collective that includes different types of land tenure, with traditionally commons-based spaces and plots under private ownership with more intensive modes of exploitation, individually or for a subgroup of the community; or individual use of certain resources such as the collection of fodder or the gathering of gum or fruit within a space used in common for other of its resources.

6. Inter-réseaux Développement rural, "Fanaye: Arrêt définitif du projet SENETHANOL," November 24, 2021, https://www.inter-reseaux.org/ressource/fanaye-arret-definitif-du-projet-senethanol/.

7. Here, the term *governance* is used in the strong sense of the "coordination of actors, social groups, and institutions to achieve collectively defined and discussed goals" (Le Galès 2019).

8. Le Roy (2011) proposes a more detailed analysis of bundles of rights through the theory of land control, which he applies to commons-based land appropriation regimes in his book *La terre de l'Autre*.

9. Neo-customary approaches refer to practices that build on customary ownership, including actors who claim to be directly or indirectly customary and sell more rights than the customary system recognizes (Durand-Lasserve, Mattingly, and Mogale 2004). Neocolonial approaches refer to practices involving the administrative recognition of possession and usage rights and the consecration of ownership into property rights (Comby 2013).

10. According to Bromley (2009), this work suffers from methodological bias.

11. See open-access platform on large-scale land acquisitions in Africa: https://landmatrix.org/.

References

Abernethy, Charles L., and M. H. Sally. 2000. "Experiences of Some Government-Sponsored Organizations of Irrigators in Niger and Burkina Faso, West Africa." *Journal of Applied Irrigation Science* 35 (2): 177–205.

Ackerley, Duncan, Ben B. B. Booth, Sylvia H. E. Knight, Eleanor J. Highwood, David J. Frame, Myles R. Allen, and David P. Rowell. 2011. "Sensitivity of Twentieth-Century Sahel Rainfall to Sulfate Aerosol and CO_2 Forcing." *Journal of Climate* 24 (19): 4999–5014. https://doi.org/10.1175/JCLI-D-11-00019.1.

AfDB, OECD, UNDP, and ECA (African Development Bank, Organisation for Economic Co-operation and Development, United Nations Development Programme, and United Nations Economic Commission for Africa). 2013. *African Economic Outlook 2013: Structural Transformation and Natural Resources.* Paris: OECD Publishing. https://www.oecd-ilibrary.org/development/african-economic-outlook-2013_aeo-2013-en.

Armitage, Derek, Ryan Plummer, Fikret Berkes, Robert Arthur, Anthony Charles, Iain Davidson-Hunt, Alan Diduck, Nancy Doubleday, Derek Johnson, Melissa Marschke, Patrick McConney, Evelyn Pinkerton, and Eva Wollenberg. 2009. "Adaptive Co-Management for Social–Ecological Complexity." *Frontiers in Ecology and the Environment* 7 (2): 95–102. Accessed October 7, 2022, from https://doi.org/10.1890/070089.

Ashukem, Jean-Claude N. 2020. "The SDGs and the Bio-Economy: Fostering Land-Grabbing in Africa." *Review of African Political Economy* 47 (164): 275–90. https://doi .org/10.1080/03056244.2019.1687086.

Aubert, Sigrid, Martine Antona, François Bousquet, Camilla Toulmin, Patrick d'Aquino, "Foncier et développement" technical committee. 2017. "Opportunités et défis d'une approche par les communs de la terre et des ressources qu'elle porte." https://www .foncier-developpement.fr/wp-content/uploads/Approche-par-les-communs-de-la -terre2.pdf.

Aubert, Sigrid, Patrick d'Aquino, François Bousquet, Martine Antona, and Camilla Toulmin. 2019. "L'approche par les communs de la terre et des ressources qu'elle porte: Illustration par six études de cas." https://www.foncier-developpe-ment.fr/wp-content/uploads/CTFD-Regards-sur-le-Foncier-6-Approche-par-les -communs.pdf.

Bachir, Amadou, Gill Vogt, and Kees Vogt. 2007. "La convention locale au Niger. L'expérience de la forêt classée de Takieta." *IIED Afrique*, no. 4. https://www.iedafrique .org/IMG/pdf/CL._Niger.pdf.

Barrière, Olivier, and Catherine Barrière. 2018. *Un droit à inventer: Foncier et environnement dans le delta intérieur du Niger.* Marseille: IRD Éditions. http://books .openedition.org/irdeditions/14471.

Beck, Tony, and Cathy Nesmith. 2001. "Building on Poor People's Capacities: The Case of Common Property Resources in India and West Africa." *World Development* 29 (1): 119–33. https://doi.org/10.1016/S0305-750X(00)00089-9.

Bergeret, Anne. 1994. "Les forestiers coloniaux français: Une doctrine et des politiques qui n'ont cessé de 'rejeter de souche.'" In *Les Sciences hors d'Occident au 20ème siècle,* edited by Yvon Chatelin and Christophe Bonneuil, 59–74. Paris: ORSTOM Éditions.

Berkes, Fikret. 2002. "Cross-Scale Institutional Linkages: Perspectives from the Bottom Up." In *The Drama of the Commons,* edited by Elinor Ostrom, Thomas Dietz, Nives Dolšak, Paul C. Stern, Susan Stonich, and Elke U. Weber, 293–321. Washington, DC: National Academy Press.

Berkes, Fikret, Johan Colding, and Carl Folke. 2000. "Rediscovery of Traditional Ecological Knowledge as Adaptive Management." *Ecological Applications* 10 (5): 1251–62. https://doi.org/10.2307/2641280.

Berkes, Fikret, Carl Folke, and Johan Colding. 2000. *Linking Social and Ecological Systems: Management Practices and Social Mechanisms for Building Resilience.* Cambridge: Cambridge University Press.

Binswanger, Hans P., Klaus Deininger, and Gershon Feder. 1993. "Agricultural Land Relations in the Developing World." *American Journal of Agricultural Economics* 75 (5): 1242–48. https://doi.org/10.2307/1243465.

Blache, Adriana. 2020. "De la 'Fortress Conservation' aux nouveaux modèles de gestion participative de la biodiversité en Tanzanie." *VertigO—La revue électronique en sciences de l'environnement* 20 (1). https://doi.org/10.4000/vertigo.27524.

Blanc-Pamard, Chantal. 1986. "Dialoguer avec le paysage ou comment l'espace écologique est vu et pratiqué par les communautés rurales des hautes terres malgaches." In *Milieux et paysages: Essai sur diverses modalités de connaissance,* edited by Yvon Chatelin and Gérard Riou, 17–36. Paris: Masson.

Boche, Mathieu. 2014. "Contrôle du foncier, agricultures d'entreprise et restructurations agraires: Une perspective critique des investissements fonciers à grande échelle: Le cas de la partie centrale du Mozambique." PhD dissertation, Paris-Sud University. https://tel.archives-ouvertes.fr/tel-01126967.

Bollig, Michael. 2016. "Adaptive Cycles in the Savannah: Pastoral Specialization and Diversification in Northern Kenya." *Journal of Eastern African Studies* 10 (1): 21–44. https://doi.org/10.1080/17531055.2016.1141568.

Bon, Bérénice, Claire Simonneau, Éric Denis, and Philippe Lavigne Delville, eds. Forthcoming. *Conversions des usages des sols liées à l'urbanisation des suds.* Vol. 2. Case study. Paris: "Foncier et développement" technical committee.

Bourgoin, Jeremy, Djibril Diop, Djiby Dia, Moussa Sall, Romaric Zagré, Quentin Grislain, and Ward Anseeuw. 2020. "Regard sur le modèle agricole sénégalais: Pratiques foncières et particularités territoriales des moyennes et grandes exploitations agricoles." *Cahiers agricultures* 29: 18. https://doi.org/10.1051/cagri/2020018.

Brockhaus, Maria, Houria Djoudi, and Hermann Kambire. 2012. "Multi-level Governance and Adaptive Capacity in West Africa." *International Journal of Commons* 6 (2): 200–32. https://doi.org/10.18352/ijc.331.

Bromley, Daniel W. 2009. "Formalising Property Relations in the Developing World: The Wrong Prescription for the Wrong Malady." *Land Use Policy* 26 (1): 20–7. https://doi.org/10.1016/j.landusepol.2008.02.003.

Brossier, Marie, Cédric Jourde, and Modibo Ghaly Cissé. 2018. "Relations de pouvoir locales, logiques de violence et participation politique en milieu peul (région de Mopti)." Rapport du projet "Stabiliser le Mali." University of Quebec in Montreal and Centre FrancoPaix.

Burnod, Perrine, Heriniaina Rakotomalala, Valérie Andriamanga, and Lydia Razanakolona, "Foncier et développement" technical committee. 2022. *Zones dédiées à l'investissement à Madagascar (ZEF, ZII, ZES, ZIA): Caractéristiques et incidences foncières.* https://www.foncier-developpement.fr/wp-content/uploads/Regards-sur-le-foncier-11_ZES-Madagascar.pdf.

Campbell, Bonnie. 2009. *Mining in Africa: Regulation and Development.* London: Pluto Press.

Campbell, Bruce, and Sheona Shackleton. 2001. *Devolution in Natural Resource Management: Institutional Arrangements and Power Shifts: A Synthesis of Case Studies from Southern Africa.* Jakarta, Indonesia: Center for International Forestry Research.

Chamberlin, Jordan, Thomas S. Jayne, and Derek D. Headey. 2014. "Scarcity amidst Abundance? Reassessing the Potential for Cropland Expansion in Africa." *Food Policy, Boserup, and Beyond: Mounting Land Pressures and Development Strategies in Africa* 48: 51–65. https://doi.org/10.1016/j.foodpol.2014.05.002.

Chang, Ching Yee, John C. H. Chiang, Michael F. Wehner, Andrew R. Friedman, and Reto Ruedy. 2011. "Sulfate Aerosol Control of Tropical Atlantic Climate over the Twentieth Century." *Journal of Climate* 24 (10): 2540–55.

Chauveau, Jean-Pierre. 2008. "Transferts fonciers et relations de tutorat en Afrique de l'Ouest." In *Ruralités nords-suds: Inégalités, conflits, innovations,* edited by Hervé Rakoto Ramiarantsoa, Bénédicte Thibaud, and Daniel Peyrusaubes, 81–95. Paris: L'Harmattan.

Chauveau, Jean-Pierre. 2017. "Les politiques de formalisation des droits coutumiers en Afrique rurale subsaharienne: Une perspective historique." In *La formalisation des droits sur la terre: Bilan des expériences et des réflexions*, 49–66. Paris: Agence française de développement.

Chauveau, Jean-Pierre, "Foncier et développement" technical committee. 2018. "Les politiques de formalisation des droits coutumiers en Afrique rurale subsaharienne: Une histoire tourmentée." https://www.foncier-developpement.fr/wp-content /uploads/2018_FR-Fiche-Chauveau.pdf.

Chene-Sanogo, Alima. 2012. "Enjeux fonciers et développement 'durable' au Mali." PhD dissertation, University of Burgundy. https://tel.archives-ouvertes.fr/tel-00839314.

Chouli, Lila. 2014. "Social Movements and the Quest for Alternatives in Burkina Faso." In *Liberalism and Its Discontents: Social Movements in West Africa*, edited by Ndongo Samba Sylla, 263–303. Berlin: Rosa Luxemburg Foundation.

Chuhan-Pole, Punam, Andrew L. Dabalen, and Bryan Christopher Land. 2017. *L'exploitation minière en afrique: Les communautés locales en tirent-elles parti?* Washington, DC: World Bank. https://doi.org/10.1596/978-1-4648-0819-7.

Colin, Jean-Philippe, and E. Bouquet. 2022. "Les marchés fonciers. Dynamiques, efficience, équité." In *Le foncier rural dans les pays du Sud. Enjeux et clés d'analyse*, edited by Jean-Philippe Colin, Philippe Lavigne Delville, and Éric Léonard, 453–522. Versailles and Marseille: QUAE and IRD.

Colin, Jean-Philippe, Philippe Lavigne Delville, and Éric Léonard, eds. 2022. *Le foncier rural dans les pays du sud. Enjeux et clés d'analyse*. Versailles and Marseille: QUAE and IRD.

Comby, Joseph. 2013. "Sortir du système foncier colonial." http://www.comby-foncier .com/sortir.pdf.

Cudworth, Erika, and Stephen Hobden. 2011. *Posthuman International Relations: Complexity, Ecologism, and Global Politics*. London: Bloomsbury Publishing.

d'Aquino, Patrick, Omar Fedior, Kader Ngom, and Aziz Sow, "Foncier et développement technical committee." 2020. "Quels mécanismes opérationnels pour faciliter la sécurisation de communs agrosylvopastoraux au Sahel? Le produit de vingt ans d'apprentissage sur la rive gauche de la vallée du fleuve Sénégal." https://www.foncier -developpement.fr/wp-content/uploads/2020_Fiche-foncier_Aquino-Fedior-Ngom -Sow-VF.pdf.

Dassetto, Felice, and Pierre-Joseph Laurent. 2006. "Ramatoullaye: Une confrérie musulmane en transition." *Recherches sociologiques et anthropologiques* 37 (2): 51–62. https:// doi.org/10.4000/rsa.564.

Delay, Étienne, Sigrid Aubert, and Aurélie Botta, "Foncier et développement" technical committee. 2020. "Définir et mettre en oeuvre une approche par les communs tissés autour de la terre et des ressources qu'elle porte." https://www.foncier-developpement .fr/wp-content/uploads/2020_Fiche-foncier_Delay-Aubert-Botta-VF.pdf.

Delors, Foyet Gankam Arsène. 2019. "Données d'observations de la terre et outils cartographiques libres à la caractérisation de la dynamique foncière face à l'accaparement des terres à grande échelle au sud-ouest Cameroun." *African Journal on Land Policy and Geospatial Sciences* 2 (2): 100–11. Accessed October 7, 2022, from https://doi .org/10.48346/IMIST.PRSM/ajlp-gs.v2i2.15974.

De Soto, Hernando, and Harry P. Diaz. 2002. "The Mystery of Capital. Why Capitalism Triumphs in the West and Fails Everywhere Else." *Canadian Journal of Latin American & Caribbean Studies* 27 (53): 172–74.

Diongue, Momar, Abdoulaye Diagne, Mamadou Bouna Timera, and Pape Sakho. 2021. "Gestion des propriétés lignagères et stratégies d'appropriation à la périphérie de Dakar: Le cas de Kounoune dans la commune de Bambilor (Sénégal)." In *Une Afrique des convoitises foncières. Regards croisés depuis le Mali*, edited by Monique Bertrand, 231–48. Toulouse: Presses Universitaires du Midi.

Djiré, Moussa. 2003. "Les conventions locales, un outil de gestion durable des ressources naturelles? Acquis et interrogations à partir d'exemples maliens." Paper presented at the workshop "Comment sécuriser les droits fonciers en milieu rural" at the Forum Praïa +9, CILSS, Bamako, Mali, November 17–21.

Djiré, Moussa, and Abdel Kader Dicko. 2007. *Les conventions locales face aux enjeux de la décentralisation au Mali*. Paris: Karthala.

Duffy, Rosaleen. 2006. "The Potential and Pitfalls of Global Environmental Governance: The Politics of Trans Frontier Conservation Areas in Southern Africa." *Political Geography* 25 (1): 89–112. https://doi.org/10.1016/j.polgeo.2005.08.001.

Durand-Lasserve, Alain, Maÿlis Durand-Lasserve, and Harris Selod. 2015. *Land Delivery Systems in West African Cities: The Example of Bamako, Mali*. Washington, DC: World Bank.

Durand-Lasserve, Alain, Michael Mattingly, and Thomas Mogale. 2004. "La nouvelle coutume urbaine. Évolution comparée des filières coutumières de la gestion foncière urbaine dans les pays d'Afrique subsaharienne." https://www.gemdev.org/old/prud/rapports/rapport19_3.pdf.

Ellis, James E., and David M. Swift. 1988. "Stability of African Pastoral Ecosystems: Alternate Paradigms and Implications for Development." *Journal of Range Management* 41 (6): 450–59. https://doi.org/10.2307/3899515.

Epstein, Richard A. 2011. "Bundle-of-Rights Theory as a Bulwark against Statist Conceptions of Private Property." *Econ Journal Watch* 8 (3): 223–35.

Fache, Elodie, Véronique Ancey, and Philippe Lavigne Delville. 2022. "Gouverner les ressources partagées." In *Le foncier rural dans les pays du Sud. Enjeux et clés d'analyse*, edited by Jean-Philippe Colin, Philippe Lavigne Delville and Éric Léonard. Versailles and Marseille: QUAE and IRD.

Faye, Papa, Tobias Haller, and Jesse Ribot. 2018. "Shaping Rules and Practice for More Justice: Local Conventions and Local Resistance in Eastern Senegal." *Human Ecology* 46: 15–25. https://doi.org/10.1007/s10745-017-9918-1.

Feder, Gershon, and Akihiko Nishio. 1998. "The Benefits of Land Registration and Titling: Economic and Social Perspectives." *Land Use Policy* 15 (1): 25–43. https://doi.org/10.1016/S0264-8377(97)00039-2.

Feder, Gershon, and Tongroj Onchan. 1987. "Land Ownership Security and Farm Investment in Thailand." *American Journal of Agricultural Economics* 69 (2): 311–20. https://doi.org/10.2307/1242281.

Fish, Robert, Andrew Church, and Michael Winter. 2016. "Conceptualizing Cultural Ecosystem Services: A Novel Framework for Research and Critical Engagement." *Ecosystem Services* 21: 208–17. https://doi.org/10.1016/j.ecoser.2016.09.002.

Folke, Carl. 2006. "Resilience: The Emergence of a Perspective for Social-Ecological Systems Analyses." *Global Environmental Change* 16 (3): 253–67. https://doi.org/10.1016/j.gloenvcha.2006.04.002.

Froger, Géraldine, and Philippe Méral. 2002. "Des mécanismes de l'action collective aux perspectives pour les politiques d'environnement." In *Gouvernance II. Action collective et politique d'environnement*, edited by Géraldine Froger and Philippe Méral, 9–24. Geneva: Helbing & Lichtenhahn.

Gagnon-Champigny, Chloé. 2020. "Les réfugiés de la conservation: Les parcs Serengeti et Ngorongoro (Tanzanie) et Thung Yai–Huai Kha Khaeng (Thaïlande) comparés au parc national Assinica (Québec)." Master's thesis, University of Sherbrooke and University of Liège. https://savoirs.usherbrooke.ca/handle/11143/17614.

Galvin, Kathleen A., Tyler A. Beeton, and Matthew W. Luizza. 2018. "African Community-Based Conservation: A Systematic Review of Social and Ecological Outcomes." *Ecology and Society* 23 (3). https://www.jstor.org/stable/26799165.

Giraut, Frédéric, Sylvain Guyot, and Myriam Houssay-Holzschuch. 2005. "La nature, les territoires et le politique en Afrique du sud." *Annales. Histoire, sciences sociales* 60 (4): 695–717.

Goldstein, Markus, Kenneth Houngbedji, Florence Kondylis, Michael O'Sullivan, and Harris Selod. 2015. "Formalisation des Droits Fonciers dans les Zones Rurales d'Afrique de l'Ouest: Résultats Initiaux d'une Étude Expérimentale au Bénin." Policy Research Working Paper, World Bank, Washington, DC. https://doi.org/10.1596/1813-9450-7435.

Goulin, Aymard Boris, Adja Ferdinand Vanga, Yao Célestin Amani, Mélécony Célestin Blé, and Blé Marcel Yoro. 2018. "Accès au foncier relatif à la pisciculture familiale au centre-ouest et au sud-ouest de la Côte d'Ivoire." *VertigO—La revue électronique en sciences de l'environnement* 18 (2). https://doi.org/10.4000/vertigo.22306.

Gyapong, Adwoa Yeboah. 2021. "Land Grabs, Farmworkers, and Rural Livelihoods in West Africa: Some Silences in the Food Sovereignty Discourse." *Globalizations* 18 (3): 339–54. https://doi.org/10.1080/14747731.2020.1716922.

Hagberg, Sten, Moustapha Gomgnimbou, and Désiré Boniface Somé. 1996. *Forêts classées et terres des ancêtres au Burkina Faso*. Department of Cultural Anthropology and Ethnology, Uppsala University. http://urn.kb.se/resolve?urn=urn:nbn:se:uu:diva-43539.

Hartmann, Betsy. 2014. "Converging on Disaster: Climate Security and the Malthusian Anticipatory Regime for Africa." *Geopolitics* 19 (4): 757–83. https://doi.org/10.1080/14650045.2013.847433.

Héritier-Izard, Françoise. 1973. "La paix et la pluie: Rapports d'autorité et rapport au sacré chez les Samo." *L'Homme* 13 (3): 121–38.

Hesse, Ced. 2011. "Ecology, Equity, and Economics: Reframing Dryland Policy." *Opinion: Lessons from Adaptation in Practice*. https://www.iied.org/17106iied.

Hesse, Ced, Simon Anderson, Lorenzo Cotula, Jamie Skinner, and Camilla Toulmin. 2013. "Managing the Boom and Bust: Supporting Climate Resilient Livelihoods in the Sahel." Issue Paper, 1–32. https://www.iied.org/sites/default/files/pdfs/migrate/11503IIED.pdf.

Hubert, Nicolas. 2018. "La nouvelle législation minière burkinabée: Quels risques en matière de développement durable?" *Canadian Journal of Development Studies* 39 (4): 500–14. https://doi.org/10.1080/02255189.2018.1460261.

Hubert, Nicolas. 2021a. "Environnement, ressources, et conflits au Burkina Faso." PhD dissertation, University of Ottawa. https://doi.org/10.20381/ruor-26093.

Hubert, Nicolas. 2021b. "The Nature of Peace: How Environmental Regulation Can Cause Conflicts." *World Development* 141 (105409). https://doi.org/10.1016/j .worlddev.2021.105409.

Izard, Michel. 1986a. "Le calendrier du Yatenga." *Systèmes de pensée en Afrique noire* 7: 45–55. https://doi.org/10.4000/span.559.

Izard, Michel. 1986b. "L'Étendue, la durée." *L'Homme* 26 (97–98): 225–37.

Izard, Michel. 1990. "De quelques paramètres de la souveraineté." *Systèmes de pensée en Afrique noire* 10: 69–92. https://doi.org/10.4000/span.875.

Juul, Kristine. 2001. "Power, Pastures, and Politics: Boreholes and the Decentralization of Local Resource Management in Northern Senegal." In *Politics, Property, and Production in West African Sahel: Understanding Natural Resource Management*, edited by Tor A. Benjaminsen and Christian Lund, 57–74. Stockholm: Elanders Gotab.

Lange, Glenn-Marie, Quentin Wodon, and Kevin Carey. 2018. *The Changing Wealth of Nations 2018: Building a Sustainable Future*. Washington, DC: World Bank.

Lavigne Delville, Philippe. 2012. "Promouvoir une gestion locale concertée et effective des ressources naturelles et foncières: Les conditions d'une gestion durable des ressources naturelles 'communes.'" *Les Notes de politique de Negos-GRN* 4.

Lavigne Delville, Philippe. 2018. "Public Policy Reform in West Africa: Between Polity, Politics, and Extraversion. Water Supply and Rural Land Tenure (Benin, Burkina Faso)." *Gouvernement et action publique* 7 (2): 53–73. https://www.cairn-int.info/journal -gouvernement-et-action-publique-2018-2-page-53.htm.

Lavigne Delville, Philippe, Jean-Philippe Colin, Ibrahima Ka, and Michel Merlet. 2017. *Étude régionale sur les marchés fonciers ruraux en Afrique de l'ouest et les outils de leur régulation*. Ouagadougou and Dakar: UEMAO/IPAR. https://www.ipar.sn/IMG/pdf /ipar-uemoa-_rapport_sur_les_marches_fonciers_ruraux_en_afrique_de_l_oues_et _les_outils_de_leurs_regulations.pdf.

Lavigne Delville, Philippe, and Moussa Djiré. 2012a. "Les conditions d'effectivité des conventions locales–Engagement des autorités et pragmatisme dans la mise en oeuvre." *Les Notes de politique de Negos-GRN* 9: 1–4.

Lavigne Delville, Philippe, and Moussa Djiré. 2012b. "Promouvoir une gestion locale concertée et effective des ressources naturelles et foncières: Les conditions d'effectivité des conventions locales." *Les notes de politique de Negos-GRN* 9.

Lavigne Delville, Philippe, and Alain Durand-Lasserve, "Foncier et développement" technical committee. 2009. "Gouvernance foncière et sécurisation des droits dans les pays du Sud (livre blanc)." https://agritrop.cirad.fr/556116/1/document_556116.pdf.

Lavigne Delville, Philippe, and Aurore Mansion. 2015. *La formalisation des droits sur la terre dans les pays du sud: Dépasser les controverses et alimenter les stratégies*. Paris: Ministère des Affaires étrangères et du Développement international (Maedi), Agence française de développement.

Le Galès, Patrick. 2019. "Gouvernance." In *Dictionnaire des politiques publiques*, edited by Laurie Boussaguet, Sophie Jacquot, and Pauline Ravinet, 297–305. Paris: Presses de SciencesPo.

Le Roy, Étienne. 2011. *La terre de l'autre. Une anthropologie des régimes d'appropriation foncière*. Paris: LGDJ Lextenso.

Le Roy, Étienne. 2016. "'Double Helix' Commons." *Droit et société* 94 (3): 603–24. https://doi.org/10.3917/drs.094.0603.

Le Roy, Étienne. 2021. *La révolution des communs et le droit. Nouveaux enjeux fonciers en Afrique, Amérique et Europe*. Quebec: Éditions science et bien commun. https://doi.org/10.5281/zenodo.5730710.

Le Roy, Étienne, Bruno Delmas, Gaël Giraud, and Philippe Bonnichon. 2019. *Les communs, aujourd'hui! Enjeux planétaires d'une gestion locale des ressources renouvelables*. Paris: Karthala. https://documentation.insp.gouv.fr/insp/doc/SYRACUSE/115230/les-communs-aujourd-hui-enjeux-planetaires-d-une-gestion-locale-des-ressources-renouvelables-sous-la.

Le Roy, Étienne, Alain Karsenty, and Alain Bertrand. 2016. *La sécurisation foncière en Afrique: Pour une gestion viable des ressources renouvelables*. Paris: Karthala.

Magnon, Yves Z. 2013. "En attendant l'aéroport: Pression marchande et vulnérabilités sociofoncières et agricoles à Glo-Djigbé (arrondissement rural du sud-Bénin)." *Autrepart* 1 (64): 107–20.

Mansion, Aurore, and Cécile Broutin. 2013. "Quelles politiques foncières en Afrique subsaharienne? Défis, acteurs, et initiatives contemporaines." In *Le Demeter 2014: Économie et stratégies agricoles*, 159–80. Paris: Club Déméter. http://publications.cirad.fr/une_notice.php?dk=570489.

Massé, Francis. 2020. "Conservation Law Enforcement: Policing Protected Areas." *Annals of the American Association of Geographers* 110 (3): 758–73. https://doi.org/10.1080/24694452.2019.1630249.

Masterson, Vanessa, Richard Stedman, Johan Enqvist, Maria Tengö, Matteo Giusti, Darin Wahl, and Uno Svedin. 2017. "The Contribution of Sense of Place to Social-Ecological Systems Research: A Review and Research Agenda." *Ecology and Society* 22 (1). https://doi.org/10.5751/ES-08872-220149.

Milleville, Pierre, and Georges Serpantié. 1994. "Intensification et durabilité des systèmes agricoles en Afrique soudano-sahélienne." *Promotion de systèmes agricoles durables dans les pays d'Afrique soudano-sahélienne* 10–14: 33–45.

Mondjannagni, Alfred Comlan. 1977. *Campagnes et villes au sud de la République populaire du Bénin*. Paris and The Hague: Mouton.

Ndione, Emmanuel, and Philippe Lavigne Delville. 2012. "Promouvoir une gestion locale concertée et effective des ressources naturelles et foncières: Institutionnaliser une gestion négociée des ressources naturelles: Un enjeu de gouvernance, une contribution au renforcement de l'action publique." *Les Notes de politique de Negos-GRN* 7. https://www.foncier-developpement.fr/wp-content/uploads/Note-politique-Negos_7.pdf.

Obura, David, and Sébastien Treyer. 2022. "A 'Shared Earth' Approach to Put Biodiversity at the Heart of the Sustainable Development in Africa." *AFD Research Papers* 265. Paris: AFD. https://www.afd.fr/en/ressources/shared-earth-approach-put-biodiversity-heart-sustainable-development-africa.

Oliveira, Gustavo de L. T., Ben M. McKay, and Juan Liu. 2021. "Beyond Land Grabs: New Insights on Land Struggles and Global Agrarian Change." *Globalizations* 18 (3): 321–38. https://doi.org/10.1080/14747731.2020.1843842.

Ostrom, Elinor. 1990. *Governing Commons: The Evolution of Institutions for Collective Action.* Cambridge: Cambridge University Press. https://doi.org/10.1017/CBO9780511807763.

Ouedraogo, Hubert M. G. 2011. "De la connaissance à la reconnaissance des droits fonciers africains endogènes." *Études rurales* 1 (187): 79–93.

Papazian, Hermine, Patrick d'Aquino, Jérémy Bourgoin, and Alpha Ba. 2016. "Jouer avec diverses sources de régulation foncière: Le pluralisme sahélien." *Économie rurale. Agricultures, alimentations, territoires* 353–54: 27–44. https://doi.org/10.4000/economierurale.4904.

Payne, Geoffrey, Alain Durand-Lasserve, and Caroline Rakodi. 2009. "The Limits of Land Titling and Home Ownership." *Environment and Urbanization* 21 (2): 443–62.

Penner, James E. 1995. "The Bundle of Rights Picture of Property." *UCLA Law Review* 43: 711–820.

Pescay, Michel. 1998. "Transformation des systèmes fonciers et 'transition foncière' au sud-Bénin." In *Quelles politiques foncières pour l'Afrique rurale? Réconcilier pratiques, légitimité et légalité,* edited by Philippe Lavigne Delville, 131–56. Paris: Karthala.

Petit, Olivier. 2019. "Contraintes, enjeux et mise en oeuvre de l'action collective pour la gouvernance des ressources naturelles et de l'environnement." In *Économie et gestion de l'environnement et des ressources naturelles,* edited by Olivier Petit, 41–55. Quebec: Institut de la Francophonie pour le développement durable and Université Senghor.

Poda, N. Evariste. 2001. "Le sacré et les lieux sacrés: Voie privilégiée de sauvegarde de l'environnement. Cas de Tio et de Negarpoulou." In *Aménagement intégré des forêts naturelles des zones tropicales sèches de l'Afrique de l'Ouest,* edited by Proseper D. Savadogo, 263–68. Ouagadougou, Burkina Faso: CNRS.

Quesnel, André, and Patrice Vimard. 1996. *Recompositions familiales et transformations agraires: Une lecture de cas africains et mexicain.* Paris: ORSTOM. https://horizon.documentation.ird.fr/exl-doc/pleins_textes/pleins_textes_6/b_fdi_45-46/010006615.pdf.

Raynaut, Claude, and Philippe Lavigne Delville. 1997. "Transformation des rapports sociaux et dynamique d'usage des ressources (2): L'émancipation de la force de travail." In *Sahels: Diversité et dynamiques des relations sociétés-nature,* edited by Claude Raynout, 315–46. Paris: Karthala.

Richebourg, Camille. 2019. "Participations citoyennes au processus de réforme foncière au Sénégal (2010–2017): TerriStories, un jeu de rôles et de simulations pour faire délibérer des paysans?" PhD dissertation, EHESS. https://www.theses.fr/2019EHES0067.

Rodary, Estienne. 2008. "Developing Conservation or Conserving Development? Some Historical Thoughts on the Two Terms and the Way Forward." *Mondes en développement* 141 (1): 81–92. https://doi.org/10.3917/med.141.0081.

Rodary, Estienne. 2011. "Crises et résistants: Les écologies politiques en Afrique." *Écologie & politique* 42 (2): 19–32. https://www.cairn.info/revue-ecologie-et-politique-sciences-cultures-societes-2011-2-page-19.htm.

Ruf, François, Marie Salvan, and Jérôme Kouamé. 2020. "Qui sont les planteurs de cacao de Côte d'Ivoire?" *Papiers de recherche,* 1–111. https://doi.org/10.3917/afd.thier.2020.01.0001.

Sachedina, Hassanali T. 2010. "Disconnected Nature: The Scaling Up of African Wildlife Foundation and Its Impacts on Biodiversity Conservation and Local Livelihoods." *Antipode* 42 (3): 603–23. Accessed October 7, 2022, from https://doi.org/10.1111/j .1467-8330.2010.00765.x.

Saradoum, Goy, Lucie Félicité Temgoua, Mbaidje Osée Mbaiakambeye, Francis Brice Silatsa Tedou, and Allaissem Behimnan. 2022. "Estimation du potentiel de séquestration de carbone des aires protégées: Cas de la forêt classée de Djoli-Kera, Tchad." *VertigO—La revue électronique en sciences de l'environnement.* https://doi.org/10.4000 /vertigo.34658.

Schlager, Edella, and Elinor Ostrom. 1992. "Property-Rights Regimes and Natural Resources: A Conceptual Analysis." *Land Economics* 68 (3): 249–62. https://doi .org/10.2307/3146375.

Schmitz, Jean. 1994. "Cités noires: Les républiques villageoises du Fuuta Tooro (Vallée du fleuve Sénégal)." *Cahiers d'études africaines* 133–35: 419–60. https://doi.org/10.3406 /cea.1994.2058.

Scoones, Ian. 1994. *Living with Uncertainty: New Directions in Pastoral Development in Africa.* West Yorkshire: Intermediate Technology Publications.

Seegers, C. 2005. *Les conventions locales, un outil fonctionnel dans la gestion forestière décentralisée? Evaluation comparative de trois expériences sénégalo-allemandes.* Dakar: PERACOD, GTZ.

Selby, Jan. 2014. "Positivist Climate Conflict Research: A Critique." *Geopolitics* 19 (4): 829–56. https://doi.org/10.1080/14650045.2014.964865.

Selby, Jan, and Clemens Hoffmann. 2014. "Rethinking Climate Change, Conflict, and Security." *Geopolitics* 19 (4): 747–56. https://doi.org/10.1080/14650045.2014.964866.

Simonneau, Claire. 2015. "Gérer la ville au Bénin: La mise en œuvre du registre foncier urbain à Cotonou, Porto-Novo et Bohicon." PhD dissertation, University of Montreal. https://papyrus.bib.umontreal.ca/xmlui/handle/1866/13501.

Sotindjo, Sébastien Dossa. 2010. *Cotonou l'explosion d'une capitale économique: (1945–1985).* Paris: L'Harmattan.

Tall, Serigne M., and Marième B. Gueye. 2003. "Les conventions locales: Un outil de co-gouvernance en gestion des ressources naturelles." IIED Sahel.

Thébaud, Brigitte, and Simon Batterbury. 2001. "Sahel Pastoralists: Opportunism, Struggle, Conflict, and Negotiation. A Case Study from Eastern Niger." *Global Environmental Change* 11 (1): 69–78. https://doi.org/10.1016/S0959-3780(00)00046-7.

Turner, Matthew D., Tanya Carney, Laura Lawler, Julia Reynolds, Lauren Kelly, Molly S. Teague, and Leif Brottem. 2021. "Environmental Rehabilitation and the Vulnerability of the Poor: The Case of the Great Green Wall." *Land Use Policy* 111 (105750). https:// doi.org/10.1016/j.landusepol.2021.105750.

Verhoeven, Harry. 2014. "Gardens of Eden or Hearts of Darkness? The Genealogy of Discourses on Environmental Insecurity and Climate Wars in Africa." *Geopolitics* 19 (4): 784–805. https://doi.org/10.1080/14650045.2014.896794.

Villette, Michel. 2021. "Des crédits carbone au service du développement africain." *Annales des mines—Responsabilité et environnement* 103 (3): 95–99. https://doi .org/10.3917/re1.103.0095.

Westervelt, Daniel M., Andrew J. Conley, Arlene M. Fiore, Jean-Francois Lamarque, Drew Shindell, Michael Previdi, Gregory Faluvegi, Gustavo Correa, and Larry W. Horowitz. 2017. "Multimodel Precipitation Responses to Removal of U.S. Sulfur Dioxide Emissions." *Journal of Geophysical Research: Atmospheres* 122 (9): 5024–38. https://doi.org/10.1002/2017JD026756.

Williams, Timothy O. 1998. "Multiple Uses of Common Pool Resources in Semi-Arid West Africa: A Survey of Existing Practices and Options for Sustainable Resource Management." https://vtechworks.lib.vt.edu/handle/10919/66582.

World Bank. 2018. *The World Bank Annual Report 2018*. Washington, DC: World Bank. https://openknowledge.worldbank.org/handle/10986/30326.

World Bank. 2019. *The World Bank Annual Report 2019: Ending Poverty, Investing in Opportunity*. Washington, DC: World Bank. https://openknowledge.worldbank.org /handle/10986/32333.

Chapter 3

Housing and the Future of Rural Land-Based Commons

Claire Simonneau, Bérénice Bon, Éric Denis,
Stéphanie Leyronas, and Issa Sory

Introduction

The African continent has the highest rate of urban growth in the world (OECD 2020).[1] The urban population has grown from 27 million in 1950 to nearly 600 million today. It is estimated that Africa's population will double by 2050 and that two-thirds of this increase will be urban. There are expected to be 950 million new city dwellers in the next three decades.

This urban growth comes with remarkable territorial transformations. Large metropolitan regions are being created, some of which surpass national borders, such as the Accra-Lagos urban corridor, which passes through four countries and is home to more than 30 million inhabitants on the coast along the Gulf of Guinea. As a result of still-rapid population growth in rural areas, there is a growing number of small and midsize cities, particularly in the interior of the continent. Villages and larger towns are being transformed into urban areas merely as a result of their natural rate of growth. Each of the continent's regions has its own particularities, so this urbanization is not a homogeneous process. Dynamic urban areas are incorporating localities that were formerly considered villages. The lines between urban and rural are increasingly unclear (OECD 2020).

This process of urbanization—and the accompanying explosion in housing demand—significantly impacts land use. The need for land to meet the increase in housing demand comes into competition with the need for agricultural land. Even before changes in land use take place, wealth polarization in cities generates pressure on rural land, increasing its financial value and disrupting local economies.

This chapter examines land dynamics in Sub-Saharan Africa in the context of massive, rapid, and diffuse urbanization. The first section focuses on the future of land-based commons (see chapter 2), particularly on the outskirts of urban areas, including the rural fringes that some actors expect to be absorbed by the urban area. The second section addresses the emergence of new types of commons designed to provide housing access to precarious and middle-class populations. This occurs in the absence of social housing policies at a time when access to urban land for housing is being cut off as its financial value and price increase. The third and final section discusses the renewal of public action—which is desirable in our view—in the face of these land use challenges.

Rural Lands versus the City: The Effects of Urbanization Dynamics on Rural Commons

Africa urbanizes rapidly and in a geographically diffuse manner (Agergaard et al. 2019; Jaglin, Didier, and Dubresson 2018; OECD 2020). The continent is seeing the greatest increase in building construction in the world. Africa's built environment has nearly doubled in area since 1990. Because population growth has remained strong in Africa, the continent is not experiencing the kind of disjunction between population growth and built-environment growth observed in other regions of the world. Still, roughly 300,000 square kilometers of land were built on from 1990 to 2015, or an average of 6,000 square kilometers per year (Denis 2020).

These processes are not limited to the kind of outward-spreading expansions of cities that were common in Europe over the past century. They are heterogeneous, hybrid, and unstable. They call for a new vocabulary that more accurately reflects the phenomena under way in the Global South generally (Denis 2015) and in Africa in particular. The substantial scientific literature seeking to name these spaces testifies to this (Meth et al. 2021): see, for example, "piecemeal urbanization" (Sawyer 2014), "new African suburbanisation" (Buire 2014), or "postcolonial suburbs" (Mercer 2017).

The changes in land use linked to this diffuse process of urbanization are unique in that they are occurring in a context of legal pluralism (see chapter 2) that both feeds and structures them. As the urban frontier advances and is expected to continue doing so, land norms are shifting away from land-based commons, which are more typical of rural spaces, toward somewhat formal configurations of private property. These changes do not always constitute a replacement or a clean break. A variety of forces are at work.

Driving Forces behind the Shifts in Land Use and Land Norms

Chapter 2 discussed the relatively recent changes that are transforming the social and political systems of land-based commons to varying degrees across the continent. These changes are associated with increases in the individualization and commodification of land rights. There are several forces at play here: demographic pressures, worsening conditions for agricultural work (e.g., input costs, climate unpredictability), younger generations' aspirations, the progression of market forces (e.g., commodification of land rights, distress sales, economic renewal strategies, breaking up of inheritances, offers from external actors), and, in certain countries, decades of land reforms favoring private property and its individualization.

In the peripheries of rapidly growing urban areas, land-based commons are also confronted with land and housing needs[2] resulting from children moving out of the parental home, the social pressure to own rather than rent, rising living standards, and the emergence of a middle class in certain Sub-Saharan African countries. The World Bank estimates that 1 billion Sub-Saharan Africans, or 50 percent of households, will be middle class by 2060 (Lall, Henderson, and Venables 2017). These households invest mainly in their children's education and in housing (Darbon and Toulabor 2014). Large areas of land are also necessary for the infrastructure and productive spaces that are developing on the peripheries of these dynamic urban areas: industries, business platforms, logistics centers, and special economic zones require vast areas of land at a controlled cost (Berger and Cotula 2021; UNCTAD 2019).

The last force driving the conversion of land-based commons into property in expanding urban areas is the fact that land is increasingly acting as a financial asset. At the household level, land is especially important as a savings vehicle, given the lack of inclusion and trust in the banking sector and of stable sources of revenue. Land—and potentially real estate—are the quintessential components of an inheritance. The difference in value between rural and urban land also encourages hoarding and opportunistic resale. Finally, land property is often a must-have asset to mortgage in order to obtain a loan to build or to start a business (Steel, Van Noorloos, and Otsuki 2019).

At the global, macroeconomic level, public policy frameworks in Sub-Saharan Africa have favored the role of the market in the production and management of cities since the early 1990s. These institutional transformations have allowed the deployment of new forms of capital accumulation in metropolitan areas and have favored the financialization of urban production—that is, the transformation of real estate into financial assets (Aalbers, Rolnik, and Krijnen 2020; Aveline-Dubach et al. 2020). Land dynamics can now only be understood in close connection with real estate and financial markets. This is particularly true of Sub-Saharan Africa's emerging economies, where a host of new cities and luxury districts are emerging, such as Eko Atlantic in Lagos, the Lake district in

Kinshasa, the Bolé district in Addis Ababa, and Konza Technopolis in Nairobi. Private actors with a financial stake in these land dynamics encourage transactions and changes in land use, sometimes going so far as to exert financial or social pressure to encourage owners to sell their land. In various regulatory and institutional forms, they are present at various stages of the sale and development of land: surveying and demarcation, property assessment, the preparation of plans for subdivisions or of designs for developments, construction, and land and real estate development.

The Dismantling of Rural Commons: Three Processes
The forces driving changes in the relationship to the land generate different processes. All of them, however, contribute to dismantling land-based commons. We identify three distinct processes (Bon et al., forthcoming).

The first is a result of development projects organized by public authorities that require a significant amount of land. This land is taken from rural commons, whose legal status is rarely secure. The development of new towns, economic activity zones, and housing developments is accompanied by different methods of dispossessing rural landowners. Local rights are rarely protected by national laws, land documentation is insufficient, and actors are not able to fully exercise their rights. Declarations of public interest and expropriation are used, with compensation often judged to be much lower than the losses generated. For example, in the Dakar region, the establishment of the new city (*pôle urbain*) of Diamniadio was authorized by decree in 2013 over a 1,664 hectare area. The easement for the new city came under a declaration of public interest and is situated on largely agricultural land (rangelands, rain-fed fields, market gardens, orchards, and chicken coops) used by those with usage rights. The land was expropriated on a case-by-case basis, and tensions arose over the amount of compensation. With respect to usage rights, the law provides for compensation only in the case of investments. In practice, however, compensation was awarded differently depending on the construction project and the project owner (the government or private developers), leading to inequalities that were hard to swallow (Lavigne Delville and Sow, forthcoming).

A second process is linked to real estate development operations and private land operations. It operates over relatively large areas, through the sale and purchase of estates by private actors. These estates are then divided into plots and parceled out. Title deeds to the plots are awarded, and construction eventually takes place. The rural landholders or local authorities can partner with these developers (Colin and Pottier, forthcoming). These commercial transfers of land are sometimes speculative, especially when they occur far from urban areas. Afterward, these estates may be fenced in while the process of awarding title deeds is under way, and they may remain uncultivated or become the site of seasonal farming and annual crop-growing (box 3.1).

BOX 3.1

Commercial Land Transactions at the Edges of Urbanization in Kenya

About 75 percent of Kenya's population resides on the 20 percent of the country's land that is considered fertile. The other 80 percent of the country's land is arid or semi-arid. The land is divided into three categories: public (12 percent), private (20 percent and growing), and communal (68 percent). The land on the outskirts of the capital, Nairobi, varies greatly in terms of use, natural environment, access to water, price, and distance from major public or private operations. The land to the north of Nairobi within a radius of about 30 kilometers is home to fertile volcanic soil that has been used since the colonial era for coffee plantations, floriculture, and market gardening. Hundreds of hectares of this land are irrigated. In 1963, individual title deeds began to be issued for freehold agricultural land that conferred the right to subdivide and sell the land. Starting in 2009, the construction of the Thika Road and bypasses greatly accelerated the pace at which land was being subdivided and parcels sold for nonagricultural use to local and foreign investors that could afford to contend with rising prices. During the first decade of the twenty-first century, the number of land transfers also began to increase 60 kilometers southeast of Nairobi, near the small town of Kitengela and the new expressways linking Tanzania and the port of Mombasa.

These transfers are occurring in rural areas on semi-arid land under what has been a communal system since Kenyan independence. In the late 1960s, the introduction of group ranches triggered the registration of individual rights. Families in this sector usually hold freehold titles that were issued when these groups of ranchers subdivided the land. Very few large estates are available for sale today. Although most Maasai families still own some land and a family home, they have sold off much of this land. The proceeds are reinvested in irrigation for agriculture, boreholes to sell water to new settlers, the construction of small apartments for rent in Kitengela, and their children's education. The buyers are socioeconomically diverse, depending on their access to financial capital, their reasons for buying, and their purchasing strategies. Certain common tendencies do stand out, however: the privatization of land through its division into parcels and small plots, the pooling of economic resources, waiting strategies, and land that is left uninhabited.

Businesspeople have thus created land-buying companies that buy an estate, obtain the title for it, subdivide the land into parcels (of 300 square meters on average), and sell these parcels off. The proceeds are then used to purchase other estates and to fund commercial projects in the city. These investors often sell to cooperatives (called *saccos* in Kenya) composed of groups of individual buyers, such as the employees of a company, civil servants, a group of friends, or members of the Kenyan diaspora. The group buys an estate or several lots of a development at below-market prices, then divides up the land among its members, each of whom is awarded a title deed. This process of pooling funds and then dividing the land among individuals is also engaged in by individuals who form interest groups that are not technically

(continued next page)

Box 3.1 (continued)

cooperatives. In these rural areas around Kitengela, very few buyers invest in building their own home. For hectares, the landscape is dotted with bollards, posts, vegetation, barbed-wire fencing, and walls—testament to the use of land as a long-term investment, whether it be as a savings device, to increase one's holdings of assets, as insurance against accidents or a downturn in business activity, as a means of accessing credit, or as a way to accumulate capital through resales.

These practices rely on the assumption that there are capital gains to be realized when services arrive and demand goes up in these areas at the edges of urbanization (Bertrand and Bon 2022).

A third and far more diverse process concerns the large market for parcels of land evictions (Colin 2004, 2017). When a family decides to divide its land into parcels, the subdivision process is sometimes formally overseen by a surveyor or the local authority through a subdivision or consolidation procedure. The decision to convert and eventually sell the land can be either defensive (e.g., distress sales, emergency sales for a large project, sales of parcels that are too small to divide among heirs) or offensive (e.g., sales to reinvest in profitable activities) (Yung and Bosc 1999). Families who divide up their land themselves before selling it keep most of the profits from the sale. Rural landholders play an active role in this market, seeking to gain from it financially, without it being either official or their main source of income. The idea is to buy and resell estates or plots at the outskirts of urban areas as land prices go up. The importance of these micro-transactions on domains divided into micro-lots is of particular note: they are carried out by a range of actors with very different degrees of capital at their disposal (rural landholders, local developers, and middle-class households). This is thus a diverse and nonlinear process that takes place plot by plot between individuals or local economic actors (box 3.2).

These three processes are bringing about changes in the way land is managed, but not necessarily—at least not immediately—in the way it is used. Hence the appearance of landscapes dotted with small-scale farms, uncultivated land, and fenced-in plots, so many subtle signs of a shift toward subdivided estates and the privatization of land rights (Bon 2022).

Forms of Resistance

We observe two forms of resistance to these changes. The first is sociopolitical: it occurs through social and partisan campaigns that combine several modes of action. For example, the evictions caused by the Diamniadio new city project in Senegal were met with intense resistance. As early as 2015, the 1,700 families who had been allocated plots of land in the Khoumbé and Khoumbé-extension communal allotments refused to give up their plots (which had been allocated

Dismantling the Collective Management of Peri-Urban Land in Burkina Faso

In Burkina Faso, the dismantling of land-based commons on the outskirts of large cities (e.g., Ouagadougou and Bobo-Dioulasso) has been driven by the public policies of the past four decades. Since the National Revolutionary Council (1983–87), inhabitants of informal settlements that are the subject of development operations have been given priority in the allocation of plots. Buying or trading plots on the outskirts of cities by settling there or by providing proof that one resides there has thus become a way to obtain land in new formal neighborhoods. This possibility increases supply as well as demand. Peri-urban land, formerly managed collectively under the aegis of a land chief, is being divided up among siblings and then sold to applicants from informal settlements. The strategy of these new landowners, who are, after all, expecting development to take place in the future, rests on the hope that there is profit to be made both by selling land to new inhabitants of informal settlements and by demanding compensation from public authorities when development does occur (Sory 2019; Traoré et al. 1986).

The shift from the collective management of land to its private appropriation was accelerated by the 2008 Loi numéro 57 portant promotion immobilière (Law 57 on real estate development) and 2009's Loi numéro 034 portant régime foncier rural (Law 034 on rural land tenure). The purpose of Law 034 was to safeguard collective property rights by dividing national land into state land, local government land, and private land. Given that Law 57 authorizes real estate developers to develop land, new landowners prefer to sell their vast estates only after obtaining a certificate of land possession. Land acquired through this channel is then developed and sold to the highest bidder, which contributes to land speculation and accelerates the dismantling of the collective management of peri-urban land.

by the state to a private company) or allow their houses to be demolished. They demanded an investigation by the State Inspectorate General. Starting in 2018, residents of Deny Malick Gueye attempted to have clear limits set on the new city's boundaries. In particular, they opposed plans for hotel developments, arguing that while they were not opposed to the development of infrastructure for the common good, they would not let their land be taken from them for the benefit of private interests (Lavigne Delville and Sow, forthcoming).

Resistance also occurs through resilient agricultural practices and hybrid economic strategies. By exploiting differences in the profitability of different areas of land and the constraints and opportunities of the agricultural sector, some farmers sell part of their land and modify their farming practices by changing what they produce or by intensifying production (box 3.3).

BOX 3.3

Madagascar—Farmers' Land Strategies to Maintain Agricultural Areas in Antananarivo

The analysis of the spatial footprint of agriculture in Antananarivo conducted by Defrise et al. (2019) shows that agriculture does not only disappear; in some areas, it is being maintained or even expanded. In less densely populated urban areas, the urban system leads to an intensification of agricultural practices, and cultivated areas are growing at the expense of pastures. In downtown Antananarivo, the area of cultivated land is decreasing, but relatively slowly: undivided land ownership slows the sale of land and helps preserve its agricultural use. In the agricultural plains on the outskirts of the city, changes in the agricultural footprint are tied to infrastructure.

In short, land issues are at the heart of the large-scale territorial transformations that Sub-Saharan Africa is experiencing today. Although urban sprawl and the commodification and individualization of land rights respond to housing demand, they also aggravate sociospatial inequalities and call into question the sustainability of metropolitan areas. Access to land for housing must be conceived of in different ways than via the peri-urban market alone. The following section examines some concrete approaches and experiences in this area through the lens of the commons.

Collective Arrangements for Access to Land and Housing in the City

Reopening Access to Urban Land for Housing

The right to adequate housing is enshrined in the 1948 Universal Declaration of Human Rights and the 1966 International Covenant on Economic, Social and Cultural Rights. It covers more than simply the material aspects of housing: it is the right "to live somewhere in security, peace and dignity" (OHCHR and UN-Habitat 2010, 3). It includes security of tenure; respect for the ability to pay; habitability; availability of services, materials, facilities, and infrastructure; accessibility; a suitable location and allowing access to employment opportunities and services; and respect for the expression of cultural identity. Housing is also explicitly addressed in Sustainable Development Goal number 11 on access for all to adequate, safe, affordable housing and basic services for all by 2030. Last, the New Urban Agenda, adopted at the Habitat III conference in 2016, develops a vision of "cities for all," one of the goals of which is to fully realize the right to adequate housing, usually through relatively conventional public policies to support private home ownership.

However, decent urban housing remains out of reach for a significant percentage of city dwellers in Sub-Saharan Africa. The risk of eviction, the insecurity of the building or the land it is built on, and a lack of access to services and employment make urban housing conditions substandard. Many households do not have access to the housing offered by the government and the market in an individual, private property system. The price of land makes it impossible to generate decent, affordable housing for low-income families, whether to rent, own, or self-build. Furthermore, the rapid rise in the exchange and financial value of urban land has steadily increased the share of speculative acquisitions, particularly in areas with weak financial inclusion and high inflation (Aalbers, Rolnik, and Krijnen 2020).

Since the early 2000s, parts of academia and of the international community have recognized the necessity of the security of land tenure systems in all their diversity. In their reflections on adequate housing, both Sustainable Development Goal 11 and the Office of the High Commissioner for Human Rights recognize the continuum of rights and the need to recognize a diverse range of solutions to housing and land tenure, including cooperative solutions and different forms of collective tenure.

In the context of rehabilitating at-risk neighborhoods and developing new housing complexes, the commons approach paves the way for thinking about modes of land ownership and access that preserve social diversity in cities.

Urban Land-Based Commons for Housing

Using the commons approach to think about access to land for low-income housing in dense urban areas, where land is commercially and financially valuable, involves making a shift in one's value system. In this case, priority is given to the land's social function, and sharing land as a resource is more important than owning it privately. The challenge lies in developing mechanisms that make it possible to resist exclusion by the market and land speculation marked by the bullish and exclusive influence of excess transnational liquidity (Simonneau and Denis 2021).

Beginning from the principle that land should serve a social function, there are various mechanisms in countries of the Global South for producing low-income housing in ways that preserve long-term access to land and housing. They are based on (a) owning land or part of the housing production process in common, (b) eliminating land value and controlling the ways housing can be resold and land value increases are distributed, and (c) governing the construction project or the management of the residential complex at a community level.

The purpose of these mechanisms is as follows:

- To establish collective use of the land or housing in order to allow the social function of the property to occur immediately. If the collective dimension of land ownership is not designed to last or can be undone, then legal land arrangements may be transitory.

- To decouple the ownership of land from the ownership of housing over the long term in a way that is not speculative. The purpose of the mechanisms' nonspeculative dimension is to guarantee the primacy of the social utility of land ownership through a low land price over the long term, even as users and owners come and go, as well as through the strict supervision of resales.

Collective and cooperative production may seem obvious in theory, but a wide range of situations exist, depending on which elements are held in common (e.g., financing, land rights, housing, open spaces and facilities, the management of the residence) (Simonneau, Denis, and Sory 2019). Situations differ in terms of how land and financing are accessed, how housing is built, how collective spaces and facilities are developed and maintained, how property transfers and realized capital gains are controlled, and how members help one another financially and more generally.

In this chapter, we focus on two forms that are being rolled out in Sub-Saharan Africa and target different social groups: West African building cooperatives (boxes 3.4 and 3.5) and the Community Land Trust (CLT) scheme that has been tested in Kenya (box 3.6). We analyze what these two approaches have to offer for land and housing access, as well as their limitations and prospects.

Housing cooperatives

Housing cooperatives are used to develop housing in several Sub-Saharan African countries[3] (Ganapati 2014). The quantity of housing developed this way remains relatively small and is aimed more at salaried workers than at the most at-risk populations. Nevertheless, given the longevity and potential of these schemes, they deserve attention.

Most of these cooperatives are "construction cooperatives" (Simonneau, Denis, and Sory 2019). The collective dimension often concerns only access to the land, the pooling of financial resources, and the negotiation for the joint purchase of an estate and construction of a residential complex. Once construction is complete, each household in the cooperative can access full ownership of its plot and dwelling.

As a point of reference, Uruguayan cooperatives, which are cited around the world as an example of the social production of housing (de Souza, Valitutto, and Simonneau 2021), collectivize every stage of the development of housing and housing districts. Ownership of land and housing remains cooperative (i.e., inhabitants have usage rights only), and community life is insisted upon, particularly when it comes to maintaining collective spaces. In comparison, then, the communal dimension of West African cooperatives appears far more limited in ambition and duration.

BOX 3.4

Housing Cooperatives in Burkina Faso

Because of natural growth, rural exodus, and more recently internal displacement resulting from Burkina Faso's security crisis, the urban region of Ouagadougou is growing at a rate of 100,000 to 110,000 people per year (Delaunay and Boyer 2017; Sory 2019). The informal land market, maintained by government subdivision practices, is generating significant urban sprawl, thereby creating a peripheral area where numerous plots are undeveloped or awaiting regularization (Guigma, Boudoux d'Hautefeuille, and Pierre-Louis 2015). Public policy since the early 2000s has been directed at deregulating the housing sector, reviving state-supervised housing construction with a focus on public–private partnerships, and a highly publicized, although rather ineffective, fight against speculative land practices on the outskirts of cities (Guigma 2017; Sory, Lingani, and Korbeogo 2015). A good example of this is the Programme national de construction de logements (PNCL) (National Housing Construction Program), launched in 2017.

The formation of housing cooperatives was first made possible in 2008 by the Loi sur la promotion immobilière (Real Estate Development Act). The PNCL, which provides for the construction of 40,000 housing units, sets a production target of 5,000 units to be built through cooperatives. Housing cooperatives are aimed at low-income households, with a view to developing formal access to land and property ownership through specially adapted bank loans. In fact, however, it is most often salaried workers who take advantage of this program.

The housing production and development activities of cooperatives are regulated by the state, similar to those of developers. Cooperatives must apply for approval from the urban planning authority. They are eligible to receive plots of land made available by the state (or acquire them on the market), and they can develop plots of land or build housing according to social housing standards (subject to a price ceiling) for direct sale or rent-to-own programs for their members.

Six cooperatives have been created since 2008. The homes are available for ownership under social housing conditions: they are sold at a ceiling price of 7.5 million CFA francs,[a] either directly or through rent-to-own agreements. In the latter case, households must obtain a bank loan on their own. The government cedes the land back to the cooperative via a "mother" title deed (which is not always issued). Households keep a housing allocation certificate attesting to their right to use the land and housing. Once a household has repaid its loan, it can apply for an urban housing permit and then for a land title. The plot of land is then normalized and can be sold at market price. The primary motivation of cooperative members seems to lie in the ease of access to land and property relative to traditional public housing programs. The cooperative can cease to serve any salient functions after the keys are handed over.

a. The minimum monthly salary is 33,000 CFA francs.

BOX 3.5

Housing Cooperatives in Senegal

A total of 3.9 million Senegalese, or half of the country's urban population, live in the Dakar region. Access to formal housing is limited by price and the fact that households who make a living through the informal economy cannot access credit (CAHF 2019). Demographic pressures, combined with soaring land prices, are generating significant urban sprawl, which the 2016 Plan de développement urbain (Urban Development Plan) attempts to manage through the creation of urban centers.

The first Senegalese housing cooperatives were founded in Dakar in the 1950s (Fall 2007; Osmont 1973). They have been legally regulated since 1983 by Loi numéro 1983/07 portant statut général des coopératives (Law 1983/07 on the general statutes of cooperatives). They are also part of the 2016 provisions to support the construction of social housing, in Law 2016-31.

These organizations are approved by the government and receive technical support and financial benefits. In 1989, the Bureau d'assistance aux collectivités pour l'habitat social (Public Housing Assistance Bureau), an administrative assistance program for social housing collectives, was set up within the urban planning ministry to facilitate the administrative and financial processes of urban land acquisition and to supervise housing construction (Sané 2013). Cooperatives benefit from reduced taxation (exemption from income tax and reduced registration rates) and preferential rates for the repayment of individual and group housing loans from the Banque de l'Habitat du Sénégal (BHS) (Housing Bank of Senegal). Since 2020, the Fonds pour l'habitat social (Social Housing Fund) has been serving as a guarantor for applicants seeking to get a loan to obtain social housing. Public housing production programs provide land and road facilities. However, cooperatives can also acquire land on the conventional market.

Cooperatives are organizations that engage in land acquisition, housing development, and mutual guarantee programs (Diop 2012). They are often organized by profession, and certain companies or government agencies act as guarantors for their employees, for whom they can get loans by financing all or part of the contributions required to join the cooperative. The land is generally acquired in the name of the cooperative, through a collective lease. The project's financing comes from members' individual savings, which are collected by the cooperative, and from loans taken out with BHS. These loans can be collective, in the name of the cooperative ("developer loan"), or individual, in the name of the members of the cooperative ("buyer loan"). Construction is carried out either by private companies contracted by the cooperative or by the members themselves.

In the early 2010s, there were more than 700 housing cooperatives totaling some 300,000 members. In 2009, 74,400 homes were built with the support of housing cooperatives. In Dakar, 3.7 percent of households resided in cooperatives in 2013, with 94.5 percent of these construction cooperatives made up of salaried workers from large public or private employers. However, the legal framework does not exclude informal workers (Cissé 2013; Sané 2013).

(continued next page)

Box 3.5 (continued)

Like other segments of formal housing production in Senegal, cooperative housing production remains constrained by the high cost of imported construction materials and by access to land. In addition, corruption and power games can undermine a project's collective dimension. Finally, projects can also fail because of developers' abusive practices toward the managers of these cooperative real estate projects, some of whom are volunteers. Nevertheless, the housing cooperative system seems to offer not only a sufficiently flexible framework to allow the development of innovative collective projects but also enough incentives to encourage residents to take advantage of it. This is what the Cité Fédération sénégalaise des habitants (FSH) (Senegalese Federation of Inhabitants) project demonstrates (box 3.7).

The Community Land Trust
The CLT is an arrangement for distributing rights to land use, land ownership, and real estate that is organized around four principles (Davis 2010):

- Ownership of land and ownership of real estate are separate. The land is owned by a third-party organization, the trust, while the housing is owned by residents.
- Residents have land use rights.
- In the case of a sale, anti-speculation provisions give the trust preemptive rights. They also allocate to the trust a portion of any capital gains that result from a sale. These provisions make it possible to keep this housing affordable in the long run.
- The housing project is organized in a collective way, one that involves residents as well as representatives from government and civil society in the CLT's management structures.

Developed in the United States in the 1960s, the CLT and its principles have been adapted to a variety of places (including Australia, Belgium, Canada, France, and the United Kingdom) (box 3.6) and functions (e.g., agriculture, housing, and economic activities) (Davis, Algoed, and Hernández-Torrales 2020; Simonneau 2018).

Alternatives to the Individualization and Commodification of Land?
Altogether, these experiments comprise a relatively small number of dwellings and households in Sub-Saharan Africa. Still, they provide a useful window into a commons-based approach to meeting housing needs in urban areas where

BOX 3.6

The Voi Community Land Trust in Kenya

The secondary city of Voi, in Kenya, is home to the only Community Land Trust (CLT) on the African continent to date.[a] It was set up in the 1990s, as part of a development project to improve living conditions in the precarious neighborhood of Tanzania-Bondeni, and was financed with the help of the German cooperation agency. Tanzania-Bondeni was occupying public land on the outskirts of the city center without authorization. It was home to some 3,000 people in precarious living conditions (i.e., substandard housing, lack of basic services, and land insecurity). The purpose of the project was to improve these conditions, with an emphasis on long-term land security.

It was with these goals in mind that the neighborhood's residents chose a CLT from among other land-regularization options, such as leasehold titles or individual titles coupled with housing cooperatives (Bassett 2001). Formally implementing the CLT required making several legal adjustments. The two owners of the land occupied by the residents, Voi Sisal Estates and Kenya Railways, ceded the land as a contribution to the project. Two institutions were created: a neighborhood organization, the Tanzania-Bondeni Settlement Society, which would represent the residents (tenants as well as presumed owners), and a trust that would hold the primary leasehold. These institutions correspond to two levels of governance: a committee of residents elected to handle day-to-day affairs and a board of trustees that manages land affairs. Finally, a general assembly meets annually and elects the representatives of these governance bodies. Soon after, several interconnected collective structures were created, including tontines and neighborhood organizations.

A quarter-century after the end of the project, the main long-term lease, the centerpiece of the land package, has still not been issued. Only a letter of allotment has been issued. As a result, residents do not benefit from subleases but only from beacon certificates, which indicate the boundaries of the plots. The CLT's once-vigorous community life has faded: representatives have been reluctant to organize the annual general assembly, and certain internal rules, such as the prohibition on selling plots or renting out houses, have not been adhered to. Nevertheless, certain material benefits of the system have been retained: the architectural quality of the houses has generally improved, plans have been respected, and urban services have been put in place.

a. CLTs have been proposed in South Africa (Klug and Klug 2019), and discussions are currently under way in Senegal with respect to the Fédération sénégalaise des habitants (FSH) (Senegalese Federation of Inhabitants) Housing Estates (CAHF, urbaMonde, and UrbaSEN 2020), but as far as we know, nothing concrete has been developed to date.

land pressures and the dynamics of individualization and commodification are most intense. They broaden the range of housing supply options, which is often limited to either difficult-to-access formal housing or precarious neighborhoods (although the latter category is in fact extremely diverse) (Deboulet 2016). They put the spotlight on actors other than just public construction agencies and private real estate developers, such as builders who are also inhabitants, their collectives, and the nongovernmental organizations (NGOs) that support them. The existence—sometimes long-standing—of these local arrangements, such as housing cooperatives, constitutes a legal framework and a useful experience for broadening the range of housing offers by pooling access to land, construction, financing, or local life.

From the perspective of land-based commons for housing, two observations should be noted. The first observation is that these collective arrangements may not be sustainable in situations where residents may be highly mobile and where real estate and financial markets are especially active (Midheme 2015, 2018; Simonneau, Bassett, and Midheme 2020):

- Existing arrangements tend not to account much for the mobility of members and are poorly equipped to deal with generational turnover in ownership (particularly upon the death of the first owners). Although, in theory, they allow for a share of rental housing to be developed, they remain largely proprietary models.

- The collectives involved in these arrangements have been fairly resistant to real estate and financial market pressures for two reasons. The first is structural: in the case of housing cooperatives in Burkina Faso and Senegal, people form cooperatives to bypass constraints on land, in order to gain full ownership of the land and property. Once this goal has been attained, the collectives fall apart (Simonneau and Denis 2021). The second reason is contextual: the Kenyan experience with CLTs is now subject to mounting land pressures, resulting in unwarranted land grabs, the use of plots for profit, and an active land market.

The second observation is that it is rarely the most precarious segments of the population that take part in these arrangements. Rather, it tends to be households with stable incomes, who can get access to mortgage credit (sometimes with the help of collective guarantees) and can afford to have their savings frozen while a project is under way, sometimes for years at a time. Housing cooperatives, for example, are essentially the preserve of formal-sector workers: just 5.5 percent of Senegalese housing cooperative members are involved in informal sector work (Fall 2007).

Nevertheless, it seems possible to strengthen the role of collective production while also including the most precarious populations, provided that actors on the ground take full ownership of the approach and that the government agrees to support it. NGOs that support housing cooperatives often have an important role to play in structuring inhabitants' demands, as well as engaging in advocacy, for example, to ensure that a cooperative's socioeconomic profile (low and irregular income, in particular) is taken into account in public housing policies.

These are the conditions that must be met in order for these arrangements to become real, long-term alternatives to the individualization and commodification of urban land in Sub-Saharan Africa. The joint project of the Fédération sénégalaise des habitants (FSH) (Senegalese Federation of Inhabitants), which brings together savings groups from low-income neighborhoods and the NGOs UrbaSEN and urbaMonde, is notable in this respect (box 3.7).

BOX 3.7

The Cité FSH Project—A Cooperative, Nonspeculative, Low-Income Housing Project on the Outskirts of Dakar

The Fédération sénégalaise des habitants (FSH) (Senegalese Federation of Inhabitants) is a federation of residents' groups from precarious neighborhoods in Senegal. Founded in 2014 in Pikine, the FSH is sponsoring a housing development project (Cité FSH) for its members, which now number over 12,000.

With the support of the nongovernmental organizations UrbaSEN and urbaMonde, as well as the Centre for Affordable Housing Finance, the FSH is building 150 dwelling units, along with community facilities, such as a clinic, a school, and places of worship, on land in the Dakar region that was acquired in 2021.

The FSH founded a cooperative in 2020. It will handle real estate development, hold the land (through a land title in the name of the FSH cooperative) with a view to preventing speculation, receive members' savings, and ensure the distribution of housing to households. By establishing itself as a cooperative, the FSH can benefit from banking services and guarantees; moreover, the government will be responsible for preparing the land for construction.

The project proposes innovative, concrete solutions to the Senegalese situation on several points. The housing estates will be part of an eco-neighborhood that uses sustainable materials and sources and will be greened throughout. Local artisans will be given preference and trained. Designing and managing the project is a participatory exercise; planning involves future residents, most of whom are women (Brant de Carvalho et al. 2020). Financing comes from a mix of socially responsible sources from the solidarity economy.

The project's collective dimension is an important feature. The Cité FSH project is founded on collective land ownership and the separation of land ownership from housing ownership. Bank loans are obtained collectively, in the name of the cooperative, with a guarantee provided by the Fonds pour l'habitat social (Social Housing Fund). In this sense, the project is similar to the Community Land Trust system.

The project is intended to set an example and promote methods of social housing production in Senegal that are accessible to precarious households. The goal is to use this pilot project to push Senegal's government to broaden the range of households targeted by social housing programs (urbaMonde 2021).

Possibilities for Public Action

Regulating Land Practices and Offering Space to Future Cities

Both the shifts in land use that result from urbanization and the dismantling of rural commons are going to continue unabated. The strategies of land acquisition and accumulation and of subdividing properties cover a vast spectrum of practices. They involve a wide range of actors that are responding to a variety of incentives and that possess varying degrees of power and different economic resources when it comes to exploiting land resources.

Support from public authorities is necessary. In terms of access to land, facilities, and services, these processes generate inequalities not only between rural landowners and newcomers (certain rights holders are less able to make their voices heard) but also among newcomers themselves, such as between the urban working class and wealthier classes. These land practices are responses to real socioeconomic situations that vary across populations. Households may be seeking to establish an inheritance (storing savings), they may be responding to inflation (a kind of social security), or they may simply need a place to live. Yet public policies rarely address the socioeconomic conditions that enable or stimulate this land market—that is, economic inequalities between households and an often overly indebted agricultural sector (Merlet, Sauzion, and El Ouaamari 2017).

The future of agricultural production and food security is also at stake. Though large farms are better protected, certain transfers of rights result in fertile land being sterilized or left to lie fallow. In some areas, farmers are resisting by adapting to urban demands or by promoting adjustments to what food is produced and how—by engaging in practices that maintain soil fertility, for example, or by selling produce to urban markets.

The environmental impacts of urbanization are also crucial when it comes to maintaining soil fertility and groundwater recharge capacity; renewing resources such as wood, stones, and water; and preserving wetlands and biodiversity reserves.

There is a balance to be struck between regulating land conversion practices in ways that promote the sustainability of these regions, on the one hand, and making it possible for people to use land for housing, savings, or sometimes as an economic asset to pursue their life plans and provide for their children's futures, on the other hand.

From this perspective, the approach of land-based commons for housing, aimed at the rational management of land assets for housing purposes, is one possible way of devising innovative systems.

Collective Measures to Meet Housing Needs

Thus, in very concrete terms, the collective housing initiatives described in the previous section are original approaches with the potential to broaden the range of methods for accessing adequate housing. Three dimensions can be identified that are consistent with the commons-based entrepreneurship approach (see chapter 1), although their real-world implementation indicates that their range is limited in terms of time and space.

First, to varying degrees and in a variety of ways, collective and cooperative production is conceived of as an alternative to individual private land ownership. It comes with different arrangements and tools (e.g., collective leases, "mother" land titles, tools for breaking up the bundle of rights, fractioning of ownership) that recenter the long-term uses of the land. Although customary land tenure norms (i.e., rural commons) are sometimes evoked by project stakeholders (Simonneau 2018), the proposed tools are more akin to what is known as modern law, and inhabitants tend to be concerned mainly with securing an individual or family home. Yet the fact remains that some members of certain neighborhoods or professional or ethnic communities display a strong sense of belonging. Note that in some countries, legal recognition of customary or collective ownership can apply in urban areas, such as in Kenya, Namibia, and Tanzania (Alden Wily 2018). Certain examples outside of Africa are inspiring in this regard, such as in Brazil, where *quilombo* properties are recognized by special land statutes (Soares-Gonçalves 2021).

Second, collective and cooperative production can include provisions that limit speculation. The purpose of such provisions is to ensure that land and housing are used to meet housing needs and not for lucrative ends in the real estate market. In certain cases, they may also serve to keep down the cost of land to households. The implementation of this principle remains uneven, and it reveals the boundaries between a housing approach based on commons and one that exploits the collective principle for the purpose of private asset accumulation. This issue is directly connected to whether collectives are temporary: ultimately, collective and cooperative production will be limited if it is simply a gateway to private property. The local economic environment also encourages this individual private appropriation if it fails to offer more in the way of economic security and insertion than simply mortgages and the capture of land and real estate rent.

Third, the texts governing cooperative arrangements often commit to participatory governance. However, long-term progress in this regard remains limited. Cooperatives that are formed for the purpose of saving in common and building and securing housing in the medium term are not always maintained over the long haul. That said, this does not prevent neighborhood life from being vibrant or other cooperatives forming for other purposes, such as saving or defending access to services.

Collective housing arrangements thus constitute commons under certain conditions. They are directly engaged with the market for urban land and reveal clear limits to what they are capable of achieving. There is no simple answer to the problem of how to reconcile the principle of "commoning" (see chapter 1) with city dwellers' individual aspirations, particularly when these include accumulating an inheritance or even retaining the right to increase the value of one's housing capital. In this regard, limiting nonspeculative commons arrangements to precarious populations who desperately need a roof over their heads would appear to only worsen inequalities. Above all, we should recall that urban land grabbing (Steel, Van Noorloos, and Otsuki 2019) also has its roots in the failure to adequately share the costs of education, health, and social security as broadly understood.

Conditions for Scaling and Long-Term Consolidation

Our analysis of the most innovative real-world experiments, particularly the nonspeculative ones, leads us to underscore the fact that few of them have surpassed experimental scale and that they struggle to sustain themselves over generations of residents. The Voi CLT in Kenya, though widely publicized in specialized international forums[4] in the first years of the twenty-first century, has never been replicated elsewhere in Kenya. The Voi CLT itself was a success for the first generation of rehoused residents, but its community governance structures have been weakened and land ownership has been dispersed because it lacks a framework to guarantee subsidized and nonspeculative access across generations. Housing cooperatives, meanwhile, constitute a discrete housing production sector in West Africa. Still in their infancy in Burkina Faso, they are more firmly established in Senegal. Because their process is arduous, they have a high rate of failure, and cooperatives often disperse once the keys are handed over. As far as we know, there has been no systematic analysis of the renewal of generations of inhabitants in these housing projects. Such analysis could provide information about the future of these cooperatives and their capacity to ensure urban housing access beyond the first generation of first-time buyers. The gray and scientific literatures list numerous collective and cooperative initiatives that are innovative in one or another aspect (such as financing, land statutes, or governance) of popular housing development or regularization in Africa[5] and the countries of the Global South[6] (urbaMonde and Royez 2015). Yet there are few in-depth empirical studies of these same initiatives over time. Only this type of analysis, however, would make it possible to evaluate how robust these cooperatives and, especially, the application of their land rules remain over time.

Through our careful observations, however, we can identify certain principles that favor initial success, the ability to scale, and the inclusive sustainability of land-based commons for low-income housing.

Local support for the model and its adoption by resident groups

As the experience of the CLT in Kenya demonstrates, support from international organizations, or even national support for the implementation of a model that has proven successful elsewhere, is not a sufficient condition to guarantee its success locally and certainly not to ensure that it grows beyond an initial trial phase. The pooling of land must be adapted to local conditions and therefore must be linked to preexisting ways of "commoning," whether they be activist or traditional. The desire to do and live in common must be met with the support of a cooperative that is sufficiently tightly knit to uphold these values in the long run. This is why starting from a preexisting set of shared values is so critical. The traditions of cooperatives and unions, or working-class savings and financing collectives, are indispensable foundations upon which to build local cooperative movements. And it is just as critical that the collective management framework for ensuring (a) the maintenance of the co-owned property, (b) the control of transactions and the sharing of capital gains, (c) handover or rental agreements, and, ultimately, (d) mutual aid among residents be clearly formalized and backed by a group of regularly elected representatives.

Strong support from public authorities

It is also a necessary, though not sufficient, condition that a favorable legislative framework emerge at the national level and that it can be put to use by residents' groups and the associations that support them, particularly when it comes to setting up a legal structure that protects these groups. Creating cooperative statutes or legal forms that make it possible to divorce land ownership from housing ownership is therefore a key step.

Local authorities also have a crucial role to play in making land available in the city center (as is the case in Uruguay, with the principle of the land portfolio) and in the collective regularization of land, in the case of the in situ rehabilitation of precarious neighborhoods (de Souza, Valitutto, and Simonneau 2021).

A regulatory framework for making urban commons for housing viable

Promising projects that were undertaken enthusiastically by residents and the associations and institutions that support them, such as the Voi CLT in Kenya, are at risk of being gradually dismantled for want of a regulatory framework.

Over time, common goods are eroded by the poorly regulated sale of individual possessions. This is why anti-speculative provisions and keeping land ownership distinct from building ownership are critical to regulating sales and inheritances in order to preserve the inclusive dimension of these commons. Procedures for sharing and limiting capital gains in the event of sale are also essential for ensuring that the social function of housing commons is maintained and that money for operations or renovations goes to the cooperative, all while ensuring that profits are shared between the cooperative and the resident selling the property.

Networking and the sharing of experiences and methods

Mutual support between residents' groups, sometimes organized by intermediaries, makes it easier to keep these experiments alive, circulate information about them, and advocate for them locally. The success of the Uruguayan cooperative experience and its knock-on effects in South America are due in large part to the Federación Uruguaya de Cooperativas de Vivienda por Ayuda Mutua (Uruguayan Federation of Mutual Aid Cooperatives), which has organized and directed peer-to-peer exchanges of experiences, first in Uruguay, then at the Latin American level, and now at the global level. That said, the way civil society organizations in Sub-Saharan Africa are structured is a major point of differentiation here.

International NGOs that are active in the housing sector (particularly those in the CoHabitat Network) have succeeded in bringing the issues of commons and the right to the city into the international debate, as well as in publicizing and promulgating pilot projects in several regions of Africa and the countries of the Global South. However, they are not a substitute for the adoption and adaptation of these projects by local stakeholders—first and foremost by the inhabitants themselves but also by economic actors in the construction sector and the public authorities.

Conclusion

This chapter has sought to explore current land dynamics in Sub-Saharan Africa and to discuss the future of land-based commons in the context of massive, rapid, and diffuse urbanization. The pressure on land to meet housing needs and the use of land as a basis for insurance and savings are both extremely significant.

On the one hand, this chapter demonstrates that access to rural land-based commons, which have roots in traditional land management, is being closed off. In the wake of societal changes and upheavals in local economies and in the conditions of agricultural production, lands that had traditionally been held in common are being divided up. Rights are being progressively individualized and sometimes transferred outside of local communities. These poorly regulated processes are generating inequalities between rural and urban dwellers and between land buyers with different financial means.

On the other hand, the chapter examines the possibilities for land access that are opening up in cities as a result of the establishment of new commons. The commons approach makes it possible to reconsider several aspects of urban housing development and to imagine, in particular, a mode of collective governance that privileges the needs of inhabitants and land that is made to serve a long-term social function and that is resistant to market pressures. The tools required to make this vision a reality do exist: nonspeculative provisions such as resale formulas, collective land statutes that protect inhabitants from exclusion by the market, and solidarity financing mechanisms. Although they may not meet the high demand for housing in these cities, they make it possible to expand the range of options for accessing land and producing housing.

We base our discussion on several real-life uses of some of these tools: housing cooperatives in Burkina Faso and Senegal and the Voi CLT in Kenya. Empirical case studies allow us to show the potential and limits of these arrangements in terms of how inclusive they are of those at the lowest end of the socio-economic spectrum, how well they are able to scale up, and to what degree they maintain the values of "commoning" beyond the first group of inhabitants. Most West African cooperatives are now temporary arrangements enabling people with stable incomes to access private property, while vulnerable populations are likely to struggle to carry out such ambitious, long-term land and real estate projects. The CLT was a rather valuable experiment when it began, but it has begun to weaken. This points to how important it is to consider procedures for allowing households to leave cooperative and collective arrangements in a timely manner, as well as procedures for modifying rules at the level of the housing project.

Since they help broaden the spectrum of housing supply and diversify financing mechanisms and modes of governance in the housing sector, cooperative and collective arrangements have the potential to help achieve Sustainable Development Goal number 11. But promising though it may be, it is simply potential: the results of these experiments, which may be highly localized (as in the case of the Voi CLT) or aimed at households that are not the most precarious (such as the housing cooperative), are still quite limited. That said, the existing cooperative movement in Africa could be supported financially, legally, technically, and in terms of governance so that it could be opened up, within the framework of public housing policies (Marot et al. 2022), to the working classes in a more radical and protected way. What access do households have to solidarity financing if they cannot access bank loans for want of a steady income? What place has been accorded to precarious households in recent public programs for social and affordable housing in Africa? How can better technical support be provided to the management bodies of cooperatives?

The CLT system also feeds into ideas about helping inhabitants stay in coveted neighborhoods or even come settle there. It also contributes to the important debate that has been running for 40 years now about the regularization of precarious neighborhoods, and it should be thoroughly examined alongside the long list of mechanisms for securing the rights of those who live in precarious neighborhoods in Sub-Saharan Africa (Gulyani and Bassett 2007) and the countries of the Global South. The collective dimension of regularizations and restrictions on the resale of land has been tested on these occasions, and these experiences deserve a second look.

In this respect, we believe that more attention should be paid to the work of international NGOs in organizing exchanges of experience between countries of the Global South and capitalizing on collective and cooperative production in the service of precarious inhabitants (Davis, Algoed, and Hernández-Torrales 2020; Gonzalez 2013; Williamson 2019). However, this work must be complemented by in-depth, long-term empirical studies in order to assess how robust commons remain over time.

Finally, we believe that it is essential to better produce and disseminate both the knowledge of inhabitants and diachronic scientific analyses according to the principles of learning communities and open-source urbanism rooted in the knowledge commons, so that local communities can adopt and adapt these systems.

Notes

1. This chapter relies on research funded by the Agence française de développement (AFD) (French Development Agency) and the Comité technique "Foncier et développement" (CTFD) (Technical Committee on "Land Tenure and Development"). We would like to thank our collaborators who handled field research, including Issa Sory (2019) in Burkina Faso, Emmanuel Midheme (2018) in Kenya, and Thomas Voldoire, with support from Momar Diongue (2022), in Senegal.
2. In 2018, Bah, Faye, and Geh estimated that Africa had a deficit of 50 million housing units (Bah, Faye, and Geh 2018).
3. Especially in Burkina Faso, Cameroon, Ghana, Kenya, Mali, and Senegal.
4. Included in Kenya's best practices at the 1996 Habitat II conference; finalist for the 2006 World Habitat Award.
5. For example, Amui Dzor Housing cooperative in Accra, Ghana (Gillespie 2018), or the Coophylos cooperative in Cameroon.
6. See the CoHabitat Network online census: https://www.co-habitat.net/en/tools/cohabitat-io.

References

Aalbers, Manuel B., Raquel Rolnik, and Marieke Krijnen. 2020. "The Financialization of Housing in Capitalism's Peripheries." *Housing Policy Debate* 30 (4): 481–85.

Agergaard, Jytte, Cecilia Tacoli, Griet Steel, and Sinne Borby Ørtenblad. 2019. "Revisiting Rural–Urban Transformations and Small Town Development in Sub-Saharan Africa." *European Journal of Development Research* 31: 2–11. https://doi.org/10.1057/s41287-018-0182-z.

Alden Wily, Liz. 2018. "The Community Land Act in Kenya Opportunities and Challenges for Communities." *Land* 7 (12). https://doi.org/10.3390/land7010012.

Aveline-Dubach, Natacha, Thibault Le Corre, Éric Denis, and Claude Napoléone. 2020. "Les futurs du foncier: Modes d'accumulation du capital, droit de propriété et production de la ville." In *Pour la recherche urbaine*, edited by Félix Adisson, Sabine Barles,

Nathalie Blanc, Olivier Coutard, Leïla Frouillou, and Fanny Rassat, 313–35. Paris: CNRS Éditions.

Bah, El-hadj, Issa Faye, and Zekebweliwai F. Geh. 2018. *Housing Market Dynamics in Africa*. London: Palgrave Macmillan. https://doi.org/10.1057/978-1-137-59792-2.

Bassett, Ellen M. 2001. "Institutions and Informal Settlements: The Planning Implications of the Community Land Trust Experiment in Kenya." PhD dissertation, The University of Wisconsin–Madison.

Berger, Thierry, and Lorenzo Cotula. 2021. "Thierry Berger et Lorenzo Cotula examen des tendance globales concernant les ZES." In *Les zones économiques spéciales et le foncier: Tendances globales et incidences locales au Sénégal et à Madagascar: Final report*, 8–31. Paris: "Foncier et développement" technical committee.

Bertrand, Monique, and Bérénice Bon. 2022. "Négocier la terre en attendant la ville: Marchés fonciers et gouvernance périurbaine en Afrique subsaharienne." *Canadian Journal of African Studies* 57 (1): 1–26. https://doi.org/10.1080/00083968 .2021.2023359.

Bon, Bérénice. 2022. "Invisible Sprawl: Land, Money and Politics at the Rural-Urban Interface in Kenya." *disP—The Planning Review* 57 (3): 33–49. https://doi.org/10.1080 /02513625.2021.2026649.

Bon, Bérénice, Claire Simonneau, Éric Denis, and Philippe Lavigne Delville, eds. Forthcoming. *Conversions des usages des sols liées à l'urbanisation des Suds: Vol. 2 Case Study*. Paris: "Foncier et développement" technical committee.

Brant de Carvalho, Gustavo, Nizar Hajar, Nicolas Myhie, Nicolas Poinsot, and Maïlys Simion. 2020. "Sama Keur. Mon toit. Perspectives d'intégration et faisabilité du projet de cité FSH dans les dynamiques urbaines de l'est dakarois." Master's report. Ecole d'urbanisme de Paris.

Buire, Chloé. 2014. "Suburbanisms in Africa? Spatial Growth and Social Transformation in New Urban Peripheries: Introduction to the Cluster." *African Studies* 73 (2): 241–44.

CAHF (Centre for Affordable Housing Finance in Africa). 2019. "Chroniques d'investissements dans le logement au Sénégal." Last modified December 2019. https:// housingfinanceafrica.org/app/uploads/Rapport-Senegal-CIL-final-1.pdf.

CAHF (Centre for Affordable Housing Finance in Africa), urbaMonde, and UrbaSEN. 2020. "Étude sur les mécanismes de financement citoyen pour la production de loge-ments abordables en Afrique." http://urbamonde.org/IMG/pdf/00_etude_sur_les _mecanismes_de_financement_citoyen_introduction_et_conclusion_juin_2020.pdf.

Cissé, Oumar. 2013. *Profil du secteur du logement au Sénégal*. Nairobi: UN-Habitat.

Colin, Jean-Philippe. 2004. "Droits fonciers, pratiques foncières et relations intra-famil-iales: les bases conceptuelles et méthodologiques d'une approche compréhensive." *Land Reform, Land Settlement and Cooperatives* 2: 55–67.

Colin, Jean-Philippe. 2017. "Émergence et dynamique des marchés fonciers ruraux en Afrique subsaharienne. Un état des lieux sélectif." *Cahiers du Pôle Foncier* 18/2017, Dakar/ Montpellier, IPAR/IRD.

Colin, Jean-Philippe, and Auréa Pottier. Forthcoming. "Dynamique de conversion de l'usage des sols dans un village du Sud Comoé (Côte d'Ivoire)." In *Conversions des usages des sols liées à l'urbanisation dans les Suds Vol. 2 Case Study*, edited by Bérénice Bon, Claire Simonneau, Éric Denis, and Philippe Lavigne Delville. Paris: "Foncier et développement" technical committee.

Darbon, Dominique, and Comi M. Toulabor, eds. 2014. *L'invention des classes moyennes africaines: Enjeux politiques d'une catégorie incertaine*. Paris: Karthala.

Davis, John Emmeus, ed. 2010. *The Community Land Trust Reader*. Cambridge, MA: Lincoln Institute of Land Policy.

Davis, John Emmeus, Line Algoed, and María Hernández-Torrales. 2020. *On Common Ground: International Perspectives on the Community Land Trust*. Madison, WI: Terra Nostra Press.

Deboulet, Agnès. 2016. *Rethinking Precarious Neighborhoods*. Paris: Agence française de développement.

Defrise, Laurence, Perrine Burnod, Jean-Philippe Tonneau, and Valérie Andriamanga. 2019. "Disparition et permanence de l'agriculture urbaine à Antananarivo." *L'Espace géographique* 48 (3): 263–81.

Delaunay, Daniel, and Florence Boyer. 2017. "Habiter Ouagadougou." In *Monographies Sud-Nord*, 1–84. Nogent sur Marne: IEDES.

Denis, Éric. 2015. "Qualifier les aires urbaines en forte expansion dans les Suds. Positionnement au prisme de travaux sur l'expansion des villes en Asie." *L'Espace géographique* 44 (4): 307–24.

Denis, Éric. 2020. "More Urban Constructions for Whom? Drivers of Urban Built-up Expansion across the World from 1990 to 2015." In *Theories and Models of Urbanization*, edited by Denise Pumain, 235–58. New York: Springer.

de Souza, Ignacio, Irene Valitutto, and Claire Simonneau. 2021. "Las cooperativas de usuarios en Uruguay. El desafío del habitat como común." *Papiers de recherche*, 1–45. Accessed October 5, 2022, from https://www.afd.fr/es/ressources/cooperativas -usuarios-uruguay-habitat-comun.

Diop, Djibril. 2012. *Urbanisation et gestion du foncier urbain à Dakar: Défis et perspectives*. Paris: L'Harmattan.

Fall, Abdou Salam. 2007. "Le renouvellement des dynamiques coopératives africaines. Les coopératives d'habitat au Sénégal." In *L'Afrique qui se refait. Initiatives socioéconomiques des communautés et développement en Afrique noire*, edited by Louis Favreau and Abdou Salam Fall, 121–39. Quebec: Presses de l'Université du Québec.

Ganapati, Sukumar. 2014. "Housing Cooperatives in the Developing World." In *Affordable Housing in the Urban Global South*, edited by Jan Bredenoord, Paul van Lindert, and Peer Smets, 102–16. London and New York: Routledge.

Gillespie, Tom. 2018. "Collective Self-Help, Financial Inclusion, and the Commons: Searching for Solutions to Accra's Housing Crisis." *Housing Policy Debate* 28 (1): 64–78.

Gonzalez, Gustavo. 2013. *Una historia de FUCVAM*. Montevideo: Ediciones Trilce.

Guigma, Léandre, Madeleine Boudoux d'Hautefeuille, and Liliane Pierre-Louis. 2015. "Gestion de l'étalement urbain informel à Ouagadougou: Le renoncement des politiques publiques?" In *Territoires périurbains. Développement, enjeux et perspectives dans les pays du sud*, edited by Jan Bogaert and Jean-Marie Halleux, 271–80. Gembloux: Les presses agronomiques de Gembloux.

Guigma, Pougdwendé Léandre. 2017. "Vivre dans le non-loti de Ouagadougou: Processus de marchandages fonciers entre citadins, chefs traditionnels et autorités publiques." PhD dissertation, Paris 8 University Vincennes-Saint-Denis. https://www.theses .fr/2017PA080113.

Gulyani, Sumila, and Ellen M. Bassett. 2007. "Retrieving the Baby from the Bathwater: Slum Upgrading in Sub-Saharan Africa." *Environment and Planning C: Government and Policy* 25 (4): 486–515.

Jaglin, Sylvy, Sophie Didier, and Alain Dubresson. 2018. "Métropolisations en Afrique subsaharienne: Au menu ou à la carte?" *Métropoles* special issue. https://doi .org/10.4000/metropoles.6065.

Klug, Heinz, and Neil Klug. 2019. "Community Land Trusts and Social Inclusion." In *Politics and Community-Based Research: Perspectives from Yeoville Studio*, edited by Claire Bénit-Gbaffou, Sarah Charlton, Sophie Didier, and Kirsten Dörmann, 179–200. Johannesburg: Wits University Press.

Lall, Somik Vinay, J. Vernon Henderson, and Anthony J. Venables. 2017. *Africa's Cities: Opening Doors to the World*. Washington, DC: World Bank. https://doi .org/10.1596/978-1-4648-1044-2.

Lavigne Delville, Philippe, and Adama Sow. Forthcoming. "Étude de cas. La ville nou-velle de Diamniadio au Sénégal." In *Conversions des usages des sols liées à l'urbanisation dans Suds: Vol. 2 Case Study*, edited by Bérénice Bon, Claire Simonneau, Éric Denis, and Philippe Lavigne Delville. Paris: "Foncier et développement" technical committee.

Marot, Bruno, Karen Lévy, Irène Salenson, and Jean-François Valette. 2022. "Les poli-tiques du logement dans les suds (2/2): Quelles alternatives à l'endettement des ménages?" *Papiers de recherche*, 1–47. https://www.cairn.info/les-politiques-du-logement -dans-les-suds-2-2-la-pr--1000000148970-page-1.htm.

Mercer, Claire. 2017. "Landscapes of Extended Ruralisation: Postcolonial Suburbs in Dar es Salaam, Tanzania." *Transactions of the Institute of British Geographers* 42 (1): 72–83. https://doi.org/10.1111/tran.12150.

Merlet, Michel, Coline Sauzion, and Samir El Ouaamari. 2017. "Étude régionale sur les marchés fonciers ruraux en Afrique de l'ouest et les outils de leur régulation." In *Fiches d'expériences de régulation des marchés fonciers dans différents pays*, edited by Michel Merlet, Coline Sauzion, and Samir El Ouaamari. Ouagadougou/Dakar: West African Economic and Monetary Union/IPAR. https://www.ipar.sn/IMG/pdf/ipar-uemoa _-_fiches_experiences___agter.pdf.

Meth, Paula, Tom Goodfellow, Alison Todes, and Sarah Charlton. 2021. "Conceptualizing African Urban Peripheries." *International Journal of Urban and Regional Research* 45 (6): 985–1007. https://doi.org/10.1111/1468-2427.13044.

Midheme, Emmanuel. 2015. "Modalities of Space Production within Kenya's Rapidly Transforming Cities. Cases from Voi and Kisumu." PhD dissertation, KU Leuven. https://lirias.kuleuven.be/1739510.

Midheme, Emmanuel. 2018. *Do Urban Land Commons Foster Urban Inclusion? Kenya Case Study*. Report on the Methodological Framework. Programme communs fonci-ers urbains. Unpublished.

OECD (Organisation for Economic Co-operation and Development). 2020. *Africa's Urbanisation Dynamics 2020. Africapolis, Mapping a New Urban Geography*. Paris: OECD.

OHCHR (Office of the High Commissioner for Human Rights) and UN-Habitat. 2010. "Le droit à un logement convenable." Fiche d'information 21. Droits de l'homme. UN-Habitat.

Osmont, Annik. 1973. "La formation d'une communauté locale à Dakar." *Cahiers d'études Africaines* 13 (51): 497–510.

Sané, Youssouph. 2013. "La politique de l'habitat au Sénégal: Une mutation permanente." *Les cahiers d'Outre-Mer* 263: 311–34. https://doi.org/10.4000/com.6913.

Sawyer, Lindsay. 2014. "Piecemeal Urbanisation at the Peripheries of Lagos." *African Studies* 73 (2): 271–89.

Simonneau, Claire. 2018. "Le community land trust aux États-Unis, au Kenya et en Belgique. Canaux de circulation d'un modèle alternatif et jeu d'intertextualité." *RIURBA Revue internationale d'urbanisme* 6. http://www.riurba.review/Revue/le -community-land-trust-aux-etats-unis-au-kenya-et-en-belgique-canaux-de-circulation -dun-modele-alternatif-et-jeu-dintertextualite/.

Simonneau, Claire, Ellen M. Bassett, and Emmanuel Midheme. 2020. "Seeding the CLT in Africa: Lessons from the Early Efforts to Establish Community Land Trusts in Kenya." In *On Common Ground. International Perspectives on the Community Land Trust*, edited by John Emmeus Davis, Line Algoed, and María E. Hernández-Torrales, 245–61. Madison, WI: Terra Nostra Press.

Simonneau, Claire, and Éric Denis. 2021. "Communs fonciers pour des villes inclusives. Produire et sécuriser l'habitat populaire autour de la propriété partagée du sol: Une diversité de modèles, leurs intérêts et leurs limites." *Papiers de recherche*, 1–81. https:// halshs.archives-ouvertes.fr/halshs-03405275/document.

Simonneau, Claire, Éric Denis, and Issa Sory. 2019. "Quel potentiel pour les approches coopératives et collectives pour l'habitat populaire en Afrique? Éléments du débat, grille d'analyse et exemples burkinabé et kenyan." *Afrique contemporaine* 269–70 (1): 155–75.

Soares-Gonçalves, Rafael. 2021. "Le pluralisme de la propriété et les communs fonciers: Le cas de la prescription acquisitive collective spéciale urbaine de la Chácara de Catumbi à Rio de Janeiro." Papiers de recherche. Agence française de développement, Paris.

Sory, Issa. 2019. "Public Land Policies at an Impasse in Ouagadougou (Burkina Faso)." *Afrique contemporaine* 269–70 (1–2): 135–54. https://doi.org/10.3917/afco.269.0135.

Sory, Issa, Salfo Lingani, and Gabin Korbeogo. 2015. "Comment loger les couches sociales à faible revenu en milieu urbain burkinabé? L'introuvable politique de 'logements sociaux' à Ouagadougou." *Revue des hautes terres* 5: 1–2.

Steel, Griet, Femke Van Noorloos, and Kei Otsuki. 2019. "Urban Land Grabs in Africa?" *Built Environment* 44 (4): 389–96.

Traoré, J.-M., Bernard Crousse, Emile Le Bris, and Etienne Le Roy. 1986. "Aménagement urbain et pratiques foncières coutumières en Haute-Volta." In *Espaces disputés en Afrique noire. Pratiques foncières locales*, edited by Bernard Crousse, Emile Le Bris, and Etienne Le Roy, 33–40. Paris: Karthala.

UNCTAD (United Nations Conference on Trade and Development). 2019. *World Investment Report: Special Economic Zones*. New York and Geneva: United Nations.

urbaMonde. 2021. "Le logement abordable. Stratégies de production coopérative à travers l'exemple de la Cité de la fédération Sénégalaise des habitants." Last modified December 2021. https://www.urbamonde.org/IMG/pdf/urbamonde_cahf_le_logement _abordable_cite-fsh_afrique_12_2021.pdf.

urbaMonde and Cyril Royez. 2015. *Production sociale de l'habitat*. Geneva: UrbaMonde. https://issuu.com/urbamonde/docs/urbabook_partner_review_small.

Williamson, Theresa. 2019. "The Favela Community Land Trust: A Sustainable Housing Model for the Global South." In *Critical Care: Architecture and Urbanism for a Broken Planet*, edited by Angelika Fitz, Elke Krasny, and Architekturzentrum Wien, 114–24. Cambridge: MIT Press.

Yung, Jean-Michel, and Pierre-Marie Bosc. 1999. "8. Schumpeter au Sahel." In *L'innovation en agriculture*, edited by Jean-Pierre Chauveau, Marie-Christine Cormier Salem, and Éric Mollard, 143–68. Marseille: IRD Éditions. https://doi.org/10.4000 /books.irdeditions.15741.

Chapter 4

Urban Commons: Reestablishing Social Ties in African Cities

Stéphanie Leyronas, Alix Françoise, Isabelle Liotard, Lola Mercier, and Guiako Obin

Introduction

Africa is simultaneously the world's least urbanized continent and the one with the highest demographic growth rate in urban areas. Its current urbanization rate is estimated at somewhere between 42.5 percent (UN 2019) and 50.4 percent (OECD and SWAC 2020) of the continent's total population. Since the 1950s, the average urban growth rate has been 4.8 percent per year. Africa's urban population therefore grew more than 16-fold between 1950 and 2018, increasing from 33 million to 548 million people. This trend is expected to continue with a tripling of the urban population by 2050, representing some 1.5 billion people (UN 2019). This rate does vary by country, and its impact is especially noticeable in countries with a low level of urbanization (such as Burundi, Lesotho, Malawi, Niger, and South Sudan). Here, the growth rate currently exceeds 7 percent, implying that the population will double every 10 years (OECD and SWAC 2020).

Most of Africa's national urban systems are dominated by large conurbations, and this trend is growing. The population of Luanda (Angola), for example, is the equivalent of that of the country's next 27 largest conurbations combined (OECD and SWAC 2020). At the same time, a network of secondary conurbations driven by national local development policies is being shaped. These medium-sized cities, often the capitals of agricultural regions, are also increasing in size because of natural growth in the population and, to a lesser extent, internal migration.

Urban development in Africa has long been a priority within the international aid community. Two significant milestones in the international governance of urban growth were the United Nation's (UN's) 2015 Sustainable Development Goal 11 to create sustainable cities accessible to all and the New Urban Agenda (UN-Habitat 2015) seeking to make cities safer, more resilient, and more sustainable, adopted at the Habitat III conference in 2016.

Public financial resources are rare so local communities must engage in new forms of governance that involve a myriad of different stakeholders from cities and the urban sector. Some consensus has been reached about the many diverse stakeholders (public, private, nonprofit, political), policy areas (land, housing, infrastructure), and scales of response (local, city, national, and international) involved in shaping cities, as well as how urban areas in Sub-Saharan Africa should be constructed and managed (Schlimmer 2022).

This chapter examines commons that have emerged in urban settings as one expression of these social, economic, political, and spatial phenomena. Its analysis draws on interviews with the stakeholders of urban commons in Sub-Saharan Africa, as well as a review of the academic literature and documentary research (websites and social networks, local and international media).

The first section sets out exactly what kind of activities can be classified as urban commons in Sub-Saharan Africa. These public or private places are shared by local residents who develop diverse uses for them. They involve a multitude of different stakeholders operating under various forms of open governance, and a variety of tangible and intangible resources from the local area are used by different groups.

The second section provides an empirical analysis of some of these places (hybrid cultural spaces, playing fields, shared gardens, fab labs[1]), while the third and final section proposes what role they could potentially have in fashioning urban environments in Sub-Saharan Africa.

Urban Commons in the Context of Sub-Saharan Africa

Urban Fragmentation and the Loss of Social Cohesion

Against a background of high demographic growth, African cities contribute to improving their country's economic performance, as well as improving living standards. In a recent report, the Organisation for Economic Co-operation and Development (OECD) revealed that urbanization in Africa has contributed to approximately 30 percent of the increase in gross domestic product (GDP) per person achieved over the past 20 years (OECD, AfDB, and ECA 2022). Moreover, living standards, the amount of time spent in education (8.5 years compared with 4.5 years on average), and professional achievements are on average higher for people living in urban areas than elsewhere in the same country. Wealth distribution by quintiles indicates that a growing share, and sometimes a majority, of the population's richest individuals live in large cities. The OECD also notes a knock-on effect in areas located near cities (OECD and SWAC 2020).

Despite these developments, in reality, Africa's urban economies have changed little over the past few years. They have not diversified to any great extent. Manufacturing has transformative potential for numerous regions in this continent (Abreha et al. 2021), but it remains underrepresented as a sector, unlike in some Asian countries (China, India, Malaysia). Urban economies must also deal with the structural challenges (such as building human capital) and operational costs of these cities.

Governance is a major challenge. Africa's local authorities struggle to plan for investments or provide essential services because of financial, institutional, and technical weaknesses. Cities are growing quickly but lack vital infrastructure investment. Some districts, particularly on the outskirts, have expanded rapidly without being connected to road networks or basic public services. More than half of the urban population in Africa lives in this kind of vulnerable neighborhood (UN-Habitat 2015). Moreover, major cities are facing significant transport challenges with high levels of pollution and congestion; government stakeholders are struggling to protect public sites, particularly green spaces; and urban dwellers, vulnerable to climate hazards, are already experiencing phenomena such as heat waves, water shortages, and flooding to a greater extent (Dodman, Hayward, and Pelling 2021).

These shortcomings are causing African cities to become spatially, socially, economically, and politically fragmented. As a result, the social fabric within communities, as well as between local populations and government institutions, is often torn (European Commission and Enabel 2021). This contributes to the severing of social ties, that is, personal relationships within the same society, mutual levels of trust, and norms of reciprocity (Colleta and Cullen 2000; Garroway 2011).

With regard to Nigerian and South African cities in particular, Fourchard suggests that, although these cities do provide jobs, they have also quickly generated "new forms of poverty and social violence (unemployment, crime, abuse, prostitution, gangsterism, and procuring), as well as problems over the integration of migrant populations" (Fourchard 2018, 7). Geographical origin (whether someone is part of the indigenous or migrant population) forms the basis for exclusion that, in some instances, has been institutionalized and politicized. These cities are "laboratories for exclusion and the use of violence" that is sometimes physical (Fourchard 2018, 8). According to the anthropologist Balandier, this leads people living in urban environments to retain close ties with their original social circles and villages so as to find support in those existing forms of solidarity. In doing so, they "return to a community, and find the material assistance they would not have found elsewhere" (Balandier 1958, 21).

The emergence in Africa's cities of commons whose remits cover a wide variety of resources is evidence of a desire to strengthen new social ties within urban communities. These commons are run by groups of different sizes and kinds (locals, residents, users, entrepreneurs, specialists) working within a broad spectrum of urban life: land, public services, welfare, and education.

From Commons in Cities to Urban Commons

In this instance, we have focused on places that are physically located within urban sites and communally managed by groups with a social, economic, and political vision for these spaces that reshapes the local area as a sociopolitical construct. Their project might focus on welfare and improving living conditions (shared gardens, playing fields, community halls) or access to art and culture. They may also specialize in science, innovation, and digital technology (spaces for technological innovation and production such as fab labs).

The urban commons we have examined overlap in numerous ways with "third places." This notion was coined by the sociologist Oldenburg in 1989 and refers to the places that sit somewhere between home and work and that contribute to urban sociability (Fabbri 2016). The people who visit them (Lofland 1998; Oldenburg 1989) create their sense of community, their accessibility by other individuals, and, thus, their collective dimension. In the context of Sub-Saharan Africa, we prefer the term *hybrid places* as the concept of "third places" is little used by African stakeholders (Besson, forthcoming).

African urban commons are multifunctional by their very nature and combine a number of different purposes:

- Services (food production in shared gardens, intermediation services, access to material and equipment, access to artistic endeavors)
- Educational and dissemination activities relating to the collective aim pursued (adult education, organization of events, lessons and workshops, gatherings)
- Activities focusing on sustainable cities and resilience (waste-to-energy conversion and renewable forms of energy)

Urban commons are also a testament to a relatively recent phenomenon, the "Africanization" of the maker movement, as evidenced by the growing number of fab labs in Sub-Saharan Africa over the past decade (Mboa Nkoudou 2017). These fab labs are diverse spaces and specialize in specific areas (agriculture, education, disability). They are local experiments that are sometimes organized informally and spontaneously. It can be difficult to grasp their significance fully because their stakeholders can only be identified through detailed field research. They mostly come from working-class and challenging social backgrounds.

Urban Commons: Theoretical Perspectives

Urban commons are not only characterized by their location or their concentration in cities (Susser and Tonnelat 2013) but also by (a) the construction of a common purpose capable of motivating stakeholder cooperation, (b) participatory systems to ensure users are included in joint deliberation and joint decision-making activities, and (c) a vision of urban areas as a communal space where individuals can create urban commons.

Urban commons emerged during a relatively recent phase of the debate about commons (Festa 2016). Their genealogy is fairly specific, forming part of the new commons that Hess proposed to map (Hess 2008). The concept was developed in Europe where several cities witnessed the development of shared management practices. In Italy, the 2011 movement to occupy cultural sites demanded the "right to the city" (Lefebvre 1996) that was supposed to produce an accessible public space. Many of these forms of urban resistance can be traced back to opposition to the confiscation of communal resources abandoned or reused speculatively (cinemas, theaters, sites for living and producing). They shone a light on how physical and symbolic urban spaces are used and questioned local governance systems and the link between citizenship rights and those relating to urban life (Gervais-Lambony 2001; Lussault and Lévy 2013). The focus was no longer on who owned the space but the function that space should have in society (Rodotà 2016).

The resources used included public or private property (parks, gardens, streets, squares, infrastructure), intangible commodities (the air), and immaterial commodities (intellectual property, information networks, social networks, cultural values and those relating to heritage). The particularity of urban commons is that they are deployed in places where certain resources are highly sought after (i.e., sites with high land and property prices, a variety of uses, or a high population density). Harvey (2012, 80) maintains that they display the same contradictions as the other commons but "in highly concentrated form."

As recalled in chapter 1, how a resource is managed is more important than its type (Bollier and Helfrich 2015). At the heart of urban commons are heterogeneous communities with open and fluid dividing lines that are sometimes very changeable. This distinguishes them from the more typical commons that were studied in great detail by Ostrom and the Bloomington School (Ostrom 1990). These urban communities form through a process of pooling their resources and can evolve in both time and space (Festa 2016). Within the community, commitment to a place can sometimes vary: small groups run the common on a day-to-day basis, while larger groups enjoy some of its uses and participate in its collective management in a more ad hoc manner. Different interests can therefore coalesce around managing commons. Some more complex urban commons involve different interest groups (civic, private, institutional) and therefore require intersectoral collaboration and long-term processes to achieve true participatory governance (Kip 2015).

African Commons Embodied by Social, Cultural, and Technological Spaces

Little detailed research exists about African urban commons (Besson 2018; Cléré 2018). We propose dividing the urban commons we studied into two types, although the line separating them remains porous: predominantly social or cultural urban commons, on the one hand, and urban commons for technological innovation and production, including fab labs, on the other.

We interviewed people from 11 social and cultural spaces (map 4.1) and 13 fab labs (map 4.2) between January and April 2017, as well as between December 2021 and May 2022. These urban sites were chosen because of the representative nature of their approach and their stage of development.

First, we examine experiences of the social and cultural spaces in Sub-Saharan Africa studied, and then we analyze urban commons for technological innovation and production.

Social and Cultural Urban Commons: Public Spaces and Hybrid Cultural Sites

Urban commons that are predominantly social and cultural in nature focus on welfare. They use art, sport, gardening, and urban agriculture as vehicles for

Map 4.1 Social and Cultural Spaces Studied

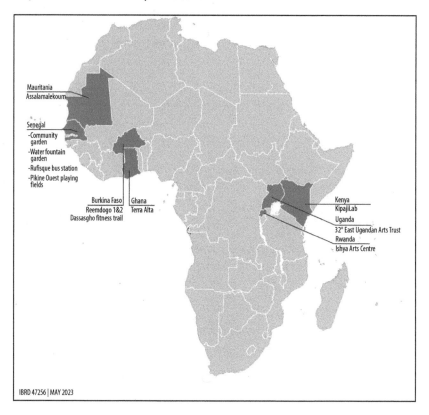

Source: World Bank.

Map 4.2 **Fab Labs Studied**

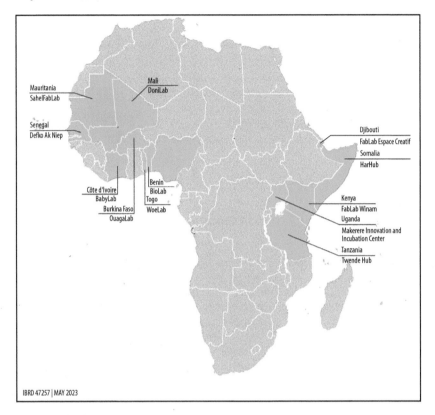

forging social ties within neighborhoods. In so doing, they address some of the social needs yet to be tackled. Hardly any creative or cultural industries are managed by government bodies in Sub-Saharan Africa, despite access to culture being considered "a way for citizens, and in particular young people, to make their voices heard in the public spaces, and thus reinforces democratic participation" (European Commission and Enabel 2021, 7). Public infrastructure for amateur sport remains insufficient,[2] despite it playing a part in maintaining public order, preventing crime, and improving young people's health.[3] Finally, and without overstating their importance in terms of the food insecurity facing African cities (Davies et al. 2021), gardening and urban agriculture do have economic worth and create employment, as well as being socially valuable (Rutt 2007).

Social and cultural urban commons in Sub-Saharan Africa fall within two main categories: public spaces used by local people, on the one hand, and spaces specifically focusing on art and artists, on the other.

In public spaces used by local people, art, sport, and gardening are deployed as vehicles for forging social ties within a neighborhood. These are public places local people can access (squares, streets, gardens, playing fields) that have been occupied by collaborative initiatives (box 4.1). They are places people pass through without necessarily stopping (Joseph 1998). Local communities in Africa struggle to plan, implement, and support these kinds of spaces, not least because of the fragmentation of cities (Navez-Bouchanine 2002) that has led to urban wastelands, vacant lots, and rubbish dumps. These public spaces are "fundamental urban materials" (Secchi 2006) for the people who take possession of them. Abandoned by the public authorities, these spaces can be occupied by groups who

---

BOX 4.1

Examples of Public Urban Commons Accessible to Local People

The Kër Thiossane Villa for Art and Multimedia School of Commons in Dakar houses a fab lab (Defko), as well as an artistic garden and a community garden. The space was created in 2002 in the Sicap neighborhood on the site of an abandoned public garden that had become a rubbish dump. The artistic garden was designed and created in 2014 by Emmanuel Louisgrand, the founder of this space. The experimental hub hosts many projects run by different people (workshops, gatherings, exhibitions). The community garden was created in 2016 to provide permaculture and urban micro-gardening training for young women.

In Burkina Faso, the Reemdogo 1 garden of music was created in 2004 in the Gounghin neighborhood of Ouagadougou as a shared garden where musicians from the neighborhood hold intimate local concerts. The space is managed by the local authorities, groups of musicians, and concert organizers. This initiative inspired the creation of the Reemdogo 2 arts and culture garden in 2018. The aim of both these spaces is to develop artistic endeavors (sculpture and music) and create neighborly bonds between artists, audiences, individuals, and businesses operating in the cultural sector through communal activities and programs.

In Dakar, the local authorities took action to refurbish some abandoned or poorly maintained public spaces (the rubbish dump in Pikine Ouest and the bus station in Rufisque). It let local groups define new public uses for these spaces. A site focusing on sport and local young people was therefore created in the district of Icotaf 1 in Pikine Ouest. At the bus station, new social areas were created, such as mobile food stands (gargotières) and spaces for chatting or resting.

As in Ouagadougou, the Dassasgho fitness trail was dreamed up and created by those who live in the neighborhood, near the Jeunesse high school. This space is used by local children and young people from primary school age to university, as well as by older people. The latter go there to meet and chat under the tree, recalling the role of the traditional village "talking" palaver tree.

develop them for communal uses focusing on sport, food production, and culture. The principal goal of collective appropriation of a place in this manner is to make it a public space where local people can stop, move around, and participate in the life of the space. Above all, it is about creating a connection between the lived urban experience and the "normal processes of existence" (Dewey 2005).

Spaces that focus on art offer artists a temporary residence in exchange for their time working with the community and their efforts to bring art closer to the city (box 4.2). In Sub-Saharan Africa, these spaces often take the form of

---

BOX 4.2

Examples of Spaces Focusing on Art and Artists

The Ishyo Arts Centre, created by eight women in Rwanda in 2007, aims to "reimagine a brutalized humanity."[a] It was created in response to a lack of cultural spaces in Rwanda. In the beginning, it operated as a mobile library that "took children hostage just as history had taken the population hostage." It aimed to construct a collective imagination from diverse stories. Once the project had permanent premises, the space was opened up to local artists, who were given free residences. The space is managed communally by the founders and the artists.

Terra Alta, on the outskirts of Accra, was created by the artist Elisabeth Efua Sutherland in 2017. This site provides a space for a number of artistic endeavors with a rehearsal room, three artist residences, a gallery, a library, and a theater. A cafe and two shared gardens have just been added. It aims to encourage local artists, residents, young people, and children to mingle and create, practice, and experiment. The space was developed by volunteer residents and artists.

The Kipaji Lab in Kenya is a cultural hub aiming "to decolonialize the African continent through visual storytelling."[b] It brings together artists, campaigners, teachers, and researchers. Training courses on screenwriting and stage production are provided, and material is shared with a view to initiating joint visual projects.

Numerous cultural centers stage festivals to promote the work of their resident artists. These initiatives are organized by spaces that focus on artists and can be adapted to public spaces open to local people so as to reach a wider audience. The KLA ART initiative run by the 32° East Ugandan Art Trust in Uganda is a good example of this approach. Its artistic festival exhibits work in public spaces across the city on an ad hoc basis with the aim of "transform[ing] relationships between artist and audience," by reflecting on issues surrounding "ownership and collectivity."[c] Another example is Assalamalekoum in Mauritania. This organization stages the annual Assalamalekoum Festival in Nouakchott. Alongside artistic performances, workshops, and training sessions, opportunities for discussion are organized with the local population to make art and artistic endeavors more accessible to a wider audience.

a. Carole Karemera at the international conference on "Cultural Third Spaces? Towards New Means of Cooperation Between France and Africa," May 16–18, 2022, Friche La Belle de Mai, Marseille.
b. Quotation from Kipaji Lab's website. Available at https://kipajilab.com/.
c. Quotation from KLA ART's website. Available at https://klaart.org/about/.

cultural centers aiming to connect art with its audiences. Such hybrid spaces (Besson, forthcoming) have emerged in response to a need for cultural facilitation (Guillon and Saez 2019) where users can become active stakeholders in the cultural program, not simply passive consumers of it (Blandin et al. 2017; Zask 2003). Art is used as a vehicle for viewing political and societal transitions through the reappropriation, reimagination, and redefinition of African culture—past, present, and future. These spaces are also drivers of specific learning processes: peer to peer, citizen empowerment, interdisciplinarity, and knowledge hybridization (Andriantsimahavandy et al. 2020).

Breathing new life into public spaces through communal use
Public spaces are a relatively recent development in Africa. They remain embryonic in many cities and are principally used for private purposes (residential use, informal economic activities) because of the inherent precariousness of life (Dahou 2005) and land speculation (Leimdorfer 1999; Steck 2006). Urban commons are developing social and cultural activities in the same spaces but on the fringes of such private uses. As such, they are exploring a form of urban life that has a foot in both camps (Durang 2000), promoting both social and functional diversity. These commons follow the entrepreneurial approach championed by their founders.

Urban commons can be developed on vacant lots (the Reemdogo 2 garden of arts and culture, the Dassasgho fitness trail in Ouagadougou) or rubbish dumps (the Kër Thiossane community and artistic gardens, the Pikine Ouest playing fields in Dakar) that they have reclaimed. They can also play a part in restoring public buildings. The Ishyo Arts Centre was set up in the former canteen of Rwanda's welfare department.

Africa's urban commons occupy public spaces as if they were a public "stage" (Habermas 1962), as well as an artistic one. The urban festivals organized by some groups are an illustration of this. The KLA ART festival staged by the 32° East Ugandan Art Trust exhibits photos in shipping containers in a number of public spaces in Kampala. In an interview with France's *Libération*[4] newspaper in 2018, Carole Karemera, cofounder of the Ishyo Arts Centre in Rwanda, explained how the mobile theater had been able to occupy streets that had been the "theater of atrocities in the past" where "people were killed, watched people being killed, or simply closed their windows." The Kipaji Lab in Kenya uses urban spaces as classrooms and places for learning.

Africa's social and cultural urban commons therefore sit at the crossroads between two of the functions that characterize public spaces: sociability in the sense of a "village community" (i.e., acquaintances, neighborhood relationships, and work relationships) (Lofland 1998) and the reciprocal observation of others and their behavior (Cornélis 2020; Goffman 2008 [1963]). At Kër Thiossane in Senegal, the women from the community garden say that before this project, they did not know one another and shared little of themselves. Carole Karemera, from the Ishyo Arts Centre, says of street theater: "People still aren't used to it so they say: 'Who can see me? Who's there? If I laugh, who will see me laugh?' People are watching themselves watching a performance."[5]

Although some commons occupy public spaces, private and public categories are so permeable that private places can also be used for communal purposes. Terra Alta in Ghana has been built on land belonging to the grandmother of its founder, the artist Elisabeth Efua Sutherland. Today, it welcomes a diverse local audience (artists, children, the public, residents, and passersby).

Transforming the audience's relationship with art

The principal goal of African cultural spaces is to change the public's relationship with art and see art as working for citizen's desires and needs. Through the buses run by the Ishyo Arts Centre in Rwanda that crisscrossed various districts, art was perceived as a tool for rebuilding society. It encouraged a process of cocreating a positive collective imagination with those living in those areas, particularly children. Each block of houses had an "ideas box" so that needs and aspirations could be heard. Each box was marked with the words "if it's in your head, it's in our program."

The way in which the public's relationship with the arts has been transformed is also evidenced through artists' desire for their work to be seen outside typical exhibition areas like galleries. The Reemdogo 2 garden of arts and culture in Ouagadougou focuses on promoting the work of local artists in public places that can be accessed by local people.

Using a different approach but with the same purpose, the first KLA ART festival in 2014 in Uganda, organized by the 32° East Ugandan Arts Trust, distributed 12 shipping containers around Kampala. Each container represented an exhibition space, with the aim of changing how the public sees art by taking it beyond the usual locations for art exhibitions. The festival's website explains that KLA ART is interested in "non-traditional audiences and artists." Its goal is to "transform Kampala into a living work of art," making the people its main protagonists so as to consider "the meaning of collective ownership, our identities, our town, our environment, our past, and our future."

Urban Commons for Technological Innovation and Production: Fab Labs in Sub-Saharan Africa

The main function of urban commons used for technological innovation and production is to stimulate innovation processes by drawing on collective intelligence methods, experimentation, and prototyping. This category includes a broad spectrum of spaces that use different and therefore potentially confusing terminology—makerspaces, fab labs, open labs, hackerspaces, Techshop, living lab, and coworking (Berrebi-Hoffmann, Bureau, and Lallement 2018). The dividing lines between these different spaces are sometimes tenuous (Capdevila 2016; Gandini 2015). The technological urban commons in Sub-Saharan Africa we identified and studied in detail define themselves as fab labs that are part of the makerspace family. Merindol et al. define the latter as "public community spaces where those who are passionate about technology can implement creative projects, exchange ideas, and learn in an environment which is often digital and designed to be open to user appropriation or reappropriation" (Merindol et al. 2016, 24).

A fab lab is a physical public collaborative space. It gives a community of nonspecialists access to sophisticated digital machines (computer-assisted design software [CAD], laser cutters, computer numerical control [CNC] milling machines, 3D printers, vinyl cutters) to design, learn, prototype, produce, and test objects or software projects or even produce them on a small scale (Bouvier-Patron 2015; Eychenne 2012; Morel and Le Roux 2016; Mortara and Parisot 2016; Rumpala 2014). The aim is to provide a production workshop in the heart of the city (Piller, Weller, and Kleer 2015; Rumpala 2014). Use of the digital tools is shared by all concerned so that anyone can make something themselves or with others (do it yourself—DIY, or do it with others—DIWO). Items produced in fab labs share the open-source philosophy and are therefore not covered by copyright.

Fab labs are makerspaces that have generally signed the Massachusetts Institute of Technology (MIT) Fab Charter (Fonda and Canessa 2016) drawn up by the Fab Foundation, an organization launched by Neil Gershenfeld, who founded the first space of this kind at the beginning of the 2000s. These production workshops can be found in both public places (universities, schools, urban spaces) and private ones (private premises, businesses). Some are open to all (using an open-lab format) without membership, while access to others is reserved for paying members. Users of fab labs come from very diverse backgrounds. They are citizens, researchers, school pupils, students, artists, and businesses.

Today, fab labs are used by large firms as part of their digital transformation process. New ideas are prototyped with a view to defining their future positioning. Local communities also support fab labs to promote digital and social inclusion in their local area.

Numerous studies have categorized the spaces that have emerged in Western countries on the basis of their legal systems, target audiences, studio type, and funding methods (Bottollier-Depois et al. 2014; Eychenne 2012; Lô 2017; Merindol et al. 2016). The following observations have been made. In terms of economic models, many spaces offer services that are either free or subject to a fee (access to a space, training). This makes them hybrid models. At the same time, for many fab labs, the aim is to support the people behind projects and guide them toward entrepreneurship, particularly by proposing a series of training and support sessions (Browder, Aldrich, and Bradley 2017; Fonda and Canessa 2016; Mortara and Parisot 2016; Rayna and Striukova 2021; Stacey 2014).

Fab labs have also been developed in Sub-Saharan Africa, alongside the emergence of other spaces for entrepreneurship and incubation (Cunningham and Cunningham 2016; De Beer et al. 2017). The success of this movement is intrinsically linked to the fact that these places have been developed as urban commons (Mboa Nkoudou 2017). They are therefore enhancing an ecosystem that can address the challenges facing African cities, particularly those connected to population growth. They are also contributing to responding to Africa's digital needs that have continued to increase over recent years (Ninot and Peyroux 2018). Fab labs are therefore agile and innovative facilities that, by judiciously and effectively placing digital technology at the very heart of their model, can provide part of the answer to many challenges.

This movement has sparked the interest of public and private international stakeholders that view fab labs as a new lever for accelerating the development of growth areas in countries in Sub-Saharan Africa, particularly jobs for young people. In 2016, the Organisation internationale de la francophonie (OIF) (International Francophone Organization) highlighted the dynamism of digital production spaces in Africa supporting the creation of digital common goods (OIF and Idest 2016). Other large international organizations, such as the International Organization for Migration (IOM), and nongovernmental organizations, such as Terre des hommes, are involved in creating fab labs. African fab labs are also supported by large firms and European support mechanisms: the Orange Foundation in Cameroon, Côte d'Ivoire, the Arab Republic of Egypt, Madagascar, Senegal, and Tunisia and the European Union's Horizon 2020 program (Cousin et al. 2017).

We have focused on 13 fab labs in particular: BabyLab (Abidjan, Côte d'Ivoire), BloLab (Cotonou, Benin), Defko Ak Niep (Kër Thiossane) (Dakar, Senegal), DoniLab (Bamako, Mali), FabLab Espace Créatif (Djibouti, Djibouti), FabLab Winam (Kisumu, Kenya), GreenLab (Akure, Nigeria), HarHub (Hargeisa, Somalia), Makerere Innovation and Incubation Center (Kampala, Uganda), OuagaLab (Ouagadougou, Burkina Faso), Sahel Fablab (Nouakchott, Mauritania), Twende Hub (Arusha, Tanzania), and WoeLab (Lomé, Togo).

The key role of founders and forming a team

The people behind these spaces play a special role in the African fab labs we studied. They organize the space, create teams, and set up partnerships and funding. They often have prior professional experience in engineering or information technology (IT), for example. Their motives are altruistic, and they often open fab labs in their own homes. They are sometimes supported by online training in the form of massive online open courses. They benefit from peer-to-peer discussions with other fab managers, particularly at conferences (box 4.3). They are generally supported in the running of their space by teams of volunteers who have often studied at the same university as the founder.

BOX 4.3

BabyLab in Côte d'Ivoire

BabyLab was founded in Côte d'Ivoire in 2014 by Guiako Obin and a dozen of his computer scientist friends. It is the first Ivorian fab lab to become part of the MIT network. The founder wanted to create a place for socializing and digital development for local residents and children who face uncertainty, poverty, and crime. With a background in information technology (IT), and having previously worked as a developer, he took the massive online open course on digital technology run by the Institut Mines-Télécom Business School and set up BabyLab at his home in the working-class district of Abobo ("Baby" refers to Abidjan). His goal is to support potential technological innovation in the neighborhood and provide training sessions that meet the needs of the local area. Thanks to his commitment, BabyLab not only is listed as an MIT fab lab but has also been certified by the Orange Foundation as a solidarity fab lab.

His fab lab is enabling a wide variety of people from every part of society (children in school and those who are not, young men and women following social reintegration schemes and those who are not, organizations for young people, artisans, schools, social centers, local communities, cooperatives, and village communities) to learn about digital technology (through training sessions on coding, electronics, and robotics). They can also learn how to use tools in their professional lives (such as furniture production using tools like 3D printers and CNC machines), develop projects (prototyping), and recycle IT waste via the circular economy. For example, the fab lab runs a Kid Lab program for children ages 8 to 15 during school hours or during their free time to encourage them to tinker and start coding using Arduino kits and Jerry computers.

The founder is now executive director of the space. He is working on creating a network of fab labs in Côte d'Ivoire, and he advises local governments on technological projects with the potential to transform the country. His work is not limited to BabyLab itself. His close relationship with the Orange Foundation, for example, has led to the "Carré lumineux" project (creation of a "smart classroom" with lighting provided by solar panels for pupils from the village of N'gorankro, 50 kilometers from Abidjan, which is not connected to the electricity network). The "Caravane Jeunesse Numérique" program also seeks to raise awareness about entrepreneurship among people living in the country's most isolated regions, in collaboration with the Ivorian Ministry for the Digital Economy.

BabyLab was particularly active during the COVID-19 (coronavirus) pandemic. Driven by its creativity and agility, 300 pedal-operated handwashing stations were produced and distributed to schools and public spaces, as well as 3,000 face shields for health care staff and customer-facing sales staff.

In Sub-Saharan Africa, fab managers are now key players in the fields of digital development involving the employment of young people and the urban transition. They act as an interface between their organizations, the media, and potential partners. Having worked on the ground and proven their leadership skills, they are natural activists for digital technology in their various countries. It should be noted that very few women belong to this network.

The prominent position of digital technology

Fab labs in Sub-Saharan Africa have digital and technological equipment that uses open-source software, mainly small tools and simple computers and printers. Open-source software and material such as Scratch and Arduino are often provided (Fagbohoun 2016) (box 4.4). More consequential equipment, such as 3D printers, depends on financing being available.

Fab labs that have received external support from the beginning, such as FabLab Espace Créatif (Djibouti), created in December 2019, are often better equipped, but they remain rare. Supported and funded by the IOM, this fab lab was initially equipped with five 3D printers, a large CNC milling machine, six computers, a 3D scanner, a laser engraver and cutter, a Dremel tool, and enough consumables to last a year.

Generally speaking, fab managers must innovate if they are to acquire equipment. They draw on local and international partnerships to salvage equipment that can be used to create new computers (like the Jerry computers deployed in schools). In this respect, fab labs implement creative, frugal, inexpensive, and easy-access solutions founded on the principle of recycling.

BOX 4.4

The Digital Creativity of African Fab Labs

African fab labs, like their Western counterparts, use open-source equipment and software that are therefore very inexpensive or even free. However, in some instances, they have taken this approach even further, using the equipment to create new digital materials. Arduino microcontrollers (small, inexpensive open-source circuit boards combined with a microcontroller to create devices interacting with their environment) are widespread. For example, this device can be used to control a field irrigation or livestock surveillance system remotely via an app. Raspberry Pi nano computers (low-cost computers the size of a credit card) are also used in agriculture, health, home automation, and communication (Piuzzi 2021). Jerry computers were also created in African fab labs. These computers are made from recycled information technology equipment reassembled in a 20-liter container (a jerrycan). They are widely used in education. Finally, some places like WoeLab in Togo can use a 3D printer to replicate at least half the parts for another 3D printer so as to provide other fab labs, for example, with this kind of equipment (the RepRap [Replication Rapid prototype] project).

There are many illustrative examples. For example, French companies, including Société Générale, provide BabyLab (Côte d'Ivoire) with IT waste. BloLab (Benin) has a similar arrangement via IT donations from international organizations. OuagaLab (Burkina Faso) has received equipment from French fab labs (Artilect, ElectroLab, and LabFab).

Shaping African Cities through the Prism of Urban Commons

African cities are developing rapidly and often informally. They are looking for new urban models and ways to construct a city that are specific to Africa (Chenal 2015). Faced with such a task, exactly how a city is fashioned day to day by those who live there needs to be understood. The initiatives described above suggest that, in the field of urban development, a route to collective and participatory methods for recycling and managing local resources does exist. The role of residents in shaping cities is an age-old theme. Our contribution is to analyze how urban commons, and the men and women who create and sustain them, can participate in shaping cities in Sub-Saharan Africa differently. In this final section, we consider what urban commons produce and what functions they fulfill, as well as the strategies they are developing to make themselves sustainable and expand. Finally, we take a look ahead, exploring two possible visions of how commons might contribute to the cities of the future.

Multifunctionality Built on Innovative Approaches to Education

All the urban commons we studied in Sub-Saharan Africa champion the values of ecological and social sustainability, as well as commitment to the local groups involved. Their role as intermediaries connecting diverse people, disciplines, scales, and worlds is essential. They also adopt experimentation and risk-taking. They develop innovative teaching practices by drawing on the dynamics of collective intelligence. This kind of upskilling enables groups to develop sustainable solutions to environmental and social challenges.

Innovative educational practices

The old African adage that "it takes a village to raise a child" is testament to the communal approach to education and training for young people in Africa. Hybrid African spaces employ learning methods that are both nonformal (noninstitutionalized methods aimed at a specific group using ad hoc tools according to need) and informal (all other noninstitutionalized forms of education) (Andriantsimahavandy et al. 2020).

Informal education covers the sociocultural aspects of a child's life: "It embraces the formation of character as much as the development of physical aptitudes, the acquisition of moral qualities, and the acquisition of knowledge and techniques required for life in all its many respects" (Andriantsimahavandy et al. 2020). Informal education is also described as "traditional" or "original" (Ngakoutou 2004). Traditional education is one of the characteristics of African villages and the rural world more widely, but the urban milieu does not lend itself to this community-based traditional education. They are "two types of society, two types of existence and culture, and consequently two types of people. On the one hand, the village, the rural milieu, where society is created alongside the individuals of which it is composed. . . . On the other, the city, the urban milieu, where society is made by members who feel united not by the natural ties of family but by the artificial bonds of work" (Elungu 1987, 124).

Urban commons are seeking to invent new teaching and educational models, reconciling the urban milieu with the sociocultural dimensions of traditional education. WoeLab (Togo) alludes to "new spaces for learning for young people."[6] For the founders of all these spaces, such educational approaches are necessary "to encourage resilience and the ability to reinvent oneself," in the face of the environmental, social, demographic, democratic, and economic challenges confronting the continent (Andriantsimahavandy et al. 2020, 30).

Skills need to be acquired in four areas (Andriantsimahavandy et al. 2020): problem solving and solution finding, creativity, cooperative work and empowerment, and leadership and entrepreneurialism. Urban commons (box 4.5) and the individuals of which they are composed who are actively engaged in finding local solutions to sustainable development acquire these skills via "blending" (Serres 1992), interdisciplinarity, knowledge hybridization, and the horizontality of exchanges.

Clear environmental and social functions

Urban commons sit at the crossroads between several functions. They combine environmental and social activities with educational work and action to spread the message about the collective aim being pursued. In terms of the environment (box 4.6), African urban commons can have a clear ecological aim: recycling, responsible consumption and supply, short food supply chains, or eco-friendly urban agriculture (permaculture, organic farming). Urban commons are one of the key elements required for sustainable local development in a given area (Mboa Nkoudou 2020). They are part of a rationale of circular urbanism through intensified collective uses of urban spaces and renovation (vacant lots, wastelands, rubbish dumps) or recycling (schools, public buildings) of existing sites and infrastructure. Some urban commons propose activities for those championing projects supporting the ecological transition.

BOX 4.5

Educational Skills and Practices Developed within African Urban Commons

Problem solving and solution finding: Be it through design prototyping (FabLab Espace Créatif in Djibouti) or face shields during the pandemic (FabLab Winam in Kenya, OuagaLab in Burkina Faso, BabyLab in Côte d'Ivoire, and BloLab in Benin), fab labs employ design thinking and design sprint methods (Knapp, Zeratsky, and Kowitz 2017).

Creativity by developing a new collective imagination and desirable narratives and futures: In Rwanda, the Ishyo Arts Centre works on trauma related to the genocide in the 1990s. In Kenya, Kipaji Lab considers *Africanness* and the decolonialization of Africa. In Nigeria, GreenLab is developing a narrative around local solutions and independence from imported products, as well as young people's abilities to invent and develop innovative solutions through prototyping.

Cooperative work: Exchanging a myriad of skills between people from diverse backgrounds and interdisciplinarity (Labrune 2018) are at the heart of various projects. The Ishyo Arts Centre in Rwanda and Terra Alta in Ghana use theater, music, stories, and photography. The founder of Terra Alta emphasizes the notion of "modularity" across the site and the hybrid nature of the spaces, stakeholders, and arts. The Réseau francophone des fablabs d'Afrique de l'Ouest (Francophone Network of West African Fab Labs) is illustrative of the desire for cooperation at the regional level.

Empowerment, leadership, and entrepreneurship: Developing these skills is the principal goal of many urban commons. Artistic training is provided at some sites: screenwriting lessons at Kipaji Lab (Kenya), awareness raising and artistic training at Terra Alta (Ghana). The Kër Thiossane community garden (Senegal) provides women with permaculture training. Central to the work of fab labs is the cultural integration of digital technology among young people from disadvantaged neighborhoods (Liotard 2020). Numerous workshops are therefore organized for children and teenagers, both boys and girls, during school hours to introduce them to programming and making simple connected objects: Dekfo (Senegal), OuagaLab (Burkina Faso) through the Jerry school program, and GreenLab (Nigeria) through the "One Student, One Arduino," "Katrina Golden Book," and "Mickey Mickey" programs. DoniLab (Mali), in collaboration with the Institut Mines-Télécom de Paris (Paris Engineering and Management Graduate School), runs a massive online open course on "How to Program an Object with Arduino" aimed particularly at students from Mali's School of Engineering, Architecture, and Urban Planning.

BOX 4.6

The Environmental Functions of African Urban Commons

Eco-friendly practices within urban commons: Defko (Senegal) provides access to a repair cafe for artisans working with metal, fabric, dye, and glass painting, the goal being "unplanned obsolescence" (Goyon 2016). In fab labs, low-cost materials and recycling lead to frugal and inexpensive technical solutions. Responsible practices (limited consumption, recycling) are also at the heart of the efforts of hybrid cultural spaces. At the Pikine Ouest playing fields and the Dassasgho fitness trail in Ouagadougou, use of concrete is minimal. Furniture is made by local artisans and benches from tree trunks on the site. This land had been abandoned by the public authorities but has been developed by those living in the neighborhood using local or recycled materials. Despite its limited means, it promotes the circular economy while creating nice places to spend time.

Support for eco-friendly projects in terms of urban agriculture: The Kër Thiossane community garden (Senegal) provides training sessions on permaculture practices. WoeLab (Togo) is developing the Urban Attic project that aims to turn unauthorized rubbish dumps into vegetable gardens for organic farming, store the food produced in the city's fab labs, and provide a local platform for purchasing organic products.

Urban commons have a broad social impact (box 4.7) on their members (employees, volunteers, and contributors), their external stakeholders directly or indirectly affected by their work (recipients, users, and clients), and society in general (Gayet and Ung 2021). Commons are first and foremost champions of shared values relating to commitment, intermediation, and connecting people, disciplines, scales, and worlds (Besson 2021). They develop projects in response to specific societal problems: juvenile delinquency, gender discrimination, humanitarian challenges, and health crises. With regard to fab labs, the creation of communities of practices also ensures that "technical activities are seen as social activities guaranteeing cohesion between individuals" and therefore strengthening the local social fabric (Mboa Nkoudou 2020, 54). Some projects target farmers or rural populations and therefore have social effects beyond the limits of the neighborhood or even the city.

Fragile Economic Models and Strategies for Dissemination via Hives

Hybrid economic models by necessity

The economic models of Africa's urban commons remain fragile and can quickly fluctuate. There is no standard template as such, but the business models of urban commons appear to be based on a variety of activities that can be

BOX 4.7

The Social Functions of African Urban Commons

Combating juvenile delinquency: For the founder of BabyLab (Côte d'Ivoire), the fab lab is a way of giving young people something to do outside school and encouraging them to imagine, create, and produce (Leyronas, Liotard, and Prié 2018). BabyLab wants to make every individual an actor for change to achieve social transformation. The founder of OuagaLab (Burkina Faso) also created the Mogtédo fab lab specifically to combat crime and small-scale gold mining by young people.

Combating gender discrimination: "Stop VBG" (Violences basées sur le genre) (Stop Gender-Based Violence), created by BloLab (Benin), is a mobile app for reporting gender-based violence. This project was developed with input from the "Imagination for People" (IP Benin) community and support from the United Nations Development Programme. Defko (Senegal) and BabyLab (Côte d'Ivoire) are involved in specific action for women, as is Sahel Fablab (Mauritania), whose managers are all women. The Kër Thiossane community garden in Senegal is exclusively reserved for women.

Humanitarian focus: FabLab Espace Créatif (Djibouti) welcomes and trains migrants from Ethiopia, Somalia, and the Republic of Yemen. Workshops focus on typing and how to use a keyboard.

Solutions during a health crisis: A number of initiatives were launched during the COVID-19 (coronavirus) health crisis. The Réseau francophone des fablabs d'Afrique de l'Ouest (Francophone Network of West African Fab Labs) launched "Makers Nord Sud contre le coronavirus" (North South Makers against Coronavirus) in 2020, in association with Réseau français des fablabs (French Fab Lab Network) and Réseau Bretagne solidaire (Brittany Solidarity Network). This project provided fab labs with the equipment to produce face shields and even ventilators. Similar initiatives were developed in East Africa. For example, FabLab Espace Créatif (Djibouti) sent FabLab Winam (Kenya) models for 3D printed face shields.

Effects beyond the city limits: BloLab (Benin) is developing the Ipatic digital app for farmers. It helps them link up with one another and includes a remote-controlled automatic crop irrigation system. BloLab has trained approximately 250 farmers. At OuagaLab (Burkina Faso), most projects also focus on farmers: a low-cost wind turbine producing 1 kilowatt-hour, a public weather station providing climate data (temperatures and humidity levels) on the city and agricultural areas sent by text message, a platform for recycling and marketing local agricultural products, and a kit for farmers to alert one another when a parasite disease is observed. Sahel Fablab (Mauritania) has designed and produced solar cookers to reduce firewood consumption in rural areas, as well as an automatic irrigation project controlled via a mobile app that includes a drip system and can also measure soil moisture. Mobile cultural initiatives, such as the Ishyo Arts Centre in Rwanda, are sometimes held outside the city.

funded from difference sources, thereby ensuring greater independence and less vulnerability (see the hybrid model defined in chapter 1).

Originally, many of the founders of these spaces wanted them to be open and free to all. However, economic reality caught up with them, and they were forced to consider an economic model that could guarantee the sustainability of their activities. Some spaces received funding from international organizations very early on in their development, especially if they were not receiving any support from local bodies (Mboa Nkoudou 2020). However, all the spaces have developed hybrid models over time. Membership, volunteering, grants, contributions to costs by local residents (to hire the space), income from activities (catering, bar), donations in cash or in kind, various services (expertise, project support, adult education), participatory funding, and partnerships are all used to help balance budgets.

Most of these spaces were founded by men and women who initially used their own funds. For example, the founder of Terra Alta in Ghana funded almost the entire renovation of her space by selling her artwork. Some were able to obtain financial support (via corporate foundations, states, and international organizations). Defko (Senegal) is an exception. When it was created, it immediately received a relief fund from the OIF to purchase equipment and then a grant from the Orange Foundation for its training program for children. Similarly, Fablab Espace Créatif (Djibouti) has been supported by the IOM from the very beginning. BabyLab (Côte d'Ivoire) received financial support as it developed. In particular, it accrued a financial grant from Orange Solidarity, part of the Orange Foundation, and funding from the French government. Among the hybrid cultural spaces, Kipaji Lab (Kenya) has received financial support from the nongovernmental organization Zuri Works.

Many of Africa's urban commons have raised money through crowdfunding (BabyLab in Côte d'Ivoire, BloLab in Benin, OuagaLab in Burkina Faso, and Terra Alta in Ghana). Some have received bursaries (Winam in Kenya) or scientific awards (BabyLab in Côte d'Ivoire). Fab labs offer membership to their users, but numbers remain very low. The Ishyo Arts Centre requires artists to pay the center a third of any revenue they earn that is connected to the sale of their work in that space. Some of the activities and services on offer involve payment of a fee. For example, fab labs provide free digital manufacturing training courses, but there are also paid versions via partnerships with either schools or universities or with incubators. For example, BabyLab (Côte d'Ivoire) provides services to the incubator Incub'Ivoir, and Defko does the same for the Senegalese incubator Cetim. Some hybrid spaces hire out part of the site for private use. Terra Alta in Ghana uses an unusual credit-based system where a contribution to the day-to-day work of the space (cleaning, childcare, art awareness, and teaching) can be exchanged for use of the rehearsal rooms. Finally, some places provide incubator spaces that give them an income. Currently, WoeLab incorporates nine startups that belong to the community under the Silicon Village banner. The young people involved are co-members. Kipaji Lab (Kenya) has an incubator space enabling artists to receive partial payment.

Most economic models for urban commons are precarious. However, they are adapting to the places where they are being developed and particularly to the legislation of countries that do not yet have a specific or appropriate status for them. The area they choose to specialize in is crucial.

Dissemination strategies: Off-shoots and hives

The founder's personality and links to national and international academic and economic communities are major assets if a space is to be sustainable. Knowledge of the environment, discussions during meetings and conferences, and trips overseas are essential for networking and forging ties with potential sources of funding. GreenLab (Nigeria) is indicative in this respect. Its founder is Nigerian but lives in Germany and works with a German fab lab. He is involved in research into innovation and how African fab labs operate and therefore benefits from the related network of contacts.

Belonging to a regional, or even international, network appears to be a necessity. The network acts simultaneously as a learning community and a vehicle for dissemination. Research conducted by Kebir and Wallet reveals that purpose and a symbolic arsenal (the narrative supporting projects) are decisive if these communities are to spread and be reproduced. The authors identify two routes for dissemination: "off-shoots" and "hives" (Kebir and Wallet 2021).

Dissemination via off-shoots requires an umbrella organization that can support the creation of initiatives implementing its goal and help give a group structure. Its goal is not expansion and management of several sites but rather to spread, reproduce, and replicate its concept and its approach across the region. In Rwanda, the Ishyo Arts Centre, a leading cultural center, has inspired 15 similar spaces.

The dynamics of hives (working as a network) is different. The umbrella organization develops a project that centers on the space where it performs its work. This site is unique, and the aim is not to reproduce it or replicate it. However, anyone wanting to develop a similar approach can take inspiration from it. Dissemination is achieved by people leaving the site (the hive) at a given moment to pursue their own activities and found their own community that is independent of the umbrella organization.

"Collaborative City" or "Commons-Invested City": Two Possible Visions for African Cities

Local authorities are struggling to address the challenges facing cities and urban areas more widely, but the dynamism of commons initiatives and the creativity of their solutions could galvanize public stakeholders to take an interest.

An entire mosaic of circumstances and relationships exists between African urban commons and state intervention mechanisms. Although some commons are part of larger projects championed by local communities, others remain specialized niche spaces for social experimentation. Kebir and Wallet propose three visions of a city where commons have a role: an "enhanced city," a "disputed city," and a "reinvested city" (Kebir and Wallet 2021). On the basis of what we have studied, we propose two of our own: a "collaborative city" and a "commons-invested city."

The first vision is that of a city "collaborating" with urban commons. In this configuration, African urban commons are islands that emerge to address welfare issues (access to resources, new local services, education, culture). This vision relies on these initiatives being viable in the long term and their ability to transform their initial experimental approach into a sustainable one. Local communities can sometimes sincerely support these initiatives. The enthusiasm generated by the Kër Thiossane community garden in Senegal, for example, encouraged the town hall to install public lighting around the space. However, state authorities can be slow to act or even pursue strategies preventing the sustainability of urban commons. The latter remain a safety valve within the dominant economic model, a refuge for those excluded from the heart of that model and confined to the margins of the system. Juxtaposing these two mechanisms (state intervention, on the one hand, and urban commons, on the other) would surely have an impact on the spatial configurations of African cities that have been "atomized [and] fragmented into sub-spaces based on function" (Mayer and Soumahoro 2014).

The second vision is a city "invested" by urban commons. It is characterized by initiatives that fill in any gaps left by city policy and have a close connection with local communities or are even initiated by them (box 4.8). This vision of a city is based on blending commons methods and state intervention mechanisms. By focusing more on collective mechanisms for creating and managing urban resources, commons enhance the local authorities' urban project by seeking greater inclusion, equity, and deliberative democracy. Some urban commons (the Ishyo Arts Centre in Rwanda, WoeLab in Togo, and the Assalamalekoum organization in Mauritania) claim to follow this approach and highlight the inspirational nature of their initiatives. In this respect, processes associated with commons complement those described in literature on territorial development by combining economic considerations with those connected to societal challenges (ecological transition, education, welfare, and gender equality) and environmental challenges (recycling and thrift).

BOX 4.8

Urban Fabric Initiatives: From Temporary Urbanism to Transitional Urbanism

In 2018, the Agence française de développement (AFD) (French Development Agency) set up a mechanism called "Pépinières urbaines" (Urban Fabric Initiatives)[a] in what was intended to be an immediately visible contribution to the participation of local residents in the development of their city and their neighborhoods (Besson 2022). Alongside drawing up 5-year and 10-year plans and offering support with their implementation, this initiative sought to experiment with and support new ways of shaping cities. By bringing together local communities, the public contracting authorities of large urban projects, and civil society stakeholders, the goal was to contribute to encouraging new practices through micro-projects.

The nature of any potential results is very broad and will be formed by the discussions between local residents and users, as well as the public contracting authorities. Support will be provided by organizations specializing in these mechanisms (such as le Gret, urbaSEN, urbaMonde, and Cabanon Vertical). These initiatives are presented as citizen initiative hubs supporting the city's stakeholders in codesigning and co-constructing innovative and participatory micro-actions for developing and reactivating public spaces.

At the beginning of 2022, urban fabric initiatives were rolled out in Burkina Faso in two central zones of Ouagadougou (Tampouy and Grand Est). In the long term, these areas will be the recipients of a larger infrastructure program (as part of the Ouagadougou Sustainable Development Project implemented by the town hall and funded by AFD during its second phase). The initiatives were also introduced in Dakar in connection with future public transport equipment, in Tunisia in neighborhoods covered by National Programs for Renovating and Integrating Districts with Insecure Housing, and in Abidjan in disadvantaged neighborhoods covered by Côte d'Ivoire's Project to Improve Abidjan's Redesigned Districts championed by the Ministère en charge de la Construction, du Logement et de l'Urbanisme (Ministry for Construction, Housing and Town Planning). The micro-actions cocreated by users and civil society organizations include interim development of sites (fitness trails, rest areas for people using public transport, roundabouts), equipment like mobile radio, and places for meeting and creativity, as well as events (e.g., sports tournaments).

This process was inspired by the urban movements known as transitional or temporary urbanism and, more widely, as co-urbanism.[b] It has been scientifically assessed and monitored,[c] providing an analysis of any benefits or issues arising from this type of "urban lab." The assessment indicates that, at the first sites, the micro-actions of urban fabric initiatives are making a decisive contribution to improving how the places chosen are used and their environment. The implementation of a participatory approach to urbanism is widely recognized and has been positively received. These urban fabric initiatives are also making a vital contribution to more horizontal organizational innovations with powerful communication and mediation tools between government

(continued next page)

Box 4.8 (continued)

authorities, nongovernmental organization stakeholders, and citizens. Cooperative processes have therefore been bolstered and the way in which management methods and the urban fabric are viewed is changing.

However, despite hubs starting to spread the idea of urban fabric initiatives, their impact on the local economy and the transformation of urban planning remains limited. These initiatives face a number of dilemmas that have still not been resolved (Besson 2022). More dialogue and greater awareness within institutions, as well as a broader scope for the initiatives, are probably necessary. They could then evolve from being part of tactical and temporary urbanism to more structured forms of transitory and transitional urbanism.[d]

a. https://pepinieres-urbaines.org/.
b. Report, Student Workshop, École d'Urbanisme de Paris (Paris School of Urban Planning): Co-urbanismes (pepurbaeup.wixsite.com).
c. Raphaël Besson (Villes Innovations, PACTE-CNRS), with scientific support from Armelle Choplin (University of Geneva) and Jérôme Lombard (IRD).
d. For definitions, see Besson (2018).

Conclusion

Urban commons are a familiar sight in Europe and North America. Confronted by the limits of neoliberalism and its excesses, citizens are engaging in numerous initiatives, testing new cooperative models, inventing new narratives, and mobilizing within wider communities and networks. Many say they belong to a "movement": a movement of fab labs, a movement of third places, a movement of commons.

Africa's situation is different. Urban commons are emerging in Sub-Saharan Africa in a more isolated manner and, like the West African fab labs, resemble an archipelago at best. They are responding to essential requirements not currently met by either government authorities or the market, while also endeavoring to rebuild strained social relations. They are the basis for innovative forms and methods of commons-based entrepreneurship (collective work and projects) founded on shared means, resources, and goals in terms of satisfying needs, without seeking a profit (see chapter 1). Africa's urban commons are raising new dilemmas (Besson 2022): how these initiatives are to be scaled up, their funding models, the role of "citizen users," how projects championed can be made more sustainable, their inclusion in very localized urban economies, and how they cooperate among themselves. It would be a mistake to view them through a homogeneous prism. Their purpose, how they operate, their motivation, and their economic models are very diverse. The reasons for people's involvement in urban commons are also varied: pragmatic, personal, professional, and sometimes political and ideological. Africa's hybrid cultural spaces and fab labs are therefore following different trajectories. For example, fab labs in West Africa display a societal vocation, while some fab labs in East Africa are seeking to become startup incubators over time.

That being the case, what potential do these African urban commons have in terms of providing a sustainable response to the needs that motivated their initial emergence, and what role can they play in reinventing urban policies? Their vulnerability is obvious: their economic models remain precarious, collective dynamics are fragile, and institutional recognition is inadequate. However, their numbers are rising and their presence is increasingly essential for local populations. Their experiments can stimulate visions of alternative futures (Graeber 2004). Is it therefore time to consider new ways of shaping and managing cities that include a role for this model, while resisting the temptation to standardize it?

Notes

1. "Fab lab" is a contraction of "fabrication laboratory."
2. "Why sports and development go hand in hand," https://blogs.worldbank.org /education/why-sports-and-development-go-hand-hand.
3. "Sport and development in Africa: What is the role of the public sector?" https:// sportencommun.org/en/actualite/sport-and-development-in-africa-what-is-the -role-of-the-public-sector/.
4. Article from *Libération*, 2018, interview with the founder of the Ishyo Arts Centre: Carole Karemera, j'irai le dire chez vous – Libération (liberation.fr).
5. Article from *Libération*, 2018, Carole Karemera, j'irai le dire chez vous – Libération (liberation.fr).
6. Les fab lab au cœur des défis numériques en Afrique (theconversation.com).

References

Abreha, Kaleb G., Woubet Kassa, Emmanuel K. K. Lartey, Taye A. Mengistae, Solomon Owusu, and Albert G. Zeufack. 2021. *Industrialization in Sub-Saharan Africa: Seizing Opportunities in Global Value Chains*. Washington, DC: World Bank Group and Agence française de développement. https://www.afd.fr/en/ressources/industrializati on-sub-Saharan-africa.

Andriantsimahavandy, Sylvia, Raphaël Besson, Laëtitia Manach, and Stéphane Natkin. 2020. *Comprendre la dynamique des écosystèmes apprenants en Afrique*. Paris: Campus AFD and Agence française de développement. https://www.afd.fr/fr/ressources/com prendre-la-dynamique-des-ecosystemes-apprenants-en-afrique.

Balandier, Georges. 1958. "Structures sociales traditionnelles et problèmes du développement." *Présence africaine* 194 (2): 131–55. https://doi.org/10.3917/presa.194.0131.

Berrebi-Hoffmann, Isabelle, Marie-Christine Bureau, and Michel Lallement. 2018. *Makers. Enquête sur les laboratoires du changement social*. Paris: Seuil.

Besson, Raphaël. 2018. "For Transitional Spaces." *Lieux infinis. Construire des bâtiments ou des lieux?* https://hal.archives-ouvertes.fr/hal-01865934/document.

Besson, Raphaël. 2021. "Role and Limits of Third Places in the Fabrication of Contemporary Cities." Translated by Richard Hillman. *Territoire en mouvement: Revue de géographie et aménagement* 51. http://journals.openedition.org/tem/8345.

Besson, Raphaël. 2022. "Les dilemmes de l'urbanisme tactique à la lumière de l'évaluation des pépinières urbaines de l'Agence française de développement." *L'Espace politique* 46.

Besson, Raphaël. Forthcoming. "Les lieux culturels hybrides africains et les tiers lieux culturels français. Quelles caractéristiques communes et perspectives de coopération?" In *Les tiers lieux culturels. Collection communication et civilisation*. Paris: L'Harmattan.

Blandin, Marie-Christine, Catherine Morin-Desailly, Sylvie Robert, and Catherine Tasca. 2017. "Les droits culturels consacrés par la loi: Et après?" *L'Observatoire* 49 (1): 9–14.

Bollier, David, and Silke Helfrich, eds. 2015. *Patterns of Commoning*. Amherst, MA: Levellers Press.

Bottollier-Depois, François, Bertrand Dalle, Fabien Eychenne, Anne Jacquelin, Daniel Kaplan, Jean Nelson, and Véronique Routin. 2014. "Etat des lieux et typologie des ateliers de fabrication numérique." http://www.newpic.fr/doc/dge-etat-des-lieux-fab labs-2014.pdf.

Bouvier-Patron, Paul. 2015. "Fab Labs and the Extension of the Network Form: Towards a New Industrial Dynamic?" *Innovations* 47 (2): 165–88. https://doi.org/10.3917 /inno.047.0165.

Browder, Russell E., Howard Aldrich, and Steven Walter Bradley. 2017. "Entrepreneurship Research, Makers, and the Maker Movement." *Academy of Management Proceedings* 2017 (1). https://doi.org/10.5465/AMBPP.2017.14361abstract.

Capdevila, Ignasi. 2016. "Une typologie d'espaces ouverts d'innovation basée sur les différents modes d'innovation et motivations à la participation." *Gestion 2000* 33 (4): 93–115. https://doi.org/10.3917/g2000.333.0093.

Chenal, Jérôme. 2015. "Les villes africaines en quête de nouveaux modèles urbanistiques." Last modified April 29, 2015. https://metropolitiques.eu/Les-villes-africaines -en-quete-de.html.

Cléré, Alexis. 2018. "Makerspace à Nairobi. Éléments de changements socio-économiques associés à une meso-fabrication numérique distribuée en Afrique urbaine contemporaine. Une étude du cas du makerspace GearBox à Nairobi." Master's thesis, Aix-Marseille University.

Colleta, Nat, and Michelle Cullen. 2000. *Violent Conflict and the Transformation of Social Capital: Lessons from Cambodia, Rwanda, Guatemala and Somalia*. Washington, DC: World Bank.

Cornélis, Tamara. 2020. "Espace public, espace commun, tiers-lieu: Clarification conceptuelle et approche empirique." Master's thesis, University of Louvain.

Cousin, Philippe, Charlotte Dupont, Sabrine Fatnassi, Congduc Pham, Ousmane Thiare, Amos Wussah, and Sename Koffi. 2017. "IoT, an Affordable Technology to Empower Africans Addressing Needs in Africa." *IST-Africa Week Conference (IST-Africa)*, 1–8. https://doi.org/10.23919/ISTAFRICA.2017.8102347.

Cunningham, Paul, and Miriam Cunningham. 2016. "Report on Innovation Spaces and Living Labs in IST-Africa Partner Countries." Last modified January 31, 2016. http://www.ist-africa.org/home/files/ist-africa_innovationspaces_ll_v2_310116.pdf.

Dahou, Tarik. 2005. "L'espace public face aux apories des études africaines." *Cahiers d'études africaines* 178: 327–49. https://doi.org/10.4000/etudesafricaines.5412.

Davies, Julia, Corrie Hannah, Zack Guido, Andrew Zimmer, Laura McCann, Jane Battersby, and Tom Evans. 2021. "Barriers to Urban Agriculture in Sub-Saharan Africa." *Food Policy, Urban Food Policies for a Sustainable and Just Future* 103: 101999. https://doi.org/10.1016/j.foodpol.2020.101999.

De Beer, Jeremy, Paula Millar, Jacquelene Mwangi, Victor Nzomo, and Isaac Rutenberg. 2017. "A Framework for Assessing Technology Hubs in Africa." *NYU Journal of Intellectual Property and Entertainment Law* 6 (2): 237–77.

Dewey, John. 2005. *Art as Experience*. New York: Penguin.

Dodman, David, Bronwyn Hayward, and Mark Pelling. 2021. "Cities, Settlements and Key Infrastructure Supplementary Material." In *Climate Change 2022: Impacts, Adaptation and Vulnerability: Contribution of Working Group II to the Sixth Assessment Report of the Intergovernmental Panel on Climate Change*, edited by Hans-Otto Pörtner, Debra C. Roberts, Melinda Tignor, Elvira Poloczanska, Katja Mintenbeck, Andrés Alegría, Marlies Craig, Stefanie Langsdorf, Sina Löschke, Vincent Möller, Andrew Okem, and Bardhyl Rama, 907–1040. Geneva: IPCC. https://www.ipcc.ch/report/ar6/wg2/downloads/report/IPCC_AR6_WGII_Chapter06.pdf.

Durang, Xavier. 2000. "La ville africaine: Entre espaces privatifs partagés et improbable espace public." Paper presented at Globalité et différenciations culturelles, Laboratoire des organisations urbaines: Espaces, sociétés, temporalités, Paris Nanterre University, Paris, France, October 25–26.

Elungu, P. E. A. 1987. *Tradition africaine et rationalité moderne*. Paris: L'Harmattan.

European Commission and Enabel. 2021. "Culture and Creativity for the Future of Cities." https://op.europa.eu/en/publication-detail/-/publication/d21cd436-d23b-11eb-ac72-01aa75ed71a1.

Eychenne, Fabien. 2012. "Tour d'horizon des Fab Labs." https://fing.org/publications/tour-d-horizon-des-fab-labs.html.

Fabbri, Julie. 2016. "Les espaces de coworking: Ni tiers-lieux, ni incubateurs, ni Fab Labs." *Entreprendre Innover* 31 (4): 8–16.

Fagbohoun, Sandra. 2016. "Frugal Innovation, Effectuation and Fab Labs: Some Practices to Combine for a New Approach to Innovation." *Innovations* 51 (3): 27–46. https://doi.org/10.3917/inno.051.0027.

Festa, Daniela. 2016. "Les communs urbains. L'invention du commun." *Tracés. Revue de sciences humaines* Hors-série 2016 (16): 233–56. https://doi.org/10.4000/traces.6636.

Fonda, Carlo, and Enrique Canessa. 2016. "Making Ideas at Scientific Fabrication Laboratories." *Physics Education* 51 (6). https://doi.org/10.1088/0031-9120/51/6/065016.

Fourchard, Laurent. 2018. *Trier, exclure et policer: Vies urbaines en Afrique du sud et au Nigeria*. Paris: Presses de SciencesPo. https://doi.org/10.3917/scpo.fourc.2018.01.

Gandini, Alessandro. 2015. "The Rise of Coworking Spaces: A Literature Review." *Ephemera, Theory & Politics in Organization* 15 (1): 193–205. http://www.ephemerajournal.org/contribution/rise-coworking-spaces-literature-review.

Garroway, Christopher. 2011. "Measuring Cross-Country Differences in Social Cohesion." Last modified January 2011. https://www.semanticscholar.org/paper/1-Measuring-cross-country-differences-in-social-Garroway/8ecde966d183a8708dde6737159a119bbe10898c.

Gayet, Laure, and Kelly Ung. 2021. "Pour un urbanisme relationnel. Analyse des impacts sociaux et urbains de l'urbanisme transitoire." http://www.ecoquartiers.logement.gouv.fr/assets/articles/documents/pour-un-urbanisme-relationnel-analyse-des-impacts-sociaux-et-urbains-de-l-urbanisme-transitoire.pdf.

Gervais-Lambony, Philippe. 2001. "La citadinité, un arbre dans la forêt ou comment un mot peut en cacher d'autres…." *Vocabulaire de la ville, Éditions du temps*, 92–108. https://core.ac.uk/download/pdf/237331441.pdf.

Goffman, Erving. 2008 (1963). *Behavior in Public Places: Notes on the Social Organization of Gatherings*. New York: The Free Press.

Goyon, Marie. 2016. "L'obsolescence déprogrammée: Fab labs, makers et repair cafés. Prendre le parti des choses pour prendre le parti des hommes." *Techniques & Culture* 65–66. https://doi.org/10.4000/tc.7981.

Graeber, David. 2004. *Fragments of an Anarchist Anthropology*. Chicago: Prickly Paradigm Press.

Guillon, Vincent, and Jean-Pierre Saez. 2019. "L'intercommunalité réinvente-t-elle (enfin) les politiques culturelles?" *L'Observatoire* 54 (2): 15–17.

Habermas, Jürgen. 1962. *L'Espace public. Archéologie de la publicité comme dimension constitutive de la société bourgeoise*. Paris: Payot.

Harvey, David. 2012. *Rebel Cities: From the Right to the City to the Urban Revolution*. London: Verso Press.

Hess, Charlotte. 2008. "Mapping the New Commons." *SSRN Electronic Journal*. https://doi.org/10.2139/ssrn.1356835.

Joseph, Isaac. 1998. *La ville sans qualités*. La Tour-d'Aigues: Éditions de l'aube.

Kebir, Leïla, and Frédéric Wallet. 2021. "Les communs à l'épreuve du projet urbain et de l'initiative citoyenne." http://www.urbanisme-puca.gouv.fr/IMG/pdf/les_communs_copie1905typookweb.pdf.

Kip, Markus. 2015. "Moving Beyond the City: Conceptualizing Urban Commons from a Critical Urban Studies Perspective." In *Urban Commons: Moving Beyond State and Market*, edited by Mary Dellenbaugh, Markus Kip, Majken Bieniok, Agnes Müller, and Martin Schwegmann, 42–59. Berlin, Munich, Boston: Birkhäuser. https://doi.org/10.1515/9783038214953-003.

Knapp, Jake, John Zeratsky, and Braden Kowitz. 2017. *Sprint—Résoudre les problèmes et trouver de nouvelles idées en cinq jours*. Paris: Eyrolles.

Labrune, Jean-Baptiste. 2018. "Tiers-lieux apprenants." Medium Blog. October 16, 2018. https://medium.com/@jeanbaptiste/nouveaux-lieux-apprenants-322ecffc35b2.

Lefebvre, Henri. 1996. "The Right to the City." In *Writings on Cities*, translated and edited by Eleonore Kofman and Elizabeth Lebas, 147–59. Oxford and Malden, MA: Blackwell. Accessed October 25, 2022, from https://chisineu.files.wordpress.com/2012/09/lefebvre-henri-writings-on-cities.pdf.

Leimdorfer, François. 1999. "The Stakes and Imaginary of Public Space in Abidjan." *Politique africaine* 74 (2): 51–75.

Leyronas, Stéphanie, Isabelle Liotard, and Gwenael Prié. 2018. "Des communs informationnels aux communs éducationnels: Les fab labs en Afrique francophone." https://encommuns.com. https://hal.archives-ouvertes.fr/hal-03407669/document.

Liotard, Isabelle. 2020. "Les fab labs, ateliers au cœur de la ville: Les spécificités des lieux d'Afrique francophone." *Innovations* 61 (1): 117–39.

Lô, Amadou. 2017. "Un Fab lab d'entreprise pour favoriser l'ambidextrie des salariés: Étude de cas chez Renault." *Revue française de gestion* 43 (164): 81–99. https://doi.org/10.3166/rfg.2017.00113.

Lofland, Lyn H. 1998. *The Public Realm: Exploring the City's Quintessential Social Territory*. Abingdon: Routledge.

Lussault, Michel, and Jacques Lévy. 2013. *Dictionnaire de la géographie et de l'espace des sociétés*. Paris: Belin.

Mayer, Raoul Etongué, and Moustapha Soumahoro. 2014. "Espaces urbains africains sub-sahariens, changements et conflits spatiaux." *Canadian Journal of Tropical Geography* 1 (1): 1–7. http://www3.laurentian.ca/rcgt-cjtg/volume1-numero1/espaces-urbains-africains-sub-sahariens-changements-et-conflits-spatiaux/.

Mboa Nkoudou, Thomas Hervé. 2017. "Benefits and the Hidden Face of the Maker Movement: Thoughts on Its Appropriation in African Context." *Liinc em Revista* 13. https://doi.org/10.18617/liinc.v13i1.3774.

Mboa Nkoudou, Thomas Hervé. 2020. "Les makerspaces en Afrique francophone, entre développement local durable et technocolonialité: Trois études de cas au Burkina Faso, au Cameroun et au Sénégal." PhD dissertation, Laval University.

Merindol, Valerie, Nadège Bouquin, David Versailles, Ignasi Capdevila, Nicolas Aubouin, Alexandra Lechaffotec, Alexis Chiovetta, and Thomas Voisin. 2016. *Le livre blanc des open labs: Quelles pratiques? Quels changements en France*. Nancy: ANRT. https://doi.org/10.13140/RG.2.2.27107.96806.

Morel, Laure, and Serge Le Roux. 2016. *Fab Labs: L'Usager-innovateur*. London: ISTE Editions.

Mortara, Letizia, and Nicolas Parisot. 2016. "How Do Fab-Spaces Enable Entrepreneurship? Case Studies of 'Makers' Entrepreneurs." *International Journal of Manufacturing Technology Management*. https://doi.org/10.2139/ssrn.2519455.

Navez-Bouchanine, Françoise, ed. 2002. *La fragmentation en question: Des villes entre fragmentation spatiale et fragmentation sociale?* Paris: L'Harmattan.

Ngakoutou, Timothée. 2004. *L'éducation africaine demain: Continuité ou rupture?* Paris: L'Harmattan.

Ninot, Olivier, and Elisabeth Peyroux. 2018. "Révolution numérique et développement en Afrique: Une trajectoire singulière." *Questions internationales* 90.

OECD, AfDB, and ECA (Organisation for Economic Co-operation and Development, African Development Bank, and Economic Commission for Africa). 2022. *Africa's Urbanisation Dynamics 2022: The Economic Power of Africa's Cities*. Paris: OECD. https://read.oecd-ilibrary.org/development/africa-s-urbanisation-dynamics-2022 _3834ed5b-en.

OECD and SWAC (Organisation for Economic Co-operation and Development and Sahel and West Africa Club). 2020. *Dynamiques de l'urbanisation africaine 2020. Africapolis, une nouvelle géographie urbaine*. Paris: OECD. https://read.oecd-ilibrary .org/development/dynamiques-de-l-urbanisation-africaine-2020_481c7f49-fr#page1.

OIF and Idest (Organisation internationale de la francophonie and Institut du droit de l'espace et des télécommunications). 2016. "Rapport 2016. La Francophonie numérique." https://www.francophonie.org/sites/default/files/2019-10/rapport-numerique-2016.pdf.

Oldenburg, Ray. 1989. *The Great Good Place: Cafés, Coffee Shops, Community Centers, Beauty Parlors, General Stores, Bars, Hangouts, and How They Get You through the Day*. London: Paragon House.

Ostrom, Elinor. 1990. *Governing the Commons: The Evolution of Institutions for Collective Action*. Cambridge: Cambridge University Press.

Piller, Frank, Christian Weller, and Robin Kleer. 2015. "Business Models with Additive Manufacturing: Opportunities and Challenges from the Perspective of Economics and Management." *Advances in Production Technology* 39–48. https://doi.org /10.1007/978-3-319-12304-2_4.

Piuzzi, François. 2021. "Les Fab Labs et 'ateliers numériques' en France." *Reflets de la physique* 68: 32–36. https://doi.org/10.1051/refdp/202168032.

Rayna, Thierry, and Ludmila Striukova. 2021. "Assessing the Effect of 3D Printing Technologies on Entrepreneurship: An Exploratory Study." *Technological Forecasting and Social Change* 164. https://econpapers.repec.org/article/eeetefoso/v_3a164_3ay _3a2021_3ai_3ac_3as0040162520313093.htm.

Rodotà, Stefano. 2016. "Vers les biens communs. Souveraineté et propriété au XXIe siècle." Translated by Guillaume Calafat. *Tracés. Revue de sciences humaines* 16: 211–32. https://doi.org/10.4000/traces.6632.

Rumpala, Yannick. 2014. "'Fab labs,' 'makerspaces': Entre innovation et émancipation?" *Revue internationale de l'économie sociale* 334: 85–97. Accessed October 7, 2022, from https://doi.org/10.7202/1027278ar.

Rutt, Rebecca L. 2007. "Community-Based Urban Agriculture in Two East African Capitals." *Urban Agriculture Magazine* 16–18: 11–13.

Schlimmer, Sina. 2022. "Gouverner les villes africaines. Panorama des enjeux et perspectives." Accessed October 7, 2022, from https://www.ifri.org/fr/publications/etudes-de -lifri/gouverner-villes-africaines-panorama-enjeux-perspectives.

Secchi, Bernardo. 2006. *Première leçon d'urbanisme*. Marseille: Editions Parenthèses.

Serres, Michel. 1992. *Le tiers-instruit*. Paris: Gallimard.

Stacey, Michael. 2014. "The FAB LAB Network: A Global Platform for Digital Invention, Education and Entrepreneurship." *Innovations: Technology, Governance, Globalization* 9 (1–2): 221–38. Accessed October 7, 2022, from https://doi.org/10.1162/inov_a _00211.

Steck, Jean-Fabien. 2006. "Qu'est-ce que la transition urbaine? Croissance urbaine, croissance des villes, croissance des besoins à travers l'exemple africain." *Revue d'économie financière* 86: 267–83. Accessed October 7, 2022, from https://doi.org/10.3406/ecofi.2006.4212.

Susser, Ida, and Stéphane Tonnelat. 2013. "Transformative Cities: The Three Urban Commons." *Focaal–Journal of Global and Historical Anthropology* 2013 (66): 105–121. Accessed October 7, 2022, from https://doi.org/10.3167/fcl.2013.660110.

United Nations. 2019. *World Urbanization Prospects: The 2018 Revision*. New York: United Nations. https://population.un.org/wup/publications/Files/WUP2018-Report.pdf.

UN-Habitat (United Nations Human Settlements Programme). 2015. "Informal Settlements." https://unhabitat.org/sites/default/files/download-manager-files/Habitat-III-Issue-Paper-22_Informal-Settlements-2.0%20%282%29.pdf.

Zask, Joëlle. 2003. *Art et démocratie*. Paris: Presses Universitaires de France. Accessed October 7, 2022, from https://doi.org/10.3917/puf.zask.2003.01.

Chapter 5

Digital Commons and Entrepreneurship: Alternative or Complementary Approaches?

Jan Krewer, Stéphanie Leyronas, and Thomas Mboa

Introduction

Digital technologies occupy an important position in development strategies in Sub-Saharan Africa today. Numerous arguments have been advanced in their support: the growing power of digital entrepreneurship, combined with the promise of a leap forward in technology, could make exponential growth possible, contribute to the transition of African economies, and transform African countries into "knowledge economies" or propel them toward the "fourth industrial revolution."

However, empirical studies demonstrate that at this stage, digital entrepreneurship does not succeed in overcoming the structural inequalities of digital economies that are faced with both local and international challenges (Friederici, Wahome, and Graham 2020). At the local level, although certain countries in Sub-Saharan Africa do stand out from the rest, most of them still wrestle with the challenges of the second and third industrial revolutions. Electricity and connectivity, for example, which are crucial for making optimal use of digital resources, are still lacking. At the international level, the African continent is confronted with the reality of a global digital economy marked by significant inequalities and divisions, as well as by methods of value capture dominated by a handful of innovation centers where intellectual property is concentrated.

In this chapter, we argue that in Sub-Saharan Africa, digital commons–based entrepreneurship is necessarily more equitable and inclusive and promotes sustainable local development of communities and regions (Mboa

Nkoudou 2017). We make use of a catalogue[1] of Sub-Saharan Africa's digital commons, along with a literature review and a series of semi-structured interviews with digital experts and members of commons. The term *Sub-Saharan African commons* refers here to digital resources—such as code, information, and digital materials—whose communities of users and contributors are located in Sub-Saharan Africa. It does not include physical commons that make use of digital resources.

The first section provides—at the risk of taking a few shortcuts—a very brief overview of the digital strategies that are currently developed in Sub-Saharan Africa and of the underlying theories. It goes on to discuss parts of the debate in the literature about the limits of this dominant view, which promotes a form of digital entrepreneurship based on privatization, the division of knowledge, and competition. The section concludes by discussing the opportunities that digital commons offer in this context.

The second section showcases the range of digital commons in Sub-Saharan Africa by analyzing content, data, and software commons separately from those based on shared physical materials or open-plan layouts. This section highlights the importance of users and contributors in Sub-Saharan Africa. It argues that there is a wide variety of digital commons on the continent and that these commons participate in the Sustainable Development Goals.

The third and final section offers an interdisciplinary analysis of the opportunities offered by digital commons in Sub-Saharan Africa. It also points to the challenges faced by these commons. The section concludes with the observation that those engaged with African digital commons tend to see them not as alternatives to the traditional model of entrepreneurship but rather as a complementary approach.

What Role Should Digital Technology Play in Commons-Based Entrepreneurship in Sub-Saharan Africa?

Since the early 2000s, a consensus has emerged among large international organizations on the benefits of digital technologies for development. The African Union's Digital Transformation Strategy for Africa (2020–2030) states that digitalization is "stimulating job creation and contributing to addressing poverty, reducing inequality, facilitating the delivery of goods and services, and contributing to the achievement of Agenda 2030 and the Sustainable Development Goals" (African Union 2020, 1). This international consensus is sustained by the promise of development that digital technology holds for the African continent.

Promises of Digital Technology in Sub-Saharan African Public Development Strategies

Digital technologies are central to many African strategies

The majority of African countries have identified digital technology as a major lever for development (World Bank Group 2016) and have largely begun their digital transformation (Nyakanini et al. 2020). Numerous arguments have been put forward (Goldfarb and Tucker 2019). These strategies include not only the transformation and optimization of all sectors of the economy but also innovation and entrepreneurship. They put emphasis on replicating the trajectories of Western startups, with rapid, exponential growth. In this way, they hold out the hope of quickly transitioning to information societies and knowledge-based economies through leapfrogging. This term refers to the idea of leaps that will allow Sub-Saharan Africa to skip over stages of development. Implementing these kinds of strategies requires the development of internet infrastructure and access to digital technologies in order to offer African populations the same opportunities to innovate and develop solutions as elsewhere in the world (box 5.1).

BOX 5.1

Digital Cameroon 2016–2020 Strategy

In Cameroon in 2015, the cell phone penetration rate was around 50 percent, while the rate of broadband internet access was around 4 percent. The communication and digital product market is still nascent but already dynamic. The Ministère des Postes et Télécommunications (Ministry of Postal and Telecommunication Services), which is responsible for sectoral policy for telecommunications and information and communication technologies (ICTs), began prioritizing the issue of the digital economy as early as 2015 (Tatchim 2018). In 2016, the government adopted the Plan stratégique de l'économie numérique (Strategic Plan for the Digital Economy), which aims to increase digital technology's contribution to gross domestic product from 5 percent in 2016 to 10 percent by 2020. It also seeks to encourage the creation of 40,000 jobs by 2020. In particular, the plan focuses on developing broadband infrastructure, increasing the production of digital content, achieving the digital transformation of all sectors of the economy, promoting digital culture by generalizing the use of ICTs in an information society, strengthening digital confidence, and developing a local digital industry (Republic of Cameroon 2020).

The plan has been only partially carried out. That said, Cameroon gives ICTs and digital technologies an important place in its Stratégie nationale de développement 2020–2030 (National Development Strategy 2020–2030), the goal of which is to make Cameroon "a new industrialized country." Its priorities include the development of digital infrastructure, the modernization of public administration, the digitization of the land registry, decentralization, and open government.

Leapfrogging: The cell phone example
The deployment of information and communication technologies (ICTs) is the first leap made by the African continent, which entered the "digital age" through widespread cell phone use (Huet 2017). Since 2010, the number of cell phone users has increased 10-fold in Sub-Saharan Africa. Today, 86 percent of the population is covered by these networks (GSMA 2020), or 930 million people in 2020 (GSMA 2021), compared with 620 million in 2011 (GSMA 2012). Forecasts predict 1.1 billion connections by 2025 (GSMA 2021). The rapid development of mobile technology represents a technological leap over the intermediate step of landline technology (Berrou and Mellet 2020). Ghana, for example, has 131 active cell phone lines for every landline.[2]

The rapid spread of mobile technology has made important African innovations possible. In particular, it has provided the continent's marginalized population with access to numerous services. The most often cited example is access to mobile financial services, particularly payments using Unstructured Supplementary Service Data technology.[3] This technology is used for 9 out of 10 mobile payment transactions in Sub-Saharan African (GSMA 2018). Today, 12 percent of Africans pay their bills, send money, or make payments using their phones (Fox and Van Droogenbroeck 2017).

In addition to payments, the African mobile revolution has gone hand in hand with the strong economic growth of African countries over the past few decades. Many sectors of the economy have used mobile technology to develop new services. For example, many mobile platforms in the agricultural sector, such as Esoko in Ghana, allow farmers to have better access to information. Significant public investment in telecommunications has aided in the development of a new economic sector that represents 10 percent of Africa's gross domestic product (GDP) and now plays a critical role in the continent's economy (GSMA 2019).

A vision based on the promises of digital entrepreneurship for development
The development of entrepreneurship, particularly entrepreneurship that is based on the Western startup model, is one of the pillars of African digital strategies. By opening up new markets and simplifying the process of scaling up a business, startups symbolize the promise of rapid, exponential growth. In Africa, this vision is bolstered by the idea that digital technologies allow anyone with an internet connection to participate in the global economy (Friederici, Wahome, and Graham 2020). The contribution of Africa's younger generations to the development of digital technology's potential on the continent is highly anticipated (Nubukpo 2019), and the youthfulness of the continent's population structure is considered "an enormous opportunity in this digital era" (African Union 2020, 1).

For investors, supporting digital entrepreneurship is a way to boost a country's economic competitiveness and to create new jobs (Hjort and Poulsen 2019) and industries. As a result, "in just a few years, hundreds of millions and maybe billions of dollars have been invested in plans for tech cities, entrepreneurship trainings, coworking spaces, innovation prizes, and investment funds" (Friederici, Wahome, and Graham 2020, 1).

The Limits of Digital Entrepreneurship: An Economy with Structural Inequalities

Digital technologies create new divisions not only between countries but also between organizations and individuals. These divisions often reflect other inequalities, particularly of income and gender, which may be compounded by the introduction of digital technologies (UNCTAD 2021). As Friederici, Wahome, and Graham (2020) point out, the development of digital entrepreneurship faces numerous structural challenges, at both the local and international levels. The world of digital technologies is rife with divisions that reflect deep inequalities between countries, organizations, and individuals in terms of access to digital technology and the capacity to seize the opportunities that they offer.

Structural challenges at the local level

The obstacles to taking advantage of these opportunities are first and foremost infrastructural. Most Sub-Saharan African countries still face the challenges of the second and third industrial revolutions. Data from the International Telecommunication Union reveal a sharp increase in internet use between 2010 and 2020 in countries such as the Democratic Republic of Congo, Ethiopia, and Guinea.[4] At around 32 percent, however, the average rate remains low. Africa is now connected to the undersea fiber-optic cables that transmit more than 99 percent of international telecommunications (Goujon and Cariolle 2019). However, the continent still lacks sufficient infrastructure to connect its interior, as well as local content infrastructure (e.g., data centers and content delivery networks). As a result, Africa remains dependent on foreign infrastructure, which results in slower network flows, higher prices, and less development of local services and content (Internet Society 2017a).

The obstacles are also social. In the Central African Republic, the cost of one month of internet access is equivalent to more than one-and-a-half times the country's per capita income (GSMA 2019). The lack of digital "literacy," or the inability to make optimal use of a computer and the internet (World Bank Group 2019), exacerbates existing inequalities and even generates new ones. African women and people who live in rural areas remain the most marginalized with respect to digital technologies (World Bank Group 2021).

The centralization of the global digital economy

The structural centralization of power and value is one of the primary characteristics of the global digital economy (UNCTAD 2019). This situation can be explained, in part, by the contemporary geography of innovation.

Innovation networks may have become globalized, but innovation itself is centralized in a handful of "innovation hubs," most of which are located in previously industrialized economies (WIPO 2019). This centralization can also be explained by the monopolistic tendencies of ICTs that lead to winner-take-all situations. Above all, however, the most famous digital platforms have managed to attain dominant positions thanks to the enormous amounts of capital available to them, which has allowed them to conquer markets by buying up the competition or by operating at a loss for years on end (UNCTAD 2019).

Only paltry amounts of financing are available to African entrepreneurs: "VCs [venture capitalists] invested $3.9 million per day in African startups in 2020; while in the US, startups received VC investment of $428 million per day" (AfricArena 2021, 6). What's more, only a few national governments can generate enough funding for research and development, in the form of grants, tax credits, or public investment, to actively support the development of startups that can compete in the world economy. As a result, African countries do not generate much value in the global digital economy.

The limited availability of financing in Sub-Saharan Africa and the unequal distribution of intellectual property rights with respect to existing technologies are structural barriers to the development of digital entrepreneurship in the region. The digital entrepreneurship that does exist is not equally distributed across the continent, nor is it undergoing rapid and exponential growth. It tends instead to be focused on local or regional markets and to incorporate local infrastructure (Friederici, Wahome, and Graham 2020).

Commons: A Different Approach to the Digital Economy

Collaborative models as alternatives to traditional forms of digital entrepreneurship

While the digital revolution has produced numerous examples of highly centralized international companies that use intellectual property rights to generate economic rents, it has also allowed digital commons, which are non-proprietary and open collaborative models, to attain unprecedented scales (Open AIR 2020).

The digital commons movement originated in the 1990s, in Western countries, in response to the increasing privatization and division of knowledge. It was seen from the start as an alternative model (Peugeot 2014; Verdier and Murciano 2017). Initially, it built on the free software movement (see definitions in box 5.2) started by the American programmer and activist Richard Stallman. The free software movement began as a reaction to the appropriation of computer code by private companies in the 1980s, which ran counter to the principles of hackers, who, at the time, were still programming openly and collaboratively (Broca and Coriat 2015). Stallman argues that the private ownership of information delays progress, obstructs scientific development, and corrupts the ethos of research. He proposes new ways of sharing software source code and new kinds of legal instruments. As opposed to the copyright, he created the "copyleft," which is founded on four fundamental freedoms: the freedom of the user to use, copy, modify, and distribute the source code (Stallman 2002).

Beyond these legal innovations, which deal with copyright, there are also specific organizational forms concerning the contribution and participation of citizens. These new forms can mobilize a large number of people through open platforms and are largely based on "peer production" (Benkler 2007). They have inspired many collaborative projects, such as Wikipedia, OpenStreetMap, and open-access scientific journals. The fact that most of the software powering the servers that host data and services in the cloud is now open source shows that it is possible to build transnational shared infrastructures through broad, collaborative efforts.

These resources generate a growing interest within international organizations (UN 2020; UNCTAD 2021; UNESCO 2017) and certain African governments.[5] In its digital transformation strategy, the African Union refers to free educational resources, open data, open access to research results, and the use of open norms and standards to foster interoperability across Africa, particularly for public digital services, such as digital identity (African Union 2020).

Concepts and definitions

Digital commons differ from land-based commons (see chapter 2) in several ways (Coriat 2015) (see box 5.2):

- Digital commons, unlike land-based commons, are made up of nonrivalrous goods,[6] and so they are not subject to, or at risk of, being overexploited.

- Digital commons that are maintained over time and become institutionalized usually set rules for the use of the resource using free licenses, so as to benefit from the opportunities of scale that digital technologies offer.

- Whether digital commons persist often depends on the existence of several groups that are engaged in the production or use of the resource and that have a variety of relationships, interests, and roles with respect to the shared resource. Because the benefits of a digital resource are often indirect, the community comprises multiple different groups. By contrast, in land-based commons, the community is often restricted to the users of the resource, who are also responsible for managing it. An open database, for example, could be set up by a group that is entirely distinct from the individuals or organizations that might make use of this data and sometimes even distinct from the group that stands to benefit from the new information or services generated from this data.

BOX 5.2

Some Definitions Related to Digital Commons

Free license: A free license allows others to reuse a creator's work freely, according to certain conditions set by the license, without needing to contact the creator. There are several standard types of licenses, and their rights and obligations for users vary in degree of permissiveness (e.g., commercial use, the right to create derivative works, share-alike, etc.).

Free software: Free software is based on a free mode of production and distribution. As opposed to proprietary software, which is developed within an organization and whose source code is confidential, the source code of free software is completely public, and it can be modified, copied, and redistributed at will. Licenses that include all of these rights are recognized by the Free Software Foundation.

Open access: This term refers to free and unrestricted access to scholarly literature, and in particular to its "free availability on the public internet, permitting any users to read, download, copy, distribute, print, search, or link to the full texts of these articles, crawl them for indexing, pass them as data to software, or use them for any other lawful purpose, without financial, legal, or technical barriers other than those inseparable from gaining access to the internet itself."[a]

Open data: Open data is data that is openly accessible and exploitable by anyone for any purpose. This data can be of private or public origin. This kind of data is transmitted under an open license that guarantees that it can be freely accessed and reused by anyone.

Open hardware: Open hardware, or open-source hardware, refers to technology related to computer hardware for which all design and manufacturing information is made available through open-source licenses in order to make it easier for others to make, reuse, or repair the object themselves.

Open-source software: Open-source software and free software are based on similar user licenses, but they should not be confused. *Free software* is a movement that preaches philosophical and political values based on Stallman's four freedoms, while *open-source* software is a method of software development and dissemination that makes it possible to reap the economic benefits of open, decentralized modes of production (Broca and Coriat 2015). Open-source licenses are recognized by the Open Source Initiative.

Open Standards: According to Free Software Foundation Europe, an Open Standard refers to a format or protocol that is

- Subject to full public assessment and use without constraints in a manner equally available to all parties
- Without any components or extensions that have dependencies on formats or protocols that do not meet the definition of an Open Standard themselves
- Free from legal or technical clauses that limit its utilization by any party or in any business model

(continued next page)

Box 5.2 (continued)

- Managed and further developed independently of any single vendor in a process open to the equal participation of competitors and third parties
- Available in multiple complete implementations by competing vendors, or as a complete implementation equally available to all parties[b]

Open Standards guarantee that systems are interoperable—that is, they allow hardware, software, and protocols to work together and share information.

Open Educational Resources: According to UNESCO, "Open Educational Resources (OER) are learning, teaching and research materials in any format and medium that reside in the public domain or are under copyright that have been released under an open license, that permit no-cost access, re-use, re-purpose, adaptation and redistribution by others."[c]

a. https://www.budapestopenaccessinitiative.org/read/.
b. https://fsfe.org/freesoftware/standards/standards.en.html.
c. https://www.unesco.org/en/communication-information/open-solutions/open-educational-resources.

In sum, the concept of the digital commons can be used to foster the development of new social dynamics that emphasize community and governance, beyond the technical apparatuses and resources involved. This governance is more or less inclusive and contributive (Broca 2021), but it allows for the development of capacity and the creation of value at the local level. It is this approach to digital commons that guided the cataloguing presented in the following section.

A Catalogue of Digital Commons in Sub-Saharan Africa: A Range of Resources and Communities Contributing to the Continent's Development

The Different Resources Associated with Digital Commons in Sub-Saharan Africa and Their Contribution to Development

This study, though it does not claim to be either exhaustive or representative, shows that numerous digital commons are a part of Africans' everyday lives. We have identified several types of digital commons in the fields of education, agriculture, rural development and biodiversity, open government, energy, digital technology and telecommunications, transport and mobility, and health. We divide them into four sections, although some appear in more than one category: content commons, data commons, free software, and a final category that includes open hardware commons and open standards and protocols commons, which are most often found in hybrid places like fab labs (Mboa Nkoudou 2020) (see chapter 4).

Content commons

The potential of content commons[7] such as AfricArXiv (box 5.3) in Sub-Saharan Africa has been recognized and documented, particularly in the fields of education and research. Advocates of open access argue that the convergence of the scientific tradition and ICTs offers an unprecedented opportunity that will "accelerate research, enrich education, share the learning of the rich with the poor and the poor with the rich, make this literature as useful as it can be, and lay the foundation for uniting humanity in a common intellectual conversation and quest for knowledge."[8] It is this preoccupation with knowledge-sharing that has motivated several international organizations to commit to promoting open educational resources. According to UNESCO, open educational resources "provide a strategic opportunity to improve the quality of learning and knowledge-sharing as well as improve policy dialogue, knowledge-sharing and capacity-building."[9] Inclusion is valued here in addition to the basic tenets of open access. Beyond the "legal and technical issues of accessibility," African digital commons make it possible to respond to demands to "develop the knowledge and skills generated in the periphery" and not to "deepen the scientific divide"—namely, the dependency on knowledge and techniques imported to Africa from abroad (Piron et al. 2017).[10]

Various initiatives have thus emerged in Sub-Saharan Africa, driven by the public and private sectors but also managed by communities of contributors (Koomar and Jull 2020). This is the case, for example, of the South African Institute for Distance Education's African Storybook Initiative. The initiative is home to more than 3,000 unique storybooks that are shared, under free licenses, by a multitude of contributors in over 200 African languages. The number of African Storybook users was estimated at nearly three million in 2021. The purpose of the initiative is to provide content that not only is adapted for a particular learning context (especially the native language) but also fosters a sense of ownership among learners.

Data commons

Since the 2000s, similar values to the creation of content commons have driven the open data and data commons[11] movement. According to the World Bank, an increase in the production and availability of data leads to increased transparency and accountability, improved public policies and services, and increased economic opportunities (World Bank Group 2021). Open data is often managed by public bodies, but it can also be handled by communities themselves (box 5.4). Such is the case of OpenStreetMap, which is attempting to use a collaborative approach to create a freely editable database of geographic data about the world.

In general, open databases managed by commons in Sub-Saharan Africa serve a variety of needs. For example, a scientific community may want to

AfricArXiv

AfricArXiv is an open digital archive for open access to African research. It was launched in 2018, in Kumasi, Ghana, at the first African Open Science and Hardware Summit, which brought together scientists from Africa and abroad. AfricArXiv is an open, decentralized repository intended for use by African populations. Its technical infrastructure is provided by the Center for Open Science, a nonprofit organization that provides researchers with open-source infrastructure.

AfricArXiv allows African researchers to publish the results of their research immediately and for free. They can thereby receive feedback on their work, improve it, and identify partners for future projects. The site helps to publicize African research, disseminate African knowledge, allow exchanges between African researchers to take place, and encourage intercontinental collaboration. AfricArXiv seeks to address the specific problems faced by African researchers: a lack of international visibility for their work, limited funding, language barriers, and bias and discrimination when it comes to working with international publications and research networks.

AfricArXiv currently has almost 400 preprints. The community of contributors is made up of African scholars based on the continent or at host institutions outside Africa, as well as of non-African scholars summarizing research that was either conducted on the continent or that is related to African issues.

AfricArXiv is managed by a group of volunteers, who share any and all information about coordinating the initiative via their website. The rules for submitting preprints are also published online. Once a preprint is submitted, two or more volunteer moderators determine whether the work meets standards for reliability and relevancy. AfricArXiv relies mainly on donations and voluntary contributions.

monitor the status of biodiversity (such as the African Bird Atlas Project). Citizens who want to make government more transparent may also contribute to the development of data commons. This was the approach, in Senegal, of Open COVID19, which was born out of a desire to publish digitized information, such as the number of cases and their geolocations, that had previously been communicated only verbally, by the government. These initiatives are also useful for journalists, researchers, civil society, citizens in general, and policy makers. The IWACU Open Data initiative in Burundi, for example, was developed by a group of journalists to address the lack of access to official data, which was stored only in paper copies. Finally, numerous academic studies have illustrated the importance of open geospatial data for the allocation of aid by governments and nongovernmental organizations (NGOs) (Grinberger et al. 2022).

BOX 5.4

Ushahidi

In 2007, violence erupted in Kenya in the wake of the Kenyan general election. A widespread media blackout prevented millions of Kenyans from accessing information about the situation in the country and from getting to safety. In a matter of days, bloggers and leading figures in the digital sphere decided to get together to build a platform to gather firsthand information from locals via SMS and the internet. More than 40,000 geolocated, time-stamped testimonies were shared on the platform. The platform served not only as an alert system for those in close proximity to the violence but also as a way to inform the rest of the world about how the situation was unfolding.

Ushahidi means "testimony" in Swahili. Ushahidi's purpose has since changed: the platform is now open to marginalized communities around the world. It is freely reusable and modifiable and is used in more than 160 countries. Some 50 million testimonies have been collected on the platform from people under threat of natural disasters, human rights violations, corruption, or harassment. These testimonies help to improve access to information, to make governments more transparent, and to better adapt government responses to crises.

Among the most active communities are contributors to the Syria Tracker, HarassMap, iWitness, Abaaraha, and Mapping Media Freedom projects. Though Ushahidi has an international team of more than 15 experts from seven African countries, it has adopted an open strategy that allows communities to participate not only in updating its platform but also in designing it and in writing user manuals. Maintenance of the Ushahidi platform is handled mainly by a nonprofit organization based in Kenya. The rules governing its management and use, particularly the data that are collected, are defined by the user communities. All that Ushahidi requires of these communities is that they respect the rules regarding personal data protection and privacy. Thanks to the publicity Ushahidi garnered in the wake of the violence in Kenya, it has received a great deal of financial support, in the form of donations and grants, from international public organizations, foundations, and private companies. Although the organization still relies in large part on this financial support, it has developed new sources of revenue by offering certain communities customization services and support for the deployment of its tool.

Free software

Because of the shared dependence on certain computer systems, a great deal of free software[12] is used around the world today by private companies, the public sector, and civil society. Companies that depend on this software also help develop it. Free software is particularly well represented in the sphere of servers and web applications. For example, the Apache HTTP Server is the most widely used software for web servers, just as WordPress is for websites and MySQL is for database management.

Several studies have pointed out the many positive externalities of free software development for the economy and employment—namely, that it makes local businesses more productive and fosters digital entrepreneurship (Wachs et al. 2022). Some companies specialize in deploying free software or in developing solutions tailored to the needs of customers. Digital services companies thus account for a large share of growth and employment in the ICT sector (UNCTAD 2019). In the course of our research, we identified several examples of free software—some of which were created in Africa, such as OpenMRS (box 5.5)—that are maintained and deployed by numerous service providers on the continent.

Open hardware commons and open standards and protocols commons
In the course of our research, we identified several examples of open hardware commons[13] and open standards and protocols commons.[14] First, these include

---

BOX 5.5

OpenMRS

OpenMRS is a software program developed in 2004 by several organizations working to improve care for patients with HIV in Kenya and Rwanda. It was originally designed as a generic medical record system that could handle all patient health information and deliver it in the form of summaries, reports, and data views that could make system users more efficient.

Before long, OpenMRS was being deployed in a host of contexts. It has developed from just a handful of founding organizations into a global community based on the principles of openness and sharing. It is used today in more than 40 countries and at over 6,000 sites, making it possible to manage the medical records of nearly 16 million patients. The community of contributors to OpenMRS is made up of small service companies that deploy the software locally, international health care organizations, and research institutions. Over the past 15 years, the number of contributors from the Global South, and from Sub-Saharan Africa in particular, has increased significantly. A growing number of companies that offer software customization and deployment services are involved in updating the core software and in sharing new features with the rest of the community.

OpenMRS is a nongovernmental organization (NGO) registered in the United States. The development of its software is carried out by "squads" of volunteer contributors. Community members can monitor the NGO's important technical and strategic decisions via committees. By constituting itself as a legal entity, OpenMRS is eligible to receive public funding. This kind of funding constitutes the bulk of its income, as it does not seek to develop services that could compete directly with the organizations that deploy and contribute to the development of its software.

---

community Wi-Fi networks (box 5.6). Access to affordable infrastructure and equipment remains a major barrier to the promotion of digital technologies. By making it possible to pool resources and costs, digital commons present an important opportunity in this context. Communities around the world have been able to establish community networks for internet access in remote areas that are not profitable for telecommunications operators. There are not many in Sub-Saharan Africa, however (Internet Society 2017b), even though the low income levels and the high cost of internet, equipment, and electricity in the region could, in theory, be a catalyst for their development. On the other hand,

---

BOX 5.6

Pamoja Net

Pamoja Net is a community Wi-Fi network established in 2016 by the nongovernmental organization (NGO) La Différence, on Idjwi Island in the Democratic Republic of Congo. The network helped several businesses and cooperatives, as well as more than 6,000 of the island's 300,000 inhabitants, get internet access. According to an evaluation conducted by the NGO, 98 percent of the network's new users feel that the project has "contributed to a positive change in their life, from a new-found ability to connect with family and friends to conducting educational research, making job applications, checking weather reports before fishing on Lake Kivu and saving money."[a] The island's foremost cooperative, the coffee growers' cooperative, has been able to expand its business and find new international clients.

The primary users and contributors to the network are local businesses, which have agreed to fund the monthly connection cost of about US$800,000. Considering the costs of installation and individual subscriptions with a conventional internet service provider, sharing the cost of Wi-Fi saves these businesses money. They also help pay for the maintenance of the network, as well as that of a small kiosk, which allows all the island's inhabitants to benefit from the bandwidth after working hours. The kiosk is located at the center of the island's main market.

The network's governance is closely linked to the island's chiefdom, headed by the king. The king has set up various commissions to discuss public policy issues, including one commission that deals with communication and handles network issues. La Différence's teams meet with this commission once a week to evaluate the evolution of the network and discuss any problems. It was therefore possible to discuss the network's management rules with all stakeholders in advance. The fact that the network is part of the existing chiefdom system is seen by locals as a way of ensuring that the project belongs to the community and remains autonomous. While the network still relies on grants and donations to fund its operation costs, 60 percent of these costs are covered by local businesses. The funds needed to set up the network were raised by the NGO from international donors and philanthropists.

a. https://www.la-difference.com/innovation-article-community-internet.

there are several barriers to their development, including a lack of awareness of the benefits of better access to information, the limited development of certain technical skills, and the lack of regulatory frameworks conducive to community initiatives.

Similarly, many urban commons, such as fab labs (see chapter 4), provide shared access to different types of equipment, such as internet-connected computers for accessing services or 3D printers for industrial prototyping. These approaches, based on a collaborative, "DIY" ethos, promote local innovation through access to open-source designs.[15] Many members of African fab labs helped design and produce health solutions in the fight against the COVID-19 pandemic.

The Different Communities Involved in Digital Commons: Dynamics of Collaboration and Participation

The communities involved in digital commons, particularly free software ones, have identified four groups that are essential to making a resource sustainable.[16] These are users, who have a use for commons; contributors, who help maintain or develop commons; administrators, who are responsible for the long-term organization of commons and who have management, exclusion, and alienation rights (see chapter 1); and funders, who help finance commons. We are concerned here with user and contributor communities located, either entirely or partially, in Sub-Saharan Africa. The very nature of digital commons, however, makes geographical belonging a thorny issue (box 5.7).

African users of digital commons

The use of digital commons has greatly increased throughout the world over the past 20 years. Sub-Saharan Africa is no exception, but it does have certain particularities.

The use of content commons, whether developed in Africa or abroad, remains lower overall in Sub-Saharan Africa than in the rest of the world, though the rates and methods of use vary from country to country. The reasons why people use them vary as well. For example, Africans who use Wikipedia tend to do so for work and learning, whereas people in industrialized countries tend to do so to check information (Lemmerich et al. 2019).

As platforms that make a great deal of data accessible are developed, and as the number of organizations and individuals with data science skills grows, the number of African users of data commons appears to be increasing. Open-data initiatives are largely driven by the media,[17] NGOs, academics, and entrepreneurs in the social economy. Intermediary entities, such as NGOs and foundations, play an essential role in Sub-Saharan Africa's data ecosystem. They often train journalists, academics, and entrepreneurs to use data, and they may finance initiatives focused on certain technologies (e.g., artificial intelligence)

Challenges of Pinning Down Digital Commons Geographically

At first glance, it appears difficult to link digital commons to particular geographic locations. The vast majority of digital commons use free licenses, which allow them to benefit from the opportunity to scale up that being digital affords them. In theory, every developer in the world could help develop software registered under a free license. This increases the chances that the software will be developed and improved but also copied and used.

We should distinguish this kind of broad de jure use from de facto use. It is possible to study the communities that contribute to different software in order to assess how diverse they are, for example, in terms of geographical origin, gender, ethnicity, or religion. Several studies have pointed out the lack of diversity among contributors to certain commons, particularly the overrepresentation of North American and European men among people who write Wikipedia articles, including articles that relate to countries of the Global South. The Wikimedia Foundation itself has set up a diversity observatory. With respect to certain digital commons, such as the technical standards that govern the internet or the Web, the low participation of African contributors is striking. Just 0.26 percent of the contributions received by the Internet Engineering Task Force are African.[a]

There are digital commons whose user groups are truly global, such as VLC media player. But it is hard to find examples of communities with an even geographic distribution of contributors. Thus, with respect to free software, although digitization facilitates remote collaboration, the persistence of regional clusters suggests that geographic location plays a decisive role in the organization of contributions to an open-source project (Wachs et al. 2022).

Among those digital commons that are considered global, such as Wikipedia or OpenStreetMap, we also observe a high number of communities organized around specific resources: for example, communities of users of Wikipedia articles dedicated to one country or language or groups organized to contribute to the cartography of a country, region, or city. While these communities are a subset of the global community of contributors, they are nevertheless geographically located and organize themselves locally according to their particular needs.

a. https://researchictafrica.net/2022/06/13/mapping-african-digital-infrastructures-part-3-understanding-the-motivations-and-challenges-of-african-contributions-to-the-internet-standards-development/.

or certain Sustainable Development Goals. This is true of projects supported by the Lacuna Fund (box 5.8) and by Outreachy, for example.

There are many users of free software in Sub-Saharan Africa, although there is a lack of data on how important free software is to African businesses. Nevertheless, our interviews confirm that the use of free software provides small businesses in the service sector and urban populations with easy

BOX 5.8

Lacuna Fund

The Lacuna Fund is a "collaborative effort to provide data scientists, researchers, and social entrepreneurs in low- and middle-income contexts globally with the resources they need to produce labeled datasets that address urgent problems in their communities."[a] The fund was created specifically to address the needs of machine learning (the contemporary methods of artificial intelligence learning enabled by access to massive amounts of data). Even though artificial intelligence seems to present huge opportunities in the way of development, in Sub-Saharan Africa, these kinds of data are either nonexistent or of poor quality, or is even discriminatory (since the most marginalized populations are underrepresented).

The Lacuna Fund now includes the Rockefeller Foundation, Google.org, the International Development Research Centre, and the German Agency for International Cooperation. The fund puts out calls for thematic project proposals and awards grants to successful applicants. The data sets generated by these projects are "locally developed and owned, and they will be openly accessible to the international community while adhering to best practices regarding ethics and privacy."[b]

a. https://lacunafund.org/about/.
b. https://lacunafund.org/about/.

access to key services at a lower cost than proprietary solutions, which can be expensive to license. Respondents cited Linux-derived operating systems, in particular, but also the free office suite LibreOffice, text-editing tools (e.g., Scribus, FontForge), audio- and video-editing tools, and 3D-creation tools (e.g., Blender) in the creative industries sector. African information technology companies rely heavily on free software for web development but also on integrated management solutions for businesses, for example, for customer relations (e.g., CRM software).

Finally, we identified several examples of community Wi-Fi networks whose users are mainly people who live in rural areas, in marginalized communities.

African contributors to digital commons

The vast majority of African contributors to global commons such as Wikimedia or OpenStreetMap are young, and they either have a degree or are in the process of obtaining one. They tend to be from urban areas, and women are still underrepresented. Few contributors receive an income, even a partial one, for their participation. Most of them are students taking part in open-source projects as part of their studies or a job search.[18] Many of them take part individually in civic engagement projects, particularly in the domain of government transparency (civic tech) or of open science. These projects, such as African Storybook, promote African languages and cultures through content creation. Others aim to produce national intangible infrastructures, such as the Digital Umuganda project in Rwanda, which mobilizes the ancestral concept of "Umuganda" (engaging once a month in work for the collective good) to collectively develop artificial intelligence voice recognition applications in Kinyarwanda.

The share of African contributions to the global digital commons remains small, with a few exceptions. According to data from GitHub (the most popular open-source code repository), contributors who identified themselves as African accounted for just 2.3 percent of active contributors in 2021 (although one-third of contributors did not declare their geographical location). The share of contributions by African developers has nevertheless increased from 0.3 percent in 2010 to 2.3 percent in 2020. The Democratic Republic of Congo, Kenya, Nigeria, and South Africa had more than 100,000 active contributors in 2021, and 2019 saw remarkable growth in the number of African projects filed on GitHub, particularly in the Arab Republic of Egypt, Kenya, and Nigeria. Some projects, such as Open Source Community Africa, see the continent as the place where the "next billion creators" will come from. Finally, the platform is also home to projects like "Made in Nigeria" and "Made in Africa."

Large international foundations are seeking to enrich the content and data commons with more African contributions, sometimes with the support of international donors. For example, local associations affiliated with the Wikimedia Foundation have been created in Sub-Saharan Africa to support the creation of content related to the countries that are the least well represented in the encyclopedia, both in the languages of these countries and by contributors that hail from them (map 5.1). They enable local communities to help build a diverse online cultural heritage. Campaigns such as Wiki Loves Africa, meanwhile, have greatly increased the number of freely reusable images from 55 countries across the continent. Images submitted between January 2016 and July 2021 have been viewed 787 million times,[19] boosting the visibility and perceived value of Africa's heritage. Similarly, initiatives such as YouthMappers, Humanitarian OpenStreetMap, Open Cities, and OpenStreetMap Microgrants have established local communities of cartographers that have helped create important geographic databases in Sub-Saharan Africa (map 5.2). OpenStreetMap communities can be found in 65 percent of African countries. Moreover, many countries, while lacking organized communities, have active contributors.[20]

Administrators and financial sponsors of digital commons in Sub-Saharan Africa

Funding models for African digital commons are often hybrid, combining donations, public subsidies, and market revenues. Relying on multiple sources

Map 5.1 **Presence in Africa of Associations Affiliated with the Wikimedia Foundation**

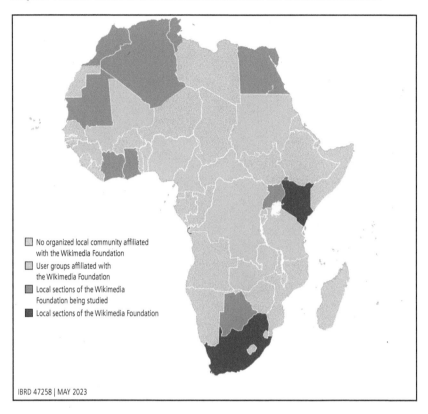

IBRD 47258 | MAY 2023

Source: Original map using Khartis software and data from meta.wikimedia.org.

of funding is seen as a way to guarantee autonomy and financial stability, but it requires the maintenance of a community of financial sponsors, which implies a legal entity, regulations, a bank account, and a staff able to write grant applications and respond to invitations to tender. Before long, these teams start to play a critical role in managing the resource, and they must be skilled at managing and evaluating projects in order to meet the criteria set by backers. As a result, most of the digital commons that we identified are legally structured entities, and these are as likely to be located in Africa as in Europe or North America. There are few informal collectives in our sample.

Map 5.2 **Density of Contributions to OpenStreetMap in Africa**

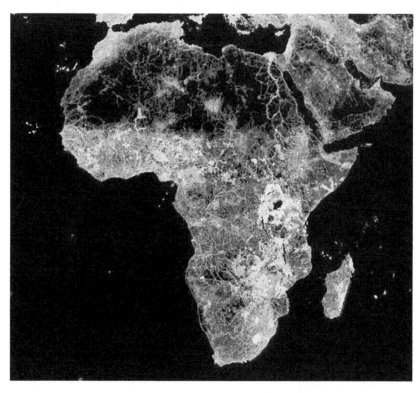

Digital Commons: Opportunities and Challenges for African Development

Digital Commons: An Opportunity for African Development

Possibilities and capacity for innovation across a wide range of application areas

Digital commons in Sub-Saharan Africa are represented in all development sectors. Their impact can be seen in both urban and rural settings, as well as in countries up and down the continent. First and foremost, they offer the private sector opportunities to cut costs, such as by using freely available images (Erickson et al. 2015). They also help to spread innovation. Any organization or company can access the resource and thus use it to invent new products and services. An open database, for example, can be used by any and all digital actors in a country to develop software and applications. These resources may be key technologies that open up the possibility for the development of applications in a wide range of fields. Digital commons thus allow entrepreneurs around the world to liberate themselves from dependence on technologies owned by companies that are usually located in the Global North.

Open digital infrastructure for an inclusive economy
The digital revolution has allowed digital commons to reach unprecedented scales.[21] As a result, many digital commons have come to be recognized as pieces of the immaterial infrastructure of systems that are now vital for digital economy actors, just like roads and bridges in the physical world.[22] Digital commons are all the more interesting as infrastructure in that they are based on modes of governance that involve multiple actors. This makes them less likely to be dependent on a single actor (whether public or private) and guarantees that access to the resource is inclusive.

In Sub-Saharan Africa, in the same way, the public and private sectors are increasingly coming to recognize the role these communities play in terms of cost sharing and innovation potential (box 5.9). Free software is playing a

BOX 5.9

WAZIHUB

WAZIHUB ("Open-Hub" in Swahili) is a project that seeks to promote African innovation in the Internet of Things (IoT) and in Big Data. Launched in 2015, with funding from the EU's Horizon 2020, its goal is to develop open software and hardware to enable African entrepreneurs to easily create solutions based on these technologies. The project offers resources and end-to-end support. It provides a free development kit for rapid prototyping of solutions that is based on free software and hardware. It also offers free access to a cloud computing platform for developing custom applications through an open interface. The project then provides access to capacity-building training for entrepreneurs and connects them with experts and researchers in the IoT field. About 48 startups have used WAZIHUB's technology to develop solutions. More than 2,000 people have used the project's resources and attended its training sessions. WAZIHUB works closely with innovation centers in countries across the continent. WAZIHUB's technology project is fully open source and is being developed on GitHub with a small community of developers. The code has already been cloned several times by other communities.

The WAZIHUB project is coordinated by the Bruno Kessler Foundation, which is based in Italy. The consortium comprises seven partners from four African countries (Burkina Faso, Ghana, Senegal, and Togo) and five partners from four European countries (France, Germany, Italy, and Portugal). It brings together developers, technology experts, and African companies. It is largely publicly funded.

growing role in the public health sector, for example. In Lesotho, the government has played a leading role in the use and development of OpenStreetMap for urban and rural planning programs.[23] Similarly, the African software development company Andela is a major contributor to the open-source projects that its business relies on, in the belief that this contributes to the training and international reputation of its employees.

Commons are also of interest to governments because solutions that were initially developed to meet local needs have been able to be deployed throughout the world. An example of this is the OpenMRS medical record system (box 5.5). This observation has helped generate new international collaborations for the development and maintenance of shared digital infrastructure, such as GovStack.

Communities of practice that act as socioeconomic connectors
Through the idea of shared resources (e.g., knowledge, information, equipment, space), digital commons are at the center of collaboration and empowerment dynamics that act as socioeconomic connectors. They offer the advantage of mixing the formal and informal sectors, the public sector with the private, industries and universities, expertise and practice, urban and rural milieux, or the African diaspora with countries of origin.

African digital commons are organized into networks by type of resource, notably at the pan-African and international levels. AfricaOSH (Africa Open Science Hardware), for example, is one of the most dynamic networks of fab labs in Africa. In contrast to interventions that are based essentially on providing digital resources developed in the Global North, these African networks make it possible to take into account all the needs and social structures at work in the production and reception of a digital resource, beyond the nature of the resource itself. Knowledge, for example, is understood as the result of a learning process—and therefore of a social process—and not as merely the digital formalization of information.

Finally, digital commons are the fruit of cooperative efforts between citizens from different countries and backgrounds, sometimes on a global scale. They are not based on a vertical transfer of knowledge but rather on mutual learning through cocreation. As a result, they pave the way for peer-to-peer partnerships that can create truly new capacities for all parties involved.[24]

Challenges to Developing the Potential of Digital Commons
Whether African digital commons contribute to sustainable local development is no longer in question, but it would be naive to think that they have no obstacles to overcome. Digital commons, like digital entrepreneurs, are faced first and foremost with Africa's traditional infrastructural challenges (i.e., electricity, connectivity, etc.). Low literacy rates and inequality of access

to digital technologies remain barriers to the deployment of digital commons. For example, a country's number of active contributors to Wikipedia is correlated with its Human Development Index (Graham, De Sabbata, and Zook 2015). The relative lack of community Wi-Fi in Sub-Saharan Africa can also be explained by the lack of awareness of the benefits of better access to information and the limited development of certain technical skills (Internet Society 2017a). However, digital commons also face unique challenges.

Digital commons are not a priority in national policies

Digital strategies in Africa are mostly focused on bringing economic activity into the formal sector and strengthening the state at the expense of African communities. As a result, digital commons in Sub-Saharan Africa are developing on fragile ground. In addition to a lack of institutional support, this is because governments, public agencies, and large- and medium-sized companies are not fully aware of the potential of digital commons. It may also be a result of the strategic priorities that have guided African public policies on digital technologies for several decades. These tend to be focused on developing connectivity, creating businesses and jobs in the ICT sector, and digitizing public services. These strategic priorities seek to formalize economic activity and strengthen states by rolling out digital civil registries, for example, or improving tax collection systems, such as through the introduction of a value-added tax. Even when digital commons initiatives flourish, they can run up against other political and economic challenges. In 2013, for example, the Central Bank of Kenya filed a lawsuit against members of the foundation Grassroots Economics (box 5.10), which had been involved in developing the Bangla-Pesa complementary currency.

Limited availability of funding and economic dependence on international partners

The financial support made available to digital commons often comes in the form of microgrants for activities related to specific projects or campaigns. This can be explained by three factors: the difficulty of estimating or measuring the value of a nonmarket, intangible resource; uncertainties about how much funding is actually needed; and a lack of information about how the developed resources might be reused. Developing a digital commons is not without risk. It is also harder to offer investors collateral or financial guaranties, since there are not usually any assets to seize if a project fails.

As a result, transitioning from an ad hoc collective that collaborates on a specific project to a community that actively manages a sustainable resource over time is not easy for many emerging civil society initiatives. Doing so requires that committed communities be able to connect with donors or international funders in order to benefit from substantial and long-term funding (box 5.11). For example, Tanzania has, with the support

Grassroots Economics

Grassroots Economics is a nonprofit foundation that aims to foster economic development by introducing local, inclusive complementary currencies. It grew out of marginalized communities in Kenya. Its first complementary-currency project, Bangla-Pesa, was implemented in 2013, in a slum on the outskirts of Mombasa called Bangladesh. The foundation is now developing complementary-currency projects in 45 localities in Kenya and 2 localities in South Africa. Its goal is to roll out such currencies across the globe.

The complementary currencies developed by Grassroots Economics function as vouchers or interest-free credit obligations. The vouchers have value because local small businesses and consumers treat them as money. The community can set its own rules for issuing and distributing the currency. According to evaluations of the foundation's programs, introducing these currencies as a complement to national currencies has created a stable medium of exchange for local development by reducing dependence on external markets and liquidity. As a result of the development of this new local financial service, the communities that have participated in these programs have seen an increase in trade, investment, and employment. The foundation itself describes the agreements made between members of the various communities as "economic commons."

The foundation has created the Grassroots Economic Commons License, an open license that defines the rights and obligations of the communities involved. It supports communities in using this license and in adapting resources and tools to their needs. Its activities are funded by grants and donations, mainly from donors and nongovernmental organizations that support development programs with a similar approach and suite of services as the foundation.

of the Humanitarian OpenStreetMap Team and the World Bank, become one of the African countries with the largest number of buildings mapped on OpenStreetMap.[25]

Proprietary or open models? A dilemma for African contributors to digital commons

Few digital-innovation spaces emphasize unorthodox systems of intellectual property. Apart from fab labs, most African digital commons are not consciously engaged in promoting a heterodox system of entrepreneurship, nor describe themselves as commons (notable exceptions include AfricArXiv and Laws.Africa).

Digital commons in Sub-Saharan Africa are usually formed in response to a specific problem. The values of openness, shared governance, or even

BOX 5.11

Energypedia

Energypedia was initially designed as an internal tool for the knowledge management of Deutsche Gesellschaft für Internationale Zusammenarbeit GmbH (GIZ) (German Agency for International Cooperation) energy projects. Interest from external partners led GIZ, in 2010, to make the wiki public and freely accessible. In 2012, the Energypedia project was spun off into an independent nongovernmental organization (NGO).

Today, Energypedia is a wiki platform for exchanging knowledge about renewable energy, energy access, and energy efficiency in developing countries. In 2021, it had more than 5,000 articles, which were consulted nearly 2 million times around the world that year. It now receives close to 90,000 monthly visits from 212 different countries. In 2021, 12,000 users were registered, mostly in the Global South. According to a 2019 survey of its users, more than half of the users identified themselves as being based in Africa. A significant number of contributors work for NGOs or in the public or private sector. The platform never pays contributors directly. On the other hand, some employers pay for writing articles.

Energypedia is an NGO based in Germany, with a small, mostly part-time team. These employees have set rules of conduct for contributors, including bans on promoting fossil or nuclear energy and on advertisements for particular business solutions. The team also maintains the writing and organizational standards of the wiki's articles, though it does not verify the quality of the content in detail. Contributors are therefore free to contribute to the wiki and submit ideas for strategic action, but they do not directly influence the NGO's direction.

Energypedia is largely publicly funded, though it does also receive donations from a limited number of individuals. The public funds are mostly grants from development agencies. A private company, Energypedia Consult, was founded in 2012. It develops consulting services for knowledge management and the evaluation of energy programs. Its profits go to the NGO. That money helps cover some recurring costs, such as the cost of maintaining the wiki, but not the platform's overall costs.

simply collaboration are grafted onto the project over time and often out of necessity, such as when a problem's solution involves mobilizing a community. Young entrepreneurs point out that community members with low incomes cannot afford to invest in long-term collective projects; they often prefer to shift to proprietary systems that make it possible to monetize their investments more quickly. For young entrepreneurs, then, commons are one of several organizational forms to be compared with a pragmatic eye. Commons tend to be favored when it comes to developing projects within and with a community (such as valorizing a region's cultural heritage or a linguistic space), which must fulfill not only economic but also social or environmental objectives.

Africans display a variety of motivations for participating in a digital commons. Most young entrepreneurs do so to acquire skills that may not be taught at universities, to increase their chances of finding a job, or to start their own business in places where formal jobs may be hard to come by.[26] For the most active members of these communities, who take on organizational roles, participating in commons can be a way of transitioning into the private sector or international organizations.

Participation in digital commons can therefore be entirely consistent with entrepreneurship; it may even be beneficial for it. Many commons administrators and contributors alternate between their contributory and private activities. Finally, the backgrounds and trajectories of digital commons contributors largely overlap with those of digital entrepreneurs.

Digital commons at risk of being grabbed

Integrating African digital commons into one's professional or entrepreneurial path can encourage the misappropriation of resources for private ends. This raises the question of which modes of governance and economic models are best suited to preventing individual entrepreneurs from diverting common resources for personal use. The same risk exists with respect to international actors, who may use community-developed local resources to develop their services.

In order to account for these risks, some commons have resorted to licenses that limit the use of the resource more strictly. Others—such as the e-Boda Co-op project, in Tanzania (box 5.12)—are developing cooperative models to ensure that common resources are maintained via democratic methods of decision-making.

Conclusion

Because they promote a more equitable distribution of the capacity for innovation and the conditions for competition, digital commons are potential catalysts for sustainable development in Sub-Saharan Africa. They allow everyone to access information, services, and tools that foster value creation at the local level. They can be seen as the intangible infrastructure of a knowledge-based economy. Finally, with communities of practice collaborating on concrete projects, digital commons act as socioeconomic connectors and drivers of cooperative learning.

In this respect, digital commons constitute a credible alternative to a model of digital entrepreneurship based on exponential growth and proprietary models that lead to the majority of wealth created in the digital economy being concentrated in the hands of a few quasi-monopolistic actors. This latter model

BOX 5.12

e-Boda Co-op in Tanzania

The e-Boda Co-op (electric boda-boda cooperative) project aims to establish worker-owned electric transportation cooperatives to empower communities to take part in the production, operation, and benefits of mobility services. It focuses on boda-boda motorcycles. The purpose of using a cooperative model is to enable local communities to derive as much of the added economic, social, and environmental value as possible from transportation and related services. Community members not only help design, produce, and maintain the electric motorcycles but also use the fleet of motorcycles to provide mobility services and the digital platform to book trips, as well as for deliveries and rentals.

The co-op is currently developing a pilot project in Tanzania's Tanga region. The goal of the project is to improve boda-boda services in three ways:

- Motorcycles with internal combustion engines will be replaced by electric motorcycles with interchangeable batteries, which will be assembled on site. This technical development will not only improve local air quality and reduce noise but also reduce the cost of purchasing vehicles. Drivers will also be trained to repair the motorcycles.

- A drivers' cooperative will be created that will share the fleet of electric motorcycles and the tools to maintain them.

- A digital platform and open-source application (based on an existing open-source resource) will be developed to make it easier to order a taxi.

The project is based on an original model of financing cooperatives through a loan, which the newly created boda-boda drivers' cooperative will be able to take out from an existing cooperative (in this case, from Robotech Labs) and repay at a low rate of interest after the first three years of operation. This model was born out of a collaboration among four organizations, two Tanzanian (Robotech Labs and Tanzania Open Innovation Organization), one Chinese (Shenzhen Open Innovation Lab), and one French (Fabrique des Mobilités, or FabMob).

currently dominates the discourses and strategies of international organizations and African states, but it has been beset by challenges at the local and international levels, as Friederici, Wahome, and Graham (2020) demonstrate. This same study also notes that, the rhetoric notwithstanding, African digital entrepreneurship today tends to be more focused on incremental innovations for local or regional markets and is associated with slow, linear growth.

A more detailed analysis of digital commons in Sub-Saharan Africa, particularly of the backgrounds and expectations of African contributors, has shown that the majority of commons participants do not see themselves as developing an alternative model. In this respect, and as is the case for many fab labs, as well (see chapter 4), African participants do not take the militant positions of their European and North American counterparts. Whether they are acting individually or collectively, they do so pragmatically, combining a commons approach with a more traditional model of entrepreneurship.

Although this combination may entail certain risks (such as the grabbing of common resources), it is seen by digital commons stakeholders themselves as an opportunity for Africa. It represents an additional opportunity for Africans who want to live and work in ways that ensure that the human communities and ecosystems that they are a part of can both be sustained. Despite structural challenges, it offers new routes for development and new multistakeholder partnerships capable of handling the realities, needs, and solutions endogenous to Africa.

Notes

1. This research was carried out in 2022 with financing from the Agence française de développement (AFD) (French Development Agency). The data can be accessed and downloaded in their entirety on Airtable at https://airtable.com/shrm Q4b9y6GSd2Tnn/tblnZ1YqqelIQJXx3. The Airtable tool can be used to filter and navigate through a collaborative catalogue. Users can add to the catalogue using an online form.
2. Data: Statistics (itu.int).
3. Unstructured Supplementary Service Data is a feature that allows the exchange of information over GSM (Global System for Mobile Communications), without internet access.
4. https://data.worldbank.org/indicator/IT.NET.USER.ZS.
5. Different terms may be used, but they all agree that access to digital resources, guaranteed by free licenses, offers opportunities for sustainable development. More specifically, in the literature, the notion of "open resources" refers to issues regarding the free circulation of information and knowledge, transparency, and support for innovation. The concept of "digital public property" refers to issues of resource sharing, efficiency, participation in the Sustainable Development Goals, and international cooperation. The use of the notion of "global digital public property" evokes the need for governments to share responsibility for protecting and even managing these resources. The concept of "digital commons" brings with it the issues of building capacity through contribution, the distribution of value creation, and developing structures that serve as alternatives to a centralized digital economy.
6. "Nonrivalrous goods" refers to those goods that can be used by an individual or group of individuals without having an effect on the supply left for other individuals.

7. Content commons catalogued in Sub-Saharan Africa: African Storybook, AfricArXiv, AgShare Planning and Pilot Project, AirGéo, Arduino, Audiopedia, Appropedia, Beautiful Trouble, BSF Thema, Energypedia, FLOSS Manuals, Ethnos Project, Grainothèque, HarassMap, Initiatives Open COVID19 Sénégal, Kiwix, Laws.Africa, Livrescolaire.fr, Local Open GovLab, Open Food Network, Precious Plastic, Project Gutenberg, Public Lab, SEOSAW, UCT Knowledge Co-op, WAZIUP Open Source IoT and Cloud platform, WeFarm, WikiFundi, Wiki Kouman, Wikimedia Community User Group Côte d'Ivoire, WikiSigns, and Wikiversité.

8. https://www.budapestopenaccessinitiative.org/read/.

9. https://www.unesco.org/en/communication-information/open-solutions/open-educational-resources.

10. Translator's note: Our translation. Unless otherwise stated, all translations of cited foreign language material are our own.

11. Data commons catalogued in Sub-Saharan Africa: AfTerFibre, Africa GeoPortal, Africa Open DEAL, African Bird Atlas Project, AirGéo, Common Voice Kinyarwanda, Data Transport, DigitalTransport4Africa, Ethnos Project, GBIF, Global Open Facility Registry (GOFR), Grainothèque, GreenAlert, Hand-in-Hand geospatial data platform, HarassMap, Initiatives Open COVID19 Sénégal, IWACU Open Data, Laws.Africa, Local Open GovLab, Masakhane, openAFRICA, Open Food Facts, Open Food Network, Open Schools Kenya, OpenStreetMap, OpenUp, Sénégal Ouvert, SEOSAW, Trufi, and Ushahidi.

12. Software commons catalogued in Sub-Saharan Africa: Apache Fineract, Arduino, Bisa Health Application, Code for Senegal, Community Exchange Systems Ltd, Data Transport, echOpen Foundation, Emmabuntüs, Gitcoin, Grassroots Economics, Hand-in-Hand geospatial data platform, Initiatives Open COVID19 Sénégal, Junebug, Kiwix, Linguere Fablab, Local Open GovLab, Masakhane, Mojaloop, Molo, MomConnect, Nubian VR, OLIP (Offline Internet Platform), Open CRVS, Open Djeliba, Open Food Network, OpenHMIS, OpenMRS, Open Robotics, Open-Sankoré, OpenSRP, OpenUp, Platform, Precious Plastic, Raspberry Pi, SatNOGS, SmartElect, SORMAS, Trufi, Ushahidi, VideoLAN, WAZIUP Open Source IoT and Cloud platform, WeFarm, and WikiFundi.

13. Hardware commons catalogued in Sub-Saharan Africa: Arduino, echOpen Foundation, Initiatives Open COVID19 Sénégal, Linguere Fablab, LowTechLab, My Human Kit, Open Food Network, Open Source Ecology, Open Source Medical Supplies (OSMS), Precious Plastic, Raspberry Pi, and WAZIUP Open Source IoT and Cloud platform.

14. Protocols and standards commons catalogued in Sub-Saharan Africa: AFRINIC's Resource Certification Program (RPKI), Akoma Ntoso, Arduino, Code for Senegal, Gitcoin, Local Open GovLab, and SEOSAW.

15. https://openair.africa/africas-maker-movement-an-overview-of-ongoing-research/.

16. https://sustainoss.org/assets/pdf/SustainOSS-west-2017-report.pdf.

17. https://archive.uneca.org/publications/africa-data-revolution-report-2018.

18. https://researchictafrica.net/2022/05/30/mapping-african-digital-infrastructures-a-qualitative-analysis-of-open-source-contributions/.

19. https://www.wikiinafrica.org/project/wiki-loves-africa/.

20. https://www.hotosm.org/updates/the-state-of-openstreetmap-in-africa/.
21. https://en.wikipedia.org/wiki/Wikipedia:Statistics.
22. https://www.fordfoundation.org/work/learning/research-reports/roads-and
    -bridges-the-unseen-labor-behind-our-digital-infrastructure/.
23. https://medium.com/@katereggal/the-state-of-openstreetmap-in-africa
    -223ecadd5556.
24. https://www.academia.edu/8235120/Peer-to-Peer_Networks_for_Knowledge
    _Sharing_in_International_Development_Cooperation.
25. https://medium.com/@katereggal/the-state-of-openstreetmap-in-africa
    -223ecadd5556.
26. https://researchictafrica.net/2022/05/30/mapping-african-digital-infrastructures-a
    -qualitative-analysis-of-open-source-contributions/.

References

African Union. 2020. *The Digital Transformation Strategy for Africa (2020–2030)*. Addis Ababa: African Union. https://au.int/sites/default/files/documents/38507-doc-dts -english.pdf.

AfricArena. 2021. "The State of Tech in Africa 2021." https://www.wired.africarena .com/_files/ugd/cdd60c_5d9debf5822c4e84940b69925d8d2ba2.pdf.

Benkler, Yochai. 2007. *The Wealth of Networks: How Social Production Transforms Markets and Freedom*. New Haven, CT: Yale University Press.

Berrou, Jean-Philippe, and Kevin Mellet. 2020. "Une révolution mobile en Afrique subsaharienne?" *Reseaux* 219 (1): 11–38.

Broca, Sébastien. 2021. "Communs et capitalisme numérique: Histoire d'un antagonisme et de quelques affinités électives." *Terminal. Technologie de l'information, culture et société* 130. https://doi.org/10.4000/terminal.7595.

Broca, Sébastien, and Benjamin Coriat. 2015. "Free Software and the Commons: Two Forms of Resistance and Alternative to Proprietary Exclusivism." *Revue internationale de droit économique* 3: 265–84. https://doi.org/10.3917/ride.293.0265.

Coriat, Benjamin, ed. 2015. *Le retour des communs. La crise de l'idéologie propriétaire*. Paris: Les Liens qui libèrent.

Erickson, Kris, Paul J. Heald, Fabian Homberg, Martin Kretschmer, and Dinusha Mendis. 2015. "Copyright and the Value of the Public Domain: An Empirical Assessment." University of Illinois College of Law Legal Studies Research Paper No. 15–16. https://papers.ssrn.com/abstract=2571220.

Fox, Mathilde, and Nathalie Van Droogenbroeck. 2017. "Les nouveaux modèles de mobile banking en Afrique: Un défi pour le système bancaire traditionnel?" *Gestion 2000* 34 (5–6): 337–60. https://doi.org/10.3917/g2000.345.0337.

Friederici, Nicolas, Michel Wahome, and Mark Graham. 2020. *Digital Entrepreneurship in Africa: How a Continent is Escaping Silicon Valley's Long Shadow*. Cambridge, MA: MIT Press.

Goldfarb, Avi, and Catherine Tucker. 2019. "Digital Economics." *Journal of Economic Literature* 57 (1): 3–43. https://doi.org/10.1257/jel.20171452.

Goujon, Michaël, and Joël Cariolle. 2019. "Infrastructure et économie numérique en Afrique subsaharienne et dans l'UEMOA: État des lieux, acteurs, et nouvelles vulnérabilités." *FERDI, Notes brèves* 186. https://ferdi.fr/publications/infrastructure-et-economie-numerique-en-afrique-subsaharienne-et-dans-l-uemoa-etat-des-lieux-acteurs-et-nouvelles-vulnerabilites.

Graham, Mark, Stefano De Sabbata, and Matthew Zook. 2015. "Towards a Study of Information Geographies: (Im)mutable Augmentations and a Mapping of the Geographies of Information." *Geo: Geography and Environment* 2 (1): 88–105. https://doi.org/10.1002/geo2.8.

Grinberger, Asher Yair, Marco Minghini, Levente Juhász, Godwin Yeboah, and Peter Mooney. 2022. "OSM Science: The Academic Study of the OpenStreetMap Project, Data, Contributors, Community, and Applications." *ISPRS International Journal of Geo-Information* 11 (4): 230.

GSMA. 2012. "Sub-Saharan Africa Mobile Observatory 2012." https://www.gsma.com/publicpolicy/wp-content/uploads/2013/01/gsma_ssamo_full_web_11_12-1.pdf.

GSMA. 2018. "L'économie mobile: L'Afrique de l'Ouest 2018." https://www.gsma.com/subsaharanafrica/wp-content/uploads/2018/11/2018-04-11-dd7760bf439236e808ea61ee986845eb.pdf.

GSMA. 2019. "L'économie mobile: Afrique de l'Ouest 2019." https://www.gsma.com/mobileeconomy/wp-content/uploads/2020/03/GSMA_MobileEconomy2020_West_Africa_FRE.pdf.

GSMA. 2020. "L'économie mobile: Afrique subsaharienne 2020." https://www.gsma.com/mobileeconomy/wp-content/uploads/2020/09/GSMA_MobileEconomy2020_SSA_Fre.pdf.

GSMA. 2021. "L'économie mobile: Afrique subsaharienne 2021." https://www.gsma.com/mobileeconomy/wp-content/uploads/2021/09/GSMA_ME_SSA_2021_French_Web_Singles.pdf.

Hjort, Jonas, and Jonas Poulsen. 2019. "The Arrival of Fast Internet and Employment in Africa." *American Economic Review* 109 (3): 1032–79. https://doi.org/10.1257/aer.20161385.

Huet, Jean-Michel. 2017. *Le digital en Afrique—Les cinq sauts numériques.* Paris: Michel Lafon.

Internet Society. 2017a. "2017 Internet Society Global Internet Report: Paths to Our Digital Future." https://future.internetsociety.org/2017/wp-content/uploads/sites/3/2017/09/2017-Internet-Society-Global-Internet-Report-Paths-to-Our-Digital-Future.pdf.

Internet Society. 2017b. "Supporting the Creation and Scalability of Affordable Access Solutions: Understanding Community Networks in Africa." https://www.internetsociety.org/wp-content/uploads/2017/08/CommunityNetworkingAfrica_report_May2017_1.pdf.

Koomar, Saalim, and Stephen Jull. 2020. "Open Educational Resources in Africa: A Curated Resource List." *EdTech Hub Helpdesk Response* 20. https://docs.edtechhub.org/lib/10.5281/zenodo.3906041.

Lemmerich, Florian, Diego Sáez-Trumper, Robert West, and Leila Zia. 2019. "Why the World Reads Wikipedia: Beyond English Speakers." *The Twelfth ACM International Conference*, 618–26. https://doi.org/10.1145/3289600.3291021.

Mboa Nkoudou, Thomas Hervé. 2017. "Benefits and The Hidden Face of the Maker Movement: Thoughts on its Appropriation in African Context." *Liinc em revista* 13 (1): 72–88. https://doi.org/10.18617/liinc.v13i1.3774.

Mboa Nkoudou, Thomas Hervé. 2020. "Les makerspaces en Afrique francophone, entre développement local durable et technocolonialité: Trois études de cas au Burkina Faso, au Cameroun et au Sénégal." PhD dissertation, Laval University.

Nubukpo, Kako. 2019. *L'urgence africaine: Changeons le modèle de croissance!* Paris: Odile Jacob.

Nyakanini, Grace, Maurice Sayinzoga, Nicholas Gates, Erik Almqvist, and Kutay Erkan. 2020. "Unlocking the Digital Economy in Africa: Benchmarking the Digital Transformation Journey." https://dial.global/wp-content/uploads/2020/10/Smart Africa-DIAL_DigitalEconomyInAfrica2020-v7_ENG.pdf.

Open AIR (Open African Innovation Research). 2020. "Scaling Innovation. How Open Collaborative Models Help Scale Africa's Knowledge-Based Enterprises." https://openair.africa/wp-content/uploads/2020/06/Scaling-Innovation-Report-1.pdf.

Peugeot, Valérie. 2014. "Les communs, une brèche politique à l'heure du numérique." In *Les débats du numérique*, edited by Maryse Carmes and Jean-Max Noyer, 77–98. Paris: Presses des Mines. http://books.openedition.org/pressesmines/1663.

Piron, Florence, Antonin Benoît Diouf, Marie Sophie Dibounje Madiba, Thomas Hervé Mboa Nkoudou, Zoé Aubierge Ouangré, Djossè Roméo Tessy, Hamissou Rhissa Achaffert, Anderson Pierre, and Zakari Lire. 2017. "Le libre accès vu d'Afrique francophone subsaharienne." *Revue française des sciences de l'information et de la communication* 11. https://doi.org/10.4000/rfsic.3292.

Republic of Cameroon. 2020. "Stratégie nationale de développement 2020-2030: Pour la transformation structurelle et le développement inclusif." http://cdnss.minsante.cm /sites/default/files/Stratégie%20Nationale%20de%20Développement%20SND30_Fench .pdf.

Stallman, Richard. 2002. *Free Software, Free Society: Selected Essays of Richard M. Stallman.* Boston, MA: GNU Press.

Tatchim, Nicanor. 2018. "The Cameroonian State and the Demand for Digital Innovation and Creativity." *Hermès, La Revue* 82 (3): 187–94. https://doi.org/10.3917/herm .082.0187.

UN (United Nations). 2020. "Roadmap for Digital Cooperation: Implementation of the Recommendations of the High-Level Panel on Digital Cooperation." https:// documents-dds-ny.un.org/doc/UNDOC/GEN/N20/102/51/PDF/N2010251. pdf?OpenElement.

UNCTAD (United Nations Conference on Trade and Development). 2019. *Trade and Development Report 2019: Financing a Global Green New Deal.* New York: United Nations. https://unctad.org/webflyer/trade-and-development-report-2019.

UNCTAD (United Nations Conference on Trade and Development. 2021. *Digital Economy Report 2021. Cross-Border Data Flows and Development: For Whom the Data Flow.* New York: United Nations." https://unctad.org/webflyer/digital-economy -report-2021.

UNESCO. 2017. "Guidelines on the Implementation of the 2005 Convention on the Protection and Promotion of the Diversity of Cultural Expressions of the Digital Environment." https://fr.unesco.org/creativity/sites/creativity/files/digital_guidelines _en_full-3.pdf.

Verdier, Henri, and Charles Murciano. 2017. "Les communs numériques, socle d'une nouvelle économie politique." *Esprit* 5: 132–45. https://doi.org/10.3917/espri .1705.0132.

Wachs, Johannes, Mariusz Nitecki, William Schueller, and Axel Polleres. 2022. "The Geography of Open-Source Software: Evidence from GitHub." *Technological Forecasting and Social Change* 176 (121478): 1–17. https://doi.org/10.1016/j .techfore.2022.121478.

WIPO (World Intellectual Property Organization). 2019. *World Intellectual Property Indicators 2019*. Geneva: World Intellectual Property Organization. https://www.wipo .int/edocs/pubdocs/en/wipo_pub_941_2019.pdf.

World Bank Group. 2016. *World Development Report 2016: Digital Dividends*. Washington, DC: World Bank. https://documents1.worldbank.org/curated/en /961621467994698644/pdf/102724-WDR-WDR2016Overview-ENGLISH-WebResBox -394840B-OUO-9.pdf.

World Bank Group. 2019. *World Development Report 2019: The Changing Nature of Work*. Washington, DC: World Bank. https://openknowledge.worldbank.org/handle /10986/30435.

World Bank Group. 2021. *World Development Report 2021. Data for Better Lives*. Washington, DC: World Bank. https://www.worldbank.org/en/publication/wdr2021.

Chapter 6

Commons, General Interest, and Public Policy: Issues for the State in Sub-Saharan Africa

Benjamin Coriat, Mamoudou Gazibo, and Stéphanie Leyronas

Introduction

In its 2017 World Development Report, *Governance and the Law*, the World Bank (2017) emphasized the fundamental role that institutions and governance have to play and, more generally, the historical trajectory of states and their relationships with society at large. Previous chapters in this book have identified a diverse range of African commons, which can be found in a variety of fields (natural resource management, housing, services of general interest, information resource management). The objective of this chapter is therefore to examine the contribution made by commons to public policy in Sub-Saharan Africa.

The hypothesis that commons in Africa can constitute sustainable actors in the formulation of collective action problems and the implementation of local solutions necessarily implies calling the state and the institutional contexts within which the activity of commons will take place into question. Indeed, whether one is interested in land-based commons (chapter 2), urban commons (chapter 4), or digital commons (chapter 5), it is often the issues of "palliative" (Olivier de Sardan 2021) or "supplementary" (Holder 2021) service provision, as well as opposition to and collaboration with the state, that are at the heart of the debate. The place of commons in public policy is thus influenced by the nature of the state, which in turn determines the nature of public policy and the type of interactions between the actors involved. To better understand this relationship, the first section reviews the different processes of state-building in Sub-Saharan Africa, the way in which they influence the implementation of public policy, and how this relates to commons.

In the second section, we firmly adopt the perspective of the state (including its constituent parts as well as municipal governments in contexts of decentralization) and the functions it can perform to contribute to securing the existence of commons, or even to their growth and deployment. There are multiple theoretical proposals on the subject (Bollier 2014; Hess and Ostrom 2006; Picavet et al. 2021), but their applicability remains to be demonstrated. The approach proposed here is therefore pragmatic and consists of drawing on the various different contexts and possible relationships between the state and commons as demonstrated in the previous empirical chapters. Despite their apparently universal nature, they can only be understood through a context-sensitive approach to both the state and commons. This analysis also brings to light three types of potential risks stemming from the adoption of an assertive relationship between the state and commons, which we detail in the third section: the risk of altering commons; the risk of instrumentalizing, assimilating, or even capturing commons; and the risk of shifting the state's responsibilities onto commons.

The fourth and final section is intended as a modest overview of the key issues in public policy. It examines the contribution of commons to the construction of distinctive trajectories for African states, breaking with the institutional inflexibility and inefficiency described in the first section. It also discusses the contribution of commons to the realization of economic and social rights, at the service of the general interest and democratic processes.

Historical Trajectories of States and Public Policy in Sub-Saharan Africa

This first section emphasizes that governance in Sub-Saharan Africa is characterized by major institutional weaknesses (Gazibo 2010), a type of "limited statehood" (Risse and Lehmkuhl 2006), the strong presence of international actors (Devarajan, Dollar, and Holmgren 2002; Lavigne Delville 2011; Olivier de Sardan 2021), and, generally, little room for maneuver being granted to social actors (Darbon and Provini 2018). This allows us to extend the frameworks provided by institutional economics that we have used extensively in the previous empirical chapters, drawing on work in development anthropology, political science, and the political sociology of public policy.

Some Specific Features of African States

An important contribution to the study of public policy is to seek to provide context for its forms, issues, and actors (Payre and Pollet 2013). This is particularly crucial in Africa, where, because of its historical trajectory (Mbembe 2001), the state is a conceptual category and a complex entity that in many ways does not conform to the Weberian model that serves as a reference for the bulk of public policy analysis. The issue here is neither the controversy surrounding whether the state existed in precolonial Africa or whether Africans are capable of producing the state (Bourmaud 1997), nor that of drawing "dubious comparisons between historical trajectories" (Mbembe 2001, 11). It is simply a matter of considering the state as a historically situated (European) political entity, one that has replaced endogenous political forms in Africa, and then observing the ways in which it has been constructed and perceived there.

In the precolonial period, many African societies functioned essentially on the basis of collective modes of organization. It is true that African societies were varied, some of them instituting powerful and centralizing bureaucratic empires such as those of Ghana, Mali, and Songhai (Ki-Zerbo 1972). But many of them were suspicious of the institutionalization of power, which was seen as an attack on equality (Clastres 1974), and the mode of management was often described by anthropologists as "ad hoc" or "ordered anarchy" (Fortes and Evans-Pritchard 1940). It is for this reason that Bourmaud (1997, 16) argues that "the ideal of self-management seems to have been realized" (box 6.1).

BOX 6.1

Community and Cooperation in Certain Precolonial African Societies

"Many [precolonial] African societies lack rulers in the sense that they do not have individuals whose exclusive function is to coordinate the activity of the group's constituent elements. Among the Boshimans and Mbuti studied by Turnbull [1983], there is no particular person in charge. Cooperation is ensured through everyone's adherence to the group's norms and values, without the need for a specific source of authority to enforce them. In fact, the imperative to cooperate is deeply internalized, because its acceptance guarantees the economic survival of the group. When an individual transgresses the code that governs this collective understanding, he is banished from society. His reintegration can take place once his fault has been publicly acknowledged. The whole social system thus tends toward the maintenance of an almost homeostatic harmony that requires reconciliation. In this context, power is not incorporated into a specific institution, whether individual or collective, but is instead a matter of a 'diffuse power' [Balandier 2013], thanks to which the group can overcome its internal tensions. However, social control does not operate in a totally mechanical and spontaneous way. The formalization of misconduct involves the use of a particular procedure that consists of bringing the whole group together, thus stigmatizing the deviant behavior. It is the whole community that constitutes itself as a deliberative body in order to perpetuate its threatened internal order. Power is in fact held by the whole group, which exercises it when social control has proved to be lacking" (Bourmaud 1997, 15–16).

The colonial process erased these differences by superimposing the European state on all societies. After independence, this logic of statehood followed four main stages that were not very conducive to the institutionalization of a culture of collectively producing public policy (with a few exceptions, such as in the case of Botswana). The first two stages consisted of, first, the "concentration of power" under the pretext of consolidating states through policies such as the establishment of single parties and the trusteeship of state and nonstate organizations and, second, the "development of power" through the establishment of bureaucracies, coercive apparatuses, and legislation. During these two phases from the 1960s to the 1970s, the autonomy of social groups and associations was reduced to a minimum (Chazan et al. 1999, 46–62). The third phase covers the 1980s, which saw the contraction of state ambitions in terms of societal penetration and redistribution due to the economic crisis and the beginning of the implementation of structural adjustment programs driven by international financial institutions (Chazan et al. 1999, 65–68). This is the period described by phrases such as "politics from the bottom up" or "popular modes of political action," during which society, thought to be totally dominated, managed to "poach" the state (Bayart, Mbembe, and Toulabor 1992). It saw the beginning of a revival of social organizations and a burgeoning of initiatives emanating from groups abandoned by the state, whether to challenge, bypass, or supplant it. Many of these organizations can easily be likened to commons when they are involved, for example, in the repair of schools, the construction of dikes, or the management of wells that are no longer maintained by the public authorities. Finally, in the fourth stage, which began in the 1990s as a result of political openness and democratization initiatives (Gazibo 2005, 2019; Ndulo and Gazibo 2016), we witnessed an increase in the complexity of state-society relations with the proliferation of national and local organizations coexisting with public bodies (Gazibo 2007), all interacting with and depending on external donors and subject to the logic of liberalization and the market.

African states place themselves both in continuity and in rupture with their colonial past. On the whole, they are still reproducing characteristics and modes of functioning resulting from the colonial and authoritarian history of the 1960s to 1990s. On the other hand, they no longer have a monopoly on public space because of the combination of internal constraints (political and associative pluralism) and external constraints (economic dependence, the influence of external actors and market logic). Under these conditions, commons play a substitutive role alongside other actors (Olivier de Sardan 2022) in a fragmented public sector in which the state is no longer the sole guarantor of the public interest, without, however, completely breaking away from the approaches that have been inherited from its past. As explained in the next section, this situation opens up the possibility for different types of relationships between the state and commons today.

States Whose Characteristics Are Generally Unfavorable to the Development of Commons

Four main characteristics of African states merit attention from the perspective of a commons' analysis.

In the first instance, states in Africa are, from a sociogenetic point of view, structures that are alien to their societies and have been imposed on them as a result of domination. Because of this, this imported structure tends to function in a way (Badie 1992) that is not inclined to base itself on (or create) a political system that is in harmony with its society. The colonial state, which completely reorganized space, social relations, modes of production, and the relationship to power in Africa, was synonymous with violence and control, not legitimacy (Young 1997). Moreover, the postcolonial state inherited most of the features of its predecessor. In most cases, contemporary states have retained the "authoritarian principle" (Mbembe 1988) and the technologies of social domination. At best, one can speak of a precarious balance between state and society, resulting in some moments of total immersion of society in the state and other moments of relative autonomy of social groups (Chazan et al. 1999). Faced with these processes of domination, actors develop principles of action based on cunning, misappropriation, and reinterpretation that reveal major gaps between official norms and the actual behavior of civil servants and the public alike (Olivier de Sardan 1995). While attempts at democratization in the 1990s opened up public space and curbed this attempt at domination, they did not fundamentally alter the situation (Cheeseman 2019; Gazibo 2019; Lynch and VonDoepp 2019).

Second, very soon after independence, African states were patrimonialized under the leadership of elites through the private monopolization of public property (Médard 1991b). The state is an organizational complex driven by actors and organizations (Levi 2002), which attempt to maximize their interests according to various opportunities and constraints. Here there is a profit motive, but also a particular type of redistribution that serves to buy the loyalty of actors that are crucial for the survival of the regimes in place (Van de Walle 2003). Patrimonialism involves corruption within the state, but also within nongovernmental organizations (NGOs) whose integrity is increasingly being called into question (May 2016). This predatory logic is present at all levels, from the distribution of positions to the capture of rents of all kinds (Hibou 2009), such as oil in Nigeria, for example (Porter and Watts 2017).

Third, African states tend to lack the capacity to extract and redistribute resources to the population. These shortcomings are themselves the result of both the structural weakness of states that have always had difficulty controlling their territory (Herbst 2000) and the patrimonial management of the available resources as described above (Bach and Gazibo 2011; Médard 1991a).

These empirical weaknesses have led some authors to express surprise that African states still manage to survive. This immediately led them to point to external factors: according to them, it is to international law and the principle of sovereignty, which de facto protects states, that they owe their survival (Jackson and Rosberg 1982). Certain authors have seen in this either the possibility of "the defeat of the state as the general technology of domination" (Mbembe 2000, 79) or that of "the emergence of new political actors in the public sphere, the proliferation of unexpected social rationalities, and the implementation of novel technologies and apparatuses, whose purpose is to control individual conduct and to make possible new modes of constituting private property and inequality" (Mbembe 2000). Others have spoken of a phenomenon of "offloading" (Hibou 1999), highlighting the state's disengagement from some of its regalian functions that are then left for the voluntary sector to take over. In both cases, we see the emergence of a form of indirect government.

Fourth, states are outward-facing in the dual sense of being entities whose policies are very often designed from the outside by international financial institutions and whose budgets are also financed in large part by bilateral and multilateral funders. As a result, they are subject to all kinds of external impacts. There are several interpretations of the aid issue in relation to public policy, development, and political regimes. The most critical of these argue that "aid kills" development opportunities and does not improve the lives of ordinary people in Africa (Moyo and Ferguson 2010) and elsewhere (Erler 1987). Other authors argue that it is when aid becomes too entrenched that we enter a situation of dependency with negative effects (Clemens et al. 2012). In most cases, African states belong to this state of affairs. In many of them, elites have developed a genuine policy of permanent crisis in order to capture international aid (Bienen and Van de Walle 1991).

In this context, it may be in the interest of commons to stay away from the state, as the latter may have adopted a posture of opposition or even predation. Chapter 2 recalls, for example, how colonization was the source of profound changes in land tenure systems imposed by administrations, or how the state can also play the role of intermediary vis-à-vis international actors in order to exploit natural resources in an industrial manner, thus weakening land-based commons. On another note, chapter 5 shows that thriving digital commons initiatives can run up against certain political and economic realities, as revealed in 2013 by the Central Bank of Kenya's complaint against members of the foundation Grassroots Economics, which had participated in the development of the Bangla-Pesa complementary currency. However, this inhibiting influence of the state over commons is not a foregone conclusion. Even though postcolonial African states are, on the whole, ill-disposed toward commons, this does not mean that it is impossible for the state to act constructively with commons.

Securing and Promoting the Development of Commons: What Is the Role of the State?

The empirical chapters of this book have shown that many commons that are developing in Sub-Saharan Africa have expectations of their governments, both to secure their existence and to receive help in promoting their growth and development. There are a wide variety of situations and possible relationships between the state (understood as the state and its constituent parts or municipal governments, depending on the circumstances of decentralization) and commons (Dongier et al. 2002). Within the framework of its functions, attributes, and prerogatives, the state can support commons with varying degrees of assertiveness as a facilitator or as a contributor.

The State as a Facilitator
In the exercise of its regalian, legislative, and regulatory functions, the state can take measures that provide commons, as well as other economic and social actors, with material or immaterial resources. Despite the characteristics described in the previous section that render the state ill-disposed toward commons, the establishment of bureaucracies, coercive apparatuses, and legislation by states in the aftermath of independence had developmental ambitions, even if this process incorporated nonstate organizations rather than empowering them. In the absence of a targeted initiative to support commons or related social experiments, it plays a "facilitating" role. These facilitative and institutional functions are central to Ostrom's work and that of theorists who have expanded upon her insights (Benkler 2013; Rose 1986) (box 6.2).

The state can thus provide information resources (e.g., data, open archives and maps, public Wi-Fi, open digital libraries) or material resources (e.g., free and open access seeds, training in agricultural techniques). Commons can make use of these resources just like other economic and social actors. The African Union's digital transformation strategy is very much along these lines (see chapter 5): it emphasizes free educational resources, open data, open access to research results, and the use of open norms and standards (African Union 2020). When the state creates the conditions for the worldwide content and data commons to be enhanced by a greater number of African contributions, possibly with support from international donors (see the example of OpenStreetMap in Tanzania described in chapter 5), it is working to provide intangible resources that commons can tap into.

Through regulatory provisions, the state can also guarantee universal access to these resources or even be an institutor by creating ad hoc structures that provide these resources.[1] Its regulatory activity can also create the legal and legislative conditions for the emergence of new commons. This is the case, for example, for the housing cooperatives presented in chapter 3. The formation of

Open Commons

Following Ostrom's work, Rose (1986) and Benkler (2013) have conducted work on the so-called open commons in which public regulation, which is in charge of ensuring the "open" character of commons, occupies a central place. Based on an investigation conducted in the nineteenth century, Rose (1986) highlights that, under the influence of common law, jurisprudence introduced into American legislation the idea that there are objects that are "inherently public property." These are essentially roads, public squares, and waterways. Regardless of who the identifiable or actual "owner" is, no easement that excludes their use by individuals (private or professional) is allowed, and the rights of use are recognized as belonging to a large "unorganized public." Hence Rose's assertion that commons are a form that promotes harmonious social development. Benkler (2013) continues in this vein, adding other "tangible" goods (bridges, sidewalks, highways) and "intangible" goods (computer protocols, unlicensed radio spectrum bands, shared standards). With open commons, it is therefore a question of making open resources available to the whole of society. It is the state that is responsible for guaranteeing the existence and integrity of these resources, as well as universal access to them, through a set of appropriate regulations.

these cooperatives has been possible in Burkina Faso since the 2008 law on real estate development and in Senegal since Law no. 1983/07 of 1983 on the general status of cooperatives. Another example is that of groundwater management, where the state can create regulatory and economic tools (taxes, licenses, and quotas, for example) on which user communities can base (with some adaptations) the definition of the rights and obligations of each party (Dumont et al. 2021). This is where the state can reliably draw on endogenous and external norms that are favorable to commons instead of acting, as is often the case, as a mere receptacle for norms that are not necessarily beneficial and that are issued by external actors as described in the previous section.

The State as a Contributor

The state can assume functions beyond those identified above by positioning itself as a "contributor," breaking with both the "offloading"-based approach and the temptation toward unrestricted domination described in the previous section. In this configuration, it enters into a direct relationship with commons. This scenario assumes that the state recognizes that commons create sustainable alternatives and that it provides them with elements of security so that they can maintain themselves in the long term and transform the initial experimental approach into a permanent one. It is based on mutual social and economic trust and assumes a mutual understanding of the limits of each party. Some African commons therefore have a strong demand for increased interaction with the state, emphasizing the inspirational nature of their initiatives for public actors. This is the case, for example, with African urban commons (Ishyo Arts Centre in Rwanda, WoeLab in Togo, or the Assalamalekoum association in Mauritania) described in chapter 4. Without necessarily having to make long-term commitments, the state provides tangible or intangible resources dedicated to commons to promote their security, stabilization, and dissemination.

The resources are of various kinds. They can, for example, be land resources. This situation is encountered in urban areas, when a local authority cedes the administration of public spaces that it owns for a defined period to communities that will use these places for various types of civic activities (e.g., artistic activities, sports facilities, meeting places for various associations that enliven the neighborhood). This is the case for the urban commons presented in chapter 4, which have developed new and open uses for neglected or poorly maintained public spaces at the request of the municipalities of Dakar and Ouagadougou. In areas of high pressure on land resources, and with a view to developing social housing in urban areas, the local authority can sell land at nonmarket prices and under favorable conditions to enable the development of common areas. This is the case, for example, with shared housing (housing cooperatives in Ouagadougou and Dakar and the Community Land Trust in Kenya), described in chapter 3.

It may be a question of structuring infrastructure for commons. This is the case, for example, with development work in rural areas (irrigation infrastructure, access roads, etc.) to create the conditions for the emergence of commons-based entrepreneurship around the exploitation of natural resources, as in the Senegal River Valley project described in chapter 2. It is also the case of the mini drinking water networks in the peripheral neighborhoods of Kinshasa, which are not served by the national company Regideso. These infrastructures were set up by the state, with international funding, and are managed by associations of drinking water users who decide how to allocate the profits from the sale of water to social activities in the neighborhood, such as libraries or community halls (Bédécarrats et al. 2019). The example of the open research platforms set up by the Drugs for Neglected Diseases Initiative,[2] located in Kinshasa in the Democratic Republic of Congo, is also interesting (see chapter 7): the state made clinical trials for a new sleeping sickness drug possible by allowing them to be conducted in local hospitals and putting the necessary regulations in place (Abecassis et al. 2019).

This may include financial resources. The empirical chapters highlighted the fragility and instability of the economic models of African commons. The question of their financing thus arises and, with it, that of the state's recognition of the social, environmental, and societal functions that commons fulfill. These functions are, for example, ecologically responsible practices or the fight against juvenile delinquency within the urban commons highlighted in chapter 4. The state has several tools at its disposal.

- The state can provide direct funding to commons in the form of grants or participation in pooled funds. The open platform Ushahidi, for example, which collects testimonies from citizens threatened by natural disasters, human rights violations, corruption, and harassment (see chapter 5), has received a significant amount of financial support in the form of grants from international government agencies thanks to the visibility it gained following the 2007 violence in Kenya. The Lacuna Fund is an example of a pooled fund. The fund supports projects through grants following calls for thematic project proposals and is funded by the Rockefeller Foundation, Google.org, the International Development Research Centre, and the German Agency for International Cooperation (GIZ).
- Beyond direct financing, the state can also act as a guarantor of commons for borrowing from public or private banks (Mazzucato 2015), support community development banks (Filho et al. 2022), create socialized investment funds (Borrits 2022), or regulate the role of public financial intermediaries (Bollier and Conaty 2015; Rigot and Plihon 2022).
- The state can also provide tax relief. One example is Niger's forestry policies, which transferred responsibility for forest resource management to village communities in 1992 and accompanied this transfer with a reform of tax regulations that allowed rural populations to collect taxes on the trade of fuelwood at the source and authorized the creation of rural wood markets, which served as village sales points for traders and transporters (Antona and Farolfi 2001; Mbairamadji 2009; Montagne et al. 2016).

This may involve human resources such as leveraging expertise within public authorities (legal, administrative, or technical support). This is the case, for example, for the housing cooperatives presented in chapter 3, which benefit from plots of land made available by the state, financial advantages (reduced taxation and preferential rates for the repayment of individual or collective housing loans from the Banque de l'Habitat du Sénégal), and technical support from the urban planning ministry.

Finally, the state can support commons in their dissemination strategy and the formation of networks. While commons movement is strong in Sub-Saharan Africa, it is mainly based on the proliferation of small sectoral or territorial initiatives. This fact determines the ways we should think about the diffusion of commons in Africa. For example, chapter 4 highlighted the networking aspect of Sub-Saharan African fab labs, which are at the heart of regional and international networks that allow for the direct sharing of ideas. Another example is the African Storybook initiative described in chapter 5: this literacy project, which provides openly licensed storybooks for early reading in African languages via an interactive website, has signed formal agreements and is working with four government departments offering the first three grades of schooling in South Africa and Kenya (the Department of Basic Education, the KwaZulu-Natal Education Library Information and Technology Services, and the Reading Support Program in South Africa, as well as the Kenya Institute of Curriculum Development in Kenya).[3]

Even if this arrangement remains rare, the state can now finally get involved beyond its traditional contributions and invest in commons over time. It can create the conditions for the emergence of collective action in the territories, by making resources available and by promoting local public spaces to encourage the intentional construction of commons. This requires that it engage in processes of adaptation, flexibility, and mutual learning. As Ostrom and Basurto (2011) remind us, its attitude is fundamental: it must fully allow for the possibility to experiment and thus to make mistakes. This is the case, for example, with the urban incubators in Dakar and Ouagadougou described in chapter 4, even though the system is not fully developed yet. These incubators consist of experimenting with and supporting new methods of shaping cities by bringing together local communities, public contracting authorities of major urban projects, and civil society stakeholders to develop new ways of doing things through the implementation of micro-projects.

Three Types of Risks to Overcome

The state's investment in an assertive relationship with commons requires two-way commitments. It is essential that the state not intervene in the establishment of the operating rules of commons and that it respect their mode of existence and their purpose. This risk is particularly important if one considers the nature of the state in Sub-Saharan Africa, as discussed in the first section. On the other hand, if they intend to secure their continuity without major clashes,[4] commons must not adopt any rules that would put them in opposition to or in contradiction with prevailing laws, regulations, and customs. This essential point appears as one of the design principles elaborated by Ostrom (see chapter 1).[5] Avoiding conflict with the law and public policy does not in any way diminish the autonomy of commons and their capacity to pursue, if necessary, different and innovative paths (see, for example, on environmental aspects [chapter 2] and on social aspects [chapter 4]).

Any assertive relationship between the state and commons must take several risks into account. We identify three types.

The Risk of Altering Commons

The first type of risk involves the possibility of altering commons in some way. Ostrom insists, for example, on the dangers that stem from the dependence of commons on external resources and the dangers of corruption, both of which are very present in African states, as described in the first section. Corruption can especially be seen when the local project is not developed according to local needs and in a location-appropriate form, and the primary motivation is instead to increase the project's chances of being included in the norms of calls for tenders and the criteria for allocating funds from funders, whether national or international (Ostrom 1999). In a similar way, Ridde and Olivier de Sardan (2022) outline risks that they describe as "conflicts of interest," in the sense that actors in commons can sometimes go against their own perceptions or knowledge in order to comply with the intervention of external actors, such as a financial backer. The financing of a commons by public authorities can have a distorting effect, for example, by integrating a logic of remuneration where the philosophy of commons might otherwise seek to avoid this altogether (Fontaine and Lebrun 2022). When they follow predetermined goals or are organized around specific themes, public funding puts commons in competition with one another and discourages initiatives that come purely from the citizens themselves, as well as synergies between preexisting initiatives in a given territory. The tools used by public authorities to account for the effectiveness of funding also raise questions (see chapter 7).

The Risk of Instrumentalization, Assimilation, and Capture of Commons

The second type of risk is that of the instrumentalization, assimilation, or even capture of commons by the state. This risk is significant in the contexts mentioned in the first section, where the elites are, in some cases, in a position to capture the income linked to international aid. This risk can also be expressed through technical and legal formalization and standardization processes. The temptation to resort to standardized solutions when the problems that arise are inevitably complex in nature leads to two pitfalls, according to Ostrom (1999): the temptation of "blueprint thinking," which consists of relying on "ready-made" solutions, and the temptation to trust in simple decision-making procedures, when deliberation must precede collective action. These processes of simplification and standardization can lead to the process of "commoning" becoming too rigid and can put the institutional flexibility of commons at risk.

The Risk of Shifting Responsibilities from the State to Commons

The third type of risk that commons can encounter was touched upon in the first section through the notion of offloading (Hibou 1999). It refers to the temptation of governments to devolve their responsibilities to these institutional forms, even though the state is still the privileged form of organization for contemporary African societies (Hervé and Gallenga 2019; Olivier de Sardan 2022). This risk of deferring state responsibilities is neither new to Sub-Saharan Africa nor specific to commons. The first section connects this trend of the deferral of state responsibilities with the proliferation, from the 1990s onward, of national and local organizations, and of development policies supported by international financial institutions in Sub-Saharan Africa advocating "participatory governance," "decentralized natural resource management," or "community development." These policies are deployed within a liberal economic framework that defends the principles of reduced public spending, private-sector development, and the extension of exclusive property rights over public or shared resources whenever possible. They are part of institutional frameworks organized by the promoters of development programs financed by funders or decision-makers, who provide the "constitutional" or even "collective" rules, leaving only the "operational" rules to be decided by the collective, according to the typology proposed by Ostrom (2005) (see chapter 1). This imported Western frame of reference does not take into account either the historical trajectories of social formations nor the specific features of the relations between the state and the different strata of society (Olivier de Sardan 2022).

To conclude this section, the state, in the exercise of its prerogatives and with its own means, can constitute a tool for securing and stabilizing commons in Sub-Saharan Africa by breaking away from the authoritarian impulses and the attempt to incorporate society inherited from its colonial origins, which was described in the first section. Beyond this, it can function as a vector for their development. The question of its positioning and the means it proposes to implement with respect to commons is eminently political. If it fails to modify some of its more traditional activities (e.g., funding through calls for projects, the proliferation of conditions and guarantees, the implementation of standardized performance criteria and norms to evaluate the effects of its funding), state support may lead commons toward practices and targets that they did not develop themselves. Conversely, if the state is aware of the specific entities that commons represent and of the values that they carry, and if it adapts its instruments and attitudes, it can then engage in a more assertive relationship with commons. To prevent the risks that have been mentioned, this relationship can be formalized and take the form of partnerships between the public sector and commons, defining the purpose of the partnership as well as the rights and obligations of each of the parties.

Beyond This, Any Opportunities for Debate?

Besides the way in which states can support African commons, the latter seem to inspire questions that public actors may or may not be able to address with regard to constructing a single developmental trajectory, in a break with the institutional rigidities and inefficiencies described in the first section. This final section therefore proposes to set out three preliminary items for debate, without claiming to be exhaustive either in the nature of the reflections proposed or in their analysis, but rather with the aim of paving the way for further work. The first item for debate concerns the contribution of commons to the realization of economic and social rights. The second item for debate addresses the question of the contribution of commons to the general interest. The third point of debate relates to the democratic character that underlies the practices of "commoning" (see chapter 1).

Realization of Economic and Social Rights

As the first section reminds us, state-society relations in Sub-Saharan Africa have been subject to liberal rationale since the 1980s. In many situations, these motivations run counter to the realization of economic and social rights such as the right to housing, the right to water, the right to food, or the right to energy, which are based on principles of access to these social goods by individuals and communities—particularly the poorest (Flauss 2002). These rights are enshrined in the 1966 International Covenant on Economic, Social and Cultural Rights, as well as at the regional level in the African Charter on Human and Peoples' Rights, which was ratified in 1981 and came into force in 1986.[6] This charter devotes several provisions to the rights of peoples, in particular the rights to existence and self-determination (Article 20) and special interest rights such as the right to the free disposal of natural resources (Article 21).

Economic and social rights as codified in declarations and applied are not sufficient to protect vulnerable populations for at least two reasons (Pousson 2005). First, they are now "secondary" to rights such as those relating to property and those relating to international trade (which are derived from property rights) (De Schutter 2013). Second, it is the nation-states that are the vehicles of these rights and who remain sovereign in the application of the rules to these populations (Salah 2002).

Commons as we have described and analyzed them throughout this book support the affirmation of economic and social rights. Indeed, their raison d'être includes the principle of the right to existence for the populations concerned. The expression of this right is affirmed through the search for the satisfaction of the common good, understood as a way of inhabiting the world that preserves communities (human and nonhuman) and ecosystems (Berque 2016; Coriat 2020; Vanuxem 2018). It incorporates not only the protection of basic social rights (food, health, education, etc.) vis-à-vis private law (Bosc 2016; Gauthier 2014) but also the recognition of the person, of their presence and their "voice" within and outside commons (see chapter 1). In mirroring this, international and regional written declarations are of prime importance for commons. They constitute a reference point for ensuring, for example, that the way in which commons are managed is sufficiently inclusive and representative of all population groups and that commons will not lead to new forms of discrimination or exclusion. Such declarations provide commons with a kind of constitutional framework to ensure that as they are utilized, commons are indeed put at the service of the interests of the greatest number of people and of future generations (box 6.3).

BOX 6.3

Commons in the Service of Fulfilling the Right to Food

The issue of food is caught in a difficult paradox. The right to food is one of the best established and most codified. However, nearly 1 billion people, or one in nine, suffer from malnutrition. Access to therapeutic food products remains ensnared in the logic of the market. The use of intellectual property is growing: the exclusive rights it defines are often considered effective drivers of innovation. Along with the rights linked to free trade treaties, intellectual property contributes to the maintenance of markets for patented products, which are highly capital intensive and unified, and which are opposed to the accessibility of essential goods in certain African countries.

Certain initiatives are subverting the classic attributes of intellectual property (Coriat et al. 2020). Without confronting them head-on, these initiatives adapt them in order to put them at the service of access to food products of a therapeutic nature. These approaches make it possible to think about and develop different legal tools that go beyond the scope of exclusive property (whether public or private) or to subvert the purely mercantile purpose of intellectual property. This is the case, for example, of Misola, a French association that has registered a trademark for a food supplement deployed in West Africa to prevent malnutrition in young children under the age of five. The flour is made entirely from locally grown ingredients and is produced and marketed in small-scale production units (UPAs—Unités de production artisanale). Most often run by women's cooperatives in villages, UPAs make no profit from their activity. The association transfers its trademark (Misola®) free of charge to the UPAs, which, in return, undertake to follow strict specifications and to accept regular checks on their practices, thus guaranteeing the nutritional quality of the products that are marketed at very low cost. This labeling makes it possible to create an open network of UPAs and to promote the distribution of the product as close to the communities as possible. Misola has been able to innovate by using intellectual property as a tool for disseminating its know-how and as a guarantee of quality for food produced in the villages. This policy has been facilitated by Misola's status as an association, whose financial stability remains highly dependent on public subsidies.

For these entities to be considered as contributing to the right to food, three major elements must be considered (Coriat et al. 2020). The first relates to the conditions (pricing policies, manufacturing, and distribution arrangements) in which food goods are physically made available. The second consideration relates to how initiatives deal with intellectual property issues concerning the products they develop and how the various attributes of property rights (see chapter 1) are, or are not, put in the service of access. Finally, the third consideration is based on the corporate form of the entities, which must give priority to the objective of providing people with access to the goods in question, rather than setting the maximization of profit as a target.

Definition and Examination of the General Interest

Today, the general interest constitutes the conceptual node that is the very object of the modern state, its law, and its legitimacy (Crétois and Roza 2017). Over time, there has been a shift from what was originally "public," considered the inalienable property of the people and citizens, to public property understood as the property of the state. The state, which for a long time only had a "right of custody" over public property, gradually saw this right transformed into the right to make use of the property entrusted to it. As such, it has become possible to alienate and privatize these assets (Orsi 2014; Xifaras 2004). This confusion is particularly strong in Sub-Saharan Africa because African society is only minimally constituted as a civil society. As the first section of this chapter reminded us, there is little public debate, little formation of interest groups, and many constraints on the possibilities for mobilizing social forces. There are therefore few spaces and processes for constructing a shared sense of purpose that could outline the contours of the general interest (Gazibo 2012; Gazibo and Moumouni 2017). The latter remains confined to its "instrumental" dimension, with the increase in items of public policy intended not for "populations" but for "users," the "justiciable," and the "creditworthy" (Darbon 2014).

This assimilation of the general interest with the interest of the state is now the subject of renewed questioning (Rochfeld, Cornu, and Martin 2021). These questions are even more fundamental in Sub-Saharan Africa because, as the first section of this chapter explained, the state is being patrimonialized under the leadership of elites through the private monopolization of public goods and is being replaced in many territories by proxies such as NGOs (Darbon 2014; Olivier de Sardan 2022).

The empirical chapters of this book have shown that some of the observed and studied commons serve the general interest when they take on the work of states (box 6.4): this is the case, for example, with the educational functions of hybrid urban spaces (chapter 4) or the transparency functions provided by digital commons (chapter 5). They also serve the general interest when they make it possible to escape the pressure of dominant capitalist norms: land commons for housing, for example, open up access to land and housing in contexts of commodification and speculation in urban land (chapter 3). Beyond that, these commons approach the general interest not as an external conception imposed on them but rather as a tool that is fully integrated into their work, serving reflexive approaches that facilitate the permanent adaptation of practices (Trosa 2017). From this perspective, the state can be the initiator of a procedural effort building "a localized 'common good' in stages" rather than public policy based on "a prior conception of 'the general interest'" (Lascoumes and Le Bourhis 1998, 40).

A Digital Commons for the General Interest—The Example of Open COVID19 in Senegal

Chapter 5 highlighted the existence of African digital commons that serve the general interest. For example, citizens who want to increase government transparency can contribute to the emergence of data commons: this was the approach taken by Open COVID19 in Senegal, which was born out of a desire to publish digitized information, such as the number of cases and their geolocation, that had previously only been communicated verbally by the government. These initiatives are also useful for journalists, researchers, civil society, citizens in general, and policy makers. The IWACU Open Data initiative in Burundi, for example, was developed by a group of journalists to address the lack of access to official data, which was only stored in paper format. Finally, numerous academic studies have shown how important open geospatial data have been for the allocation of aid by governments and nongovernmental organizations (Grinberger et al. 2022).

Democratic Processes

As the first section illustrated, African states are largely made up of imported structures that are not inclined to be based on, or to create, a political order in balance with their societies. Besides the single source of authority inherent in the exercise of administrative power, they are based, in most cases, on an "authoritarian principle," despite the democratization experiments under way in various countries in the region (Darbon 2009; Gazibo 2010). Particularly in West Africa, this situation is now being met with strong criticism, which is leveled against "democracy" and the practices to which it gives rise: it is criticized for not keeping its promises and for being incapable of "changing people's lives" (Villalón and Idrissa 2020). There is thus a critique of both the effectiveness of democracy and its legitimacy (Bayart 2009; Gazibo 2005; Mbembe 2019). This is evidenced by the political transition in Chad and the recent coups in Burkina Faso, Guinea, and Mali. As the popular support for these practices shows, this is not a minor or marginal phenomenon.[7]

In this context, commons, which in their very essence have the potential to revitalize democracy[8] and offer protection of the common good, appear as a set of mechanisms and supports that can provide fresh perspectives for public authorities. If their voice is heard and conveyed, they have the power to renew both the concept and the practice of democracy on key issues by introducing a deliberative and participatory dimension into public affairs (Bourcier, Hériard-Dubreuil, and Lavelle 2013; Lucarelli 2013).

Beyond that, if their role is recognized and supported by the state and local governments at different scales of action, it is possible to imagine commons finding a place in the forms of polycentric governance that Ostrom called for (Ostrom 2012).[9] Building on Ostrom's work, Aligica and Tarko (2012) define polycentric governance as a set of institutional arrangements in which a plurality of autonomous decision-making centers, each with its own sphere of action, operates under a single set of rules and objectives.[10] Ostrom's work on policing and water management concludes that the existence of multiple units under different authorities (national, regional, municipal, local) leads, despite the risk of duplication, to more effective systems (e.g., in terms of user and beneficiary satisfaction) than a vertical (top-down) approach to governance in which local entities must submit to centrally defined injunctions. These reflections are particularly relevant in the case of multiscalar issues, such as the fight against climate change or the governance of biodiversity (Obura and Treyer 2022). In the Policy Research Working Paper she proposed for the World Bank's 2010 World Development Report, Ostrom writes about climate change (Ostrom 2009, 28): "Given the severity of the threat, simply waiting for resolution of these issues at a global level, without trying out policies at multiple scales because they lack a global scale, is not a reasonable stance."

Conclusion

Because of its historical trajectory, the characteristics of the postcolonial African state (authoritarian modes of operation, institutional weaknesses, patrimonialization, the strong influence of international actors, little room for maneuver granted to social actors) are unfavorable to commons on the whole. However, as the previous empirical chapters have shown, there are many situations in which the state, within the framework of its proper functions, can and does act as a facilitator or contributor to commons. In this regard, it responds to a "demand" from commons, which have difficulties in guaranteeing their sustainability having been born out of citizens' initiatives.

Beyond that, if we take a step back from current events to look toward the future, two sets of facts should be noted. On the one hand, faced with its internal constraints (political and associative pluralism), its external constraints (economic dependence, the influence of external actors and market logic), and the economic, social, and environmental challenges it faces, the state no longer has a monopoly on public space or on the pursuit of the general interest. On the other hand, commons, like other actors, assume the role of substitutes at their own scale for states that are failing in their duties in many respects. In this context, taking into account commons, both as practices in territories and as bearers of demands for the common good and the right to existence, might prove to be an opportunity for African states to alter their trajectories.

In this light, working to promote the development of commons, creating the conditions for them to flourish, and even engaging with them in policies that seek to collectively construct the common good can enable states to adopt new positions, opening up spaces for debate on the realization of economic and social rights, the definition and pursuit of the general interest, and democratic processes. These topics, which remain underdeveloped, are all potential avenues for future work.

Notes

1. Ostrom uses the example of the US Geological Survey, an American institution that produces free and open access to hydrological and geological data for the United States. For Ostrom, this type of institution plays an essential role for commons and communities in their research and management of water resources (Ostrom 2020).
2. https://dndi.org/.
3. https://www.saide.org.za/documents/2017_03_29_ASb_accountability_evaluation .pdf.
4. Commons can indeed emerge from the occupation of public spaces that have an undetermined status or are considered as such (vacant lots, buildings, squares). The examples of the "Asilo Filangieri" and of the seven places occupied and transformed into common goods in the city of Naples (Italy) show that relationships with the owners and managers of these spaces can become more peaceful and give rise to stabilized forms of coexistence over time (Festa 2021; Micciarelli 2014).
5. Design principle 7 stipulates that the self-organization of the community must follow rules that are accepted and recognized by the authorities at a higher level.
6. https://au.int/sites/default/files/treaties/36390-treaty-0011_-_african_charter_on _human_and_peoples_rights_f.pdf.
7. Reflections from a series of seminars organized in February and March 2022 by the Agence française de développement (French Development Agency), the Centre d'analyse, de prévision et de stratégie (Center for Analysis, Forecasting and Strategy) of the French Ministry for Europe and Foreign Affairs, and the Institute for Strategic Research of the École Militaire.
8. As we have emphasized several times in the book, the expression of "voice" must be qualified in certain situations, notably when rules of a magico-religious nature (which are not debated) are imposed or when users do not seek to participate in the definition of either the rules of access and use or the mechanisms of control and sanction (Colin, Lavigne Delville, and Léonard 2022).
9. The definition proposed by Aligica and Tarko (2012, 1) is as follows: "A structural feature of social systems of many decision centers having limited and autonomous prerogatives and operating under an overarching set of rules."
10. Polycentric governance plays out along two intersecting axes (Weinstein 2013). On the horizontal axis, different "action arenas" can either cooperate or compete,

depending on the environment in which they operate. On the vertical axis, the different levels of rules interact, from the micro-institutional level (a community managing a resource) to the macro-institutional level, which has constitutional value (like the laws of a given country).

References

Abecassis, Philippe, Jean-François Alesandrini, Benjamin Coriat, Nathalie Coutinet, and Stéphanie Leyronas. 2019. "DNDi, a Distinctive Illustration of Commons in the Area of Public Health." AFD Research Papers 93. https://dndi.org/wp-content/uploads/2019/02/CommonsAreaPublicHealth_AFDResearchPaper_2019.pdf.

African Union. 2020. *The Digital Transformation Strategy for Africa (2020–2030)*. Addis Ababa: African Union. https://au.int/sites/default/files/documents/38507-doc-dts-english.pdf.

Aligica, Paul D., and Vlad Tarko. 2012. "Polycentricity: From Polanyi to Ostrom, and Beyond." *Governance* 25 (2): 237–62. https://doi.org/10.1111/j.1468-0491.2011.01550.x.

Antona, Martine, and Stefano Farolfi. 2001. "Décision et négociation des politiques environnementales: L'application de la fiscalité dans les pays du Nord et du Sud." In "Colloque PIREE: Les instruments des politiques environnementales," Sophia Antipolis (France). Available from http://cormas.cirad.fr/pdf/piree.pdf.

Bach, Daniel, and Mamoudou Gazibo, eds. 2011. *Neopatrimonialism in Africa and Beyond*. London: Routledge. https://doi.org/10.4324/9780203145623.

Badie, Bertrand. 1992. *L'Etat importé: L'occidentalisation de l'ordre politique*. Paris: Fayard.

Balandier, Georges. 2013. *Anthropologie politique. Quadrige*. Paris: Presses Universitaires de France.

Bayart, Jean-François. 2009. "La démocratie à l'épreuve de la tradition en Afrique subsaharienne." *Pouvoirs* 129 (2): 27–44. https://doi.org/10.3917/pouv.129.0027.

Bayart, Jean-François, Achille Mbembe, and Comi Toulabor. 1992. *Le politique par le bas en Afrique noire: Contribution à une problématique de la démocratie*. Paris: Karthala.

Bédécarrats, Florent, Oriane Lafuente-Sampietro, Martin Leménager, and Dominique Lukono Sowa. 2019. "Building Commons to Cope with Chaotic Urbanization? Performance and Sustainability of Decentralized Water Services in the Outskirts of Kinshasa." *Journal of Hydrology* 573: 1096–108. https://doi.org/10.1016/j.jhydrol.2016.07.023.

Benkler, Yochai. 2013. "Commons and Growth: The Essential Role of Open Commons in Market Economies." *University of Chicago Law Review* 80 (3): 1499–556. https://chicagounbound.uchicago.edu/uclrev/vol80/iss3/12.

Berque, Augustin. 2016. *Ecoumène. Introduction à l'étude des milieux humains*. Paris: Belin.

Bienen, Henry, and Nicolas Van de Walle. 1991. *Of Time and Power: Leadership Duration in the Modern World*. Stanford, CA: Stanford University Press.

Bollier, David. 2014. *La Renaissance des communs: Pour une société de coopération et de partage*. Paris: Éditions Charles Léopold Mayer.

Bollier, David, and Pat Conaty. 2015. "Democratic Money and Capital for the Commons: Strategies for Transforming Neoliberal Finance through Commons-Based Alternatives." https://base.socioeco.org/docs/democratic_money_and_capital_for_the_commons_report.pdf.

Borrits, Benoît. 2022. "Sécurité économique et fonds socialisé d'investissement: Des communs de mutualisation pour financer les communs." *Finance et communs: Pour une réappropriation collective de la finance*. https://www.ritimo.org/Securite-economique-et-Fonds-socialise-d-investissement-des-communs-de.

Bosc, Yannick. 2016. "Thomas Paine as a Theorist of the Right to Existence." *Journal of Early American History* 6 (2–3): 113–23. https://doi.org/10.1163/18770703-00603002.

Bourcier, Danièle, Gilles Hériard-Dubreuil, and Sylvain Lavelle. 2013. *La société en action: Une méthode pour la démocratie*. Paris: Hermann.

Bourmaud, Daniel. 1997. *La politique en Afrique*. Paris: Montchrestien.

Chazan, Naomi, Robert Mortimer, Donald Rothchild, Peter Lewis, and Stephen John Stedman. 1999. *Politics and Society in Contemporary Africa*. London: Bloomsbury Publishing.

Cheeseman, Nic. 2019. *The Oxford Encyclopedia of African Politics*. Oxford: Oxford University Press.

Clastres, Pierre. 1974. *La Société contre l'Etat: Recherches d'anthropologie politique*. Paris: Minuit.

Clemens, Michael A., Steven Radelet, Rikhil R. Bhavnani, and Samuel Bazzi. 2012. "Counting Chickens When They Hatch: Timing and the Effects of Aid on Growth." *Economic Journal* 122 (561): 590–617.

Colin, Jean-Philippe, Philippe Lavigne Delville, and Eric Léonard. 2022. *Le foncier rural dans les pays du Sud: Enjeux et clés d'analyse*. Montpellier: IRD Éditions.

Coriat, Benjamin. 2020. *La pandémie, l'anthropocène, et le Bien commun*. Paris: Les Liens qui libèrent.

Coriat, Benjamin, Nadège Legroux, Nicolas Le Guen, Stéphanie Leyronas, and Magali Toro. 2020. "Making Food a 'Common Good': Lessons from Three Experiences to Fight Malnutrition." Research Papers n°114. Paris: AFD éditions. https://www.afd.fr/en/ressources/making-food-common-good-lessons-three-experiences-fight-malnutrition.

Crétois, Pierre, and Stéphanie Roza. 2017. "De l'intérêt général: Introduction." *Astérion. Philosophie, histoire des idées, pensée politique* 17. https://journals.openedition.org/asterion/2996.

Darbon, Dominique. 2009. *La politique des modèles en Afrique: Simulation, dépolitisation et appropriation*. Paris: Karthala.

Darbon, Dominique. 2014. "Politiques publiques sectorielles dans les États et sociétés fragiles et science politique." In *Une action publique éclatée? Production et institutionnalisation de l'action publique dans les secteurs de l'eau potable et du foncier (APPI). Burkina Faso, Niger, Bénin*, edited by Héloïse Valette, Catherine Baron, François Enten, Philippe Lavigne Delville, and Alicia Tsitsikalis, 121–26. Nogent sur Marne: GRET.

Darbon, Dominique, and Olivier Provini. 2018. "'Penser l'action publique' en contextes africains. Les enjeux d'une décentration." *Gouvernement et action publique* 7 (2): 9–29. https://doi.org/10.3917/gap.182.0009.

De Schutter, Olivier, ed. 2013. *Economic, Social, and Cultural Rights as Human Rights*. Cheltenham: Edward Elgar Publishing.

Devarajan, Shantayan, David R. Dollar, and Torgny Holmgren. 2002. "Aid and Reform in Africa." https://doi.org/10.1596/0-8213-4669-5.

Dongier, Philippe, Julie Van Domelen, Elinor Ostrom, Andrea Rizvi, Wendy Wakeman, Anthony Bebbington, Sabina Alkire, Talib Esmail, and Margaret Polski. 2002. "Community-Driven Development." In *Poverty Reduction Strategy Sourcebook*, edited by Jeni Klugman, 301–32. Washington, DC: World Bank. https://documents1 .worldbank.org/curated/en/156931468138883186/pdf/298000018213149 7813.pdf.

Dumont, Aurélien, Stéphanie Leyronas, Olivier Petit, and Quentin Ballin. 2021. "Agir en commun pour un usage durable de l'eau agricole. Propositions pour prévenir la dégradation et la surexploitation des eaux souterraines." AFD Policy Paper 8. https:// www.afd.fr/fr/ressources/usage-durable-eau-agricole.

Erler, Brigitte. 1987. *L'aide qui tue: Récit de ma dernière mission d'aide au développement*. Lausanne: Lausanne Éditions d'en bas.

Festa, Daniela Anna. 2021. "Les biens culturels en Italie. De l'"assaut' à la mise en commun." *In Situ. Au regard des sciences sociales*. https://journals.openedition.org /insituarss/1148#quotation.

Filho, Genauto Carvalho de França, Isabelle Guérin, Isabelle Hillenkamp, and Ósia Vasconcelos. 2022. "Une gestion démocratique et solidaire des communs? Banques communautaires de développement au Brésil." *Finance et communs. Pour une réappropriation collective de la finance*, 23. https://www.ritimo.org/Une-gestion -democratique-et-solidaire-des-communs-Banques-communautaires-de.

Flauss, Jean-François. 2002. "Le droit international des droits de l'homme face à la globalisation économique." *Les Petites Affiches* 104: 4–20.

Fontaine, Geneviève, and Amandine Lebrun. 2022. "Financer les communs sans abîmer le commun." *Finance et communs: Pour une réappropriation collective de la finance*. https://www.ritimo.org/Financer-les-communs-sans-abimer-le-commun.

Fortes, Meyer, and Edward Evan Evans-Pritchard. 1940. *African Political Systems*. Oxford: Oxford University Press.

Gauthier, Florence. 2014. *Triomphe et mort de la révolution des droits de l'homme et du citoyen (1789-1795-1802)*. Paris: Éditions Syllepse.

Gazibo, Mamoudou. 2005. *Les paradoxes de la démocratisation en Afrique: Analyse institutionnelle et stratégique*. Montreal: Presses de l'Université de Montréal.

Gazibo, Mamoudou. 2007. "Mobilisations citoyennes et émergence d'un espace public au Niger depuis 1990." *Sociologie et sociétés* 39 (2): 19–37.

Gazibo, Mamoudou. 2010. *Introduction à la politique africaine. 2ème édition*. Montreal: Presses de l'Université de Montréal.

Gazibo, Mamoudou. 2012. "Vers des processus plus légitimes: L'exemple de la réforme constitutionnelle au Niger." In *La gouvernance en révolution(s)*, 257–63. Paris: Éditions Charles Léopold Mayer.

Gazibo, Mamoudou. 2019. "Electoral administration." In *Routledge Handbook of Democratization in Africa*, edited by Gabrielle Lynch and Peter VonDoepp, 174–87. London: Routledge. https://doi.org/10.4324/9781315112978.

Gazibo, Mamoudou, and Charles Moumouni. 2017. *Repenser la légitimité de l'État africain à l'ère de la gouvernance partagée.* Quebec: Presses de l'Université du Québec.

Grinberger, Asher Yair, Marco Minghini, Levente Juhász, Godwin Yeboah, and Peter Mooney. 2022. "OSM Science: The Academic Study of the OpenStreetMap Project, Data, Contributors, Community, and Applications." *International Journal of Geo-Information* 11 (4). https://www.researchgate.net/publication/359625703_OSM _Science-The_Academic_Study_of_the_OpenStreetMap_Project_Data_Contributors _Community_and_Applications/citations.

Herbst, Jeffrey. 2000. *States and Power in Africa: Comparative Lessons in Authority and Control.* Princeton, NJ: Princeton University Press. https://www.jstor.org/stable/j .ctt9qh05m.

Hervé, Caroline, and Ghislaine Gallenga. 2019. "Services publics: L'Etat face au commun." *Anthropologie et sociétés* 43 (2): 9–21.

Hess, Charlotte, and Elinor Ostrom. 2006. *Understanding Knowledge as a Commons: From Theory to Practice.* Cambridge, MA: MIT Press. https://doi.org/10.7551 /mitpress/6980.001.0001.

Hibou, Béatrice. 1999. "La 'décharge', nouvel interventionnisme." *Politique africaine* 73 (1): 6–15. https://doi.org/10.3917/polaf.073.0006.

Hibou, Béatrice. 2009. "The 'Social Capital' of the State as an Agent of Deception, or the Ruses of Economic Intelligence." In *The Criminalization of the State in Africa*, edited by Jean-François Leguil-Bayart, Stephen Ellis, and Béatrice Hibou, 69–113. Bloomington, IN: Indiana University Press.

Holder, Gilles. 2021. "Les services publics ambulants (SPA): Une solution pour le Sahel? (Burkina Faso, Mali, Mauritanie)." *Contract. PASAS IRD.* https://hal.archives-ouvertes .fr/hal-03515316.

Jackson, Robert H., and Carl G. Rosberg. 1982. "Why Africa's Weak States Persist: The Empirical and the Juridical in Statehood." *World Politics* 35 (1): 1–24. https://doi .org/10.2307/2010277.

Ki-Zerbo, Joseph. 1972. *Histoire de l'Afrique noire, d'hier à demain.* Paris: Hatier.

Lascoumes, Pierre, and Jean-Pierre Le Bourhis. 1998. "Le bien commun comme construit territorial. Identités d'action et procédures." *Politix. Revue des sciences sociales du politique* 42: 37–66. https://doi.org/10.3406/polix.1998.1724.

Lavigne Delville, Philippe. 2011. "Vers une socio-anthropologie des interventions de dével-oppement comme action publique." PhD dissertation, Lumière University Lyon 2.

Levi, Margaret. 2002. "The State of the Study of the State." In *Political Science: The State of the Discipline*, edited by Ira Katznelson and Helen Milner, 33–55. New York: Norton.

Lucarelli, Alberto. 2013. *La democrazia dei beni comuni.* Roma-Bari: Laterza Edizione.

Lynch, Gabrielle, and Peter VonDoepp, eds. 2019. *Routledge Handbook of Democratization in Africa.* London: Routledge. https://doi.org/10.4324/9781315112978.

May, Oliver. 2016. *Fighting Fraud and Corruption in the Humanitarian and Global Development Sector.* London: Routledge. https://doi.org/10.4324/9781315558301.

Mazzucato, Mariana. 2015. "The Green Entrepreneurial State." Working Paper 2015-28, University of Sussex. https://www.sussex.ac.uk/webteam/gateway/file.php?name =2015-28-swps-mazzucato.pdf&site=25.

Mbairamadji, Jérémie. 2009. "De la décentralisation de la gestion forestière à une gouvernance locale des forêts communautaires et des redevances forestières au Sud-est Cameroun." *VertigO—la revue électronique en sciences de l'environnement* 9 (1). https://doi.org/10.4000/vertigo.8614.

Mbembe, Achille. 1988. *Afriques indociles*. Paris: Karthala.

Mbembe, Achille. 2000. *On Private Indirect Government*. Dakar: CODESRIA.

Mbembe, Achille. 2001. *On the Postcolony*. Berkeley, CA: University of California Press.

Mbembe, Achille. 2019. *Necropolitics*. Durham, NC: Duke University Press.

Médard, Jean-François. 1991a. *Etats d'Afrique noire: Formation, mécanismes et crise*. Paris: Karthala.

Médard, Jean-François. 1991b. "L'Etat néo-patrimonial en Afrique noire." In *Etats d'Afrique noire. Formations, mécanismes et crise*, edited by Jean-François Médard, 323–53. Paris: Karthala.

Micciarelli, Giuseppe. 2014. "I beni comuni e la partecipazione democratica. Da un 'altro modo di possedere' ad un 'altro modo di governare.'" *Jura Gentium* XI (1): 58–83.

Montagne, Pierre, Mamisoa Rakotoarimanana, François Pinta, and Serge Razafimahatratra. 2016. *Hazavana. Électrification rurale décentralisée par combustion de biomasse: Expérience des projets Gesforcom et Bioenergelec à Madagascar, de 2008 à 2015*. Antsakaviro: Homme et environnement. https://agritrop.cirad.fr/580951/.

Moyo, Dambisa, and Niall Ferguson. 2010. *Dead Aid: Why Aid Is Not Working and How There Is a Better Way for Africa*. New York: Farrar, Straus, and Giroux.

Ndulo, Muna, and Mamoudou Gazibo. 2016. *Growing Democracy in Africa: Elections, Accountable Governance, and Political Economy*. Newcastle upon Tyne: Cambridge Scholars Publishing.

Obura, David, and Sébastien Treyer. 2022. "A 'Shared Earth' Approach to Put Biodiversity at the Heart of the Sustainable Development in Africa." *AFD Research Papers* 265. Paris: AFD. https://www.afd.fr/en/ressources/shared-earth-approach-put-biodiversity-heart-sustainable-development-africa.

Olivier de Sardan, Jean-Pierre. 1995. "La politique du terrain. Sur la production des données en anthropologie." *Enquête. Archives de la revue Enquête* 1: 71–109. https://doi.org/10.4000/enquete.263.

Olivier de Sardan, Jean-Pierre. 2021. *La revanche des contextes. Des mésaventures de l'ingénierie sociale en Afrique et au-delà*. Paris: Karthala. https://www.academia.edu/47765745/La_revanche_des_contextes_Des_m%C3%A9saventures_de_l_ing%C3%A9nierie_sociale_en_Afrique_et_au_del%C3%A0.

Olivier de Sardan, Jean-Pierre. 2022. "La délivrance des biens d'intérêt général en Afrique. Pratiques palliatives, réformes de l'Etat et communs." Papiers de Recherche AFD 264. Paris: AFD. https://www.afd.fr/fr/ressources/la-delivrance-des-biens-dinteret-general-en-afrique-pratiques-palliatives-reformes-de-letat-et-communs.

Orsi, Fabienne. 2014. "Réhabiliter la propriété comme bundle of rights: Des origines à Elinor Ostrom, et au-delà?" *Revue internationale de droit économique* 3: 371–85.

Ostrom, Elinor. 1999. "Design Principles and Threats to Sustainable Organizations That Manage Commons." Working paper. https://hdl.handle.net/10535/5465.

Ostrom, Elinor. 2005. *Understanding Institutional Diversity.* Princeton, NJ: Princeton University Press. https://digitalcommons.usu.edu/unf_research/54.

Ostrom, Elinor. 2009. *A Polycentric Approach for Coping with Climate Change.* Washington, DC: World Bank. https://documents1.worldbank.org/curated /en/480171468315567893/pdf/WPS5095.pdf.

Ostrom, Elinor. 2012. "Agir à plusieurs échelles pour faire face au changement climatique et à d'autres problèmes d'action collection." *Institut Veblen pour les réformes économiques.* https://www.veblen-institute.org/IMG/pdf/agir_contre_changement _climatique_ostrom2.pdf.

Ostrom, Elinor. 2020. "Elinor Ostrom Speaks about Property Rights." *Journal of Private Enterprise* 35 (3): 7–12.

Ostrom, Elinor, and Xavier Basurto. 2011. "Crafting Analytical Tools to Study Institutional Change." *Journal of Institutional Economics* 7 (3): 317–43.

Payre, Renaud, and Gilles Pollet. 2013. *Socio-histoire de l'action publique.* Paris: La Découverte. https://doi.org/10.3917/dec.payre.2013.01.

Picavet, Emmanuel, Danièle Bourcier, Jacques Chevallier, Gilles Hériard-Dubreuil, and Sylvain Lavelle. 2021. *Dynamiques du commun: Entre etat, marché et société.* Paris: Éditions de la Sorbonne. https://halshs.archives-ouvertes.fr/halshs-03230331.

Porter, Doug, and Michael Watts. 2017. "Righting the Resource Curse: Institutional Politics and State Capabilities in Edo State, Nigeria." *Journal of Development Studies* 53 (2): 249–63. https://doi.org/10.1080/00220388.2016.1160062.

Pousson, Alain. 2005. "L'effectivité des droits sociaux fondamentaux dans une économie de marché globalisée." In *Le Droit saisi par la Morale,* edited by Jacques Krynen, 83–112. Toulouse: Presses de l'Université Toulouse 1 Capitole. https://doi.org/10.4000 /books.putc.1680.

Ridde, Valéry, and Jean-Pierre Olivier de Sardan. 2022. "The Development World: Conflicts of Interest at All Levels." *Revue internationale des études du développement* 249: 247–69. https://doi.org/10.4000/ried.1530.

Rigot, Sandra, and Dominique Plihon. 2022. "Le rôle stratégique des intermédiaires financiers publics face à la transition énergétique." *Finance et communs: Pour une réappropriation collective de la finance.* https://www.ritimo.org/Le-role-strategique -des-intermediaires-financiers-publics-face-a-la-transition.

Risse, Thomas, and Ursula Lehmkuhl. 2006. "Governance in Areas of Limited Statehood—New Modes of Governance? Research Program of the Research Center (SFB) 700." https://doi.org/10.17169/refubium-22684.

Rochfeld, Judith, Marie Cornu, and Gilles J. Martin. 2021. "L'échelle de communalité. Propositions de réforme pour intégrer les biens communs en droit." *IRJS* 17–34. https:// www.researchgate.net/publication/352694162_L%27echelle_de_communalite _-_Propositions_de_reformes_pour_integrer_les_biens_communs_en_droit.

Rose, Carol. 1986. "The Comedy of the Commons: Custom, Commerce, and Inherently Public Property." *University of Chicago Law Review* 53 (3): 711–81. https://doi .org/10.2307/1599583.

Salah, Mahmoud Mohamed. 2002. *Les contradictions du droit mondialisé.* Paris: Presses Universitaires de France.

Trosa, Sylvie. 2017. "L'intérêt général: Une réalité introuvable?" *Gestion & Finances Publiques* 3: 82–7. https://doi.org/10.3166/gfp.2017.00053.

Turnbull, Colin M. 1983. *The Mbuti Pygmies: Change and Adaptation.* Orlando, FL: Harcourt Brace Jovanovich College Publishers. https://ehrafworldcultures.yale.edu/document?id=fo04-005.

Van de Walle, Nicolas. 2003. "Presidentialism and Clientelism in Africa's Emerging Party Systems." *Journal of Modern African Studies* 41 (2): 297–321. https://doi.org/10.1017/S0022278X03004269.

Vanuxem, Sarah. 2018. *La propriété de la terre.* Marseille: Éditions wildproject.

Villalón, Leonardo A., and Rahmane Idrissa. 2020. "Democratic Struggle, Institutional Reform, and State Resilience in the African Sahel." https://www.africabib.org/rec.php?RID=A00006075.

Weinstein, Olivier. 2013. "Comment comprendre les 'communs': Elinor Ostrom, la propriété et la nouvelle économie institutionnelle." *Revue de la régulation. Capitalisme, institutions, pouvoirs* 14. https://doi.org/10.4000/regulation.10452.

World Bank. 2017. *World Development Report 2017: Governance and the Law.* Washington, DC: World Bank. https://www.worldbank.org/en/publication/wdr2017.

Xifaras, Mikhaïl. 2004. *La propriété. Etude de philosophie du droit.* Paris: Presses Universitaires de France.

Young, Crawford. 1997. *The African Colonial State in Comparative Perspective.* New Haven, CT: Yale University Press.

Chapter 7

Funders' Attitudes, Perceptions, and Actions: Taking Inspiration from the Commons-Based Approach

Stéphanie Leyronas and Sophie Salomon

Introduction

In this final chapter, we take the discussion a step further by analyzing our practices as funders. It seems necessary for us to examine our epistemological preconceptions and to ask ourselves why we encounter difficulties and resistances when trying to support commons that are facing complex social dilemmas in Sub-Saharan Africa. By and large, we are bound by dominant universalist norms, despite substantial efforts to take local contexts into account (see chapter 2). In concrete terms, we are obliged to confront our "managerialist" approaches (Dar and Cooke 2013; Gulrajani 2011), which are manifest in the pressing need to achieve results, the emphasis placed on deliverables, the pressure to disburse funds, short-term time horizons, and the widespread use of conceptual frameworks defined ex ante that are not reexamined before the funding comes to an end.

African intellectuals are calling for a new founding narrative of African development from Africans themselves (Alao 2019; Mbembe 2021; Ngozi Adichie 2013; Nubukpo 2022; Sarr 2019; Wiredu 2004). However, governance in Sub-Saharan Africa is strongly under the influence of actors from abroad (Devarajan, Dollar, and Holmgren 2002; Lavigne Delville 2011). Between 2000 and 2020, official development assistance allocated to Sub-Saharan Africa more than tripled, from US$20 billion to over US$66 billion.[1] This subregion is the largest recipient of global official development assistance, with its share accounting for 41 percent of the total amount (OECD 2022). We are aware of the various critiques of aid, which are not new. These center on risks of interference, conflicts of values, the asymmetry of the relationship, its questionable effectiveness, and the potential presence of concealed geopolitical and economic intentions (Andrews 2009; Ferguson 2006; Lavigne Delville and Abdoulkader 2010; Mosse 2004; Moyo and Ferguson 2010; Olivier de Sardan 2021 in particular). We are also familiar with the principles of renewed commitment, which are relatively widely accepted. These involve taking the context into account, starting from the needs on the ground, working toward the long term, accepting risks, and adopting flexible and tailored approaches (Mélonio, Naudet, and Rioux 2022; World Bank 2017). Despite this, it remains unclear how these principles should be implemented, and changes prove limited.

We do not pretend to be able to offer a comprehensive solution here. On the other hand, it seems to us that the collective action at the heart of African commons opens up a field of thought, or at least avenues of inquiry and forms of inspiration, for development aid actors. It is therefore on the basis of the reflections in this book and the field experience of the Agence française de développement (AFD) (French Development Agency) that we examine the underlying principles and scope of a "commons-based approach" for funders working in Sub-Saharan Africa.

The commons-based approach for funders has three objectives. The first objective is to enable us to support existing African commons without undermining them (see chapter 6). The second objective is to create the conditions for the emergence of new commons in Sub-Saharan Africa. The third and final objective is to enable the emergence of "commoning" based around complex societal issues that are currently only being dealt with by public authorities or by the market, or not being dealt with at all. This is a pragmatic approach that does not seek to idealize commons or present them as the ultimate solution to the continent's challenges. In fact, it has already been thought out and experimented with by development actors.

The strength of this approach stems from the critical analysis it draws on, which is based on identifying a relationship between resources, actors, and rules for governance. This is not seen as something that is fixed in advance. By starting from commons-based practices that are already in use, it becomes possible to assess the collective action problem, to define what "commoning" really means, and to identify the resources concerned and the actors who depend on them. It creates spaces for action that follow a polycentric logic (see chapter 6) that empowers stakeholders to carry out their tasks in their own surroundings and provides them with the human and material means to accomplish them (Delay, Aubert, and Botta 2020). In this way, the commons-based approach focuses on the process of taking action. It complements two approaches that we have been promoting for several decades by taking the opposite tack. The first is participatory governance, which is mostly carried out within institutional frameworks, organized by the promoters of "development projects"[2] or decision-makers who lay down the rules (who is to participate and how, on what collective problem, with what resources). Then there are community development policies that are based on processes of decentralizing the management of a certain number of resources in the territories, independently of the historical trajectories of the social formations themselves. These approaches are the subject of a large body of critical literature on the "injunction to participate" and "associationalism" that are prevalent in Sub-Saharan Africa (Cooke and Kothari 2001; Kumar 2003; Mansuri and Rao 2013; Olivier de Sardan 2022).

The commons-based approach is first and foremost a reflexive approach with regard to our attitudes and practices (Aubert and Botta 2022; Fontaine 2021). This approach is capable of generating not only new forms of knowledge but also innovative ideas and a better understanding of the issues related to collective action. It is based on the idea that people within institutions (commons actors, public actors, funders) can adopt multiple positions (participation in action, a reflexive attitude, knowledge construction, formalization of tools) and that this multipositioning makes mutual learning possible (Perrin 2019). It is based on a prior understanding of the assumptions or even prejudices (whether they are conscious or not) that guide our activities and that come into conflict with the expectations and needs of commons in a context of social change (Fontaine 2022; Leyronas, forthcoming).

The commons-based approach can in no way be prescriptive. It is not about dictating what to do or how to do it, but rather about allowing each person to seize these questions and these sources of inspiration on a case-by-case basis and to experiment with alternative (or simply different) ways of doing things. Some issues may well lend themselves to this, others not so much. This also goes for the contexts. Beyond the positioning of the institutions themselves (funding institutions or local public institutions), it is the people involved with these institutions who will determine how experimental the approach is, whether they are "reformers from within" (Olivier de Sardan 2022) or "development artists" (Naudet 1999). This chapter thus proposes four sources of inspiration that can be applied independently. They address changes in attitudes, interpretations, methods, and tools. Each of these sources of inspiration is illustrated with concrete examples that embody principles specific to commons.

Source of Inspiration 1—Moving Away from an Assumption of Institutional Uniformity to the Recognition of the Diversity of Practices

Our actions are based on a predominant concept of rationality, one based on individualization, utilitarianism, formalism, and predictability. This form of rationality is directly linked to the possibility of profitability or return on investment (economic rationality), to a legal formalism linked to modern law and its codification (legal rationality), and to bureaucratic political administration (political rationality) (Weber 2019). This rationality translates directly into our relationship to institutions, with a tendency toward isomorphism (DiMaggio and Powell 2000), and into our relationship to property, understood in its exclusive and individual dimensions (Xifaras 2004). It is values such as progress, mastery of nature, and economic efficiency (Santos 2016) that are at the heart of the interpretive frameworks, analyses, diagnoses, and evaluations that we make use of in adopting a normative perspective (Rist 2007). These values form our frameworks for acting, and we tend to consider behaviors whose underlying goals and representations do not fit into them to be "irrational," even though these frameworks are supposed to provide a collective understanding of the activity (Trosa 2017). These values and references are propagated on a daily basis in the lives of Sub-Saharan African populations, either through the presence of public agents in the field, or the presence of proxies such as local nongovernmental organizations, or through the daily practices of increasingly urbanized, educated, and interconnected populations (Darbon 2014).

Commons are developed on the basis of a procedural and context-aware rationality (Chanteau and Labrousse 2013). It is procedural, or instrumental (Lévi-Strauss 2021), because actors engage in "bricolage" (forms of tinkering), not according to a goal and a trajectory defined ex ante but by proceeding along paths that include processes of constant trial and error to adjust to unforeseen consequences. It is context aware, because commons presuppose a deliberative dimension (see chapter 1) that involves requirements, which vary in the extent to which they can be formalized, such as ethics, politics, tradition, solidarity, reciprocity, trust, commitment, and reputation. This does not mean that there are no individual strategies or forms of utilitarianism. Nonetheless, decision-making patterns are based on considerations and objectives that fall under the right to exist (see chapter 6), and economic activities and market mechanisms are thus subordinated to social relations and interdependent ecological relationships (Aubert et al. 2017). Property is viewed not as an exclusive right of the owner, whether public or private, but as a bundle of distributed rights. This therefore takes the social function of property into account (Orsi 2014).

A commons-based approach may involve the following (box 7.1):

- Preventing the tendency toward institutional isomorphism that funder activity can create by making it possible to explore flexible and pragmatic institutional arrangements that recognize the diversity of existing forms of commons
- Questioning the relationship with property by considering it as a bundle of distributed rights and obligations, which may or may not be formalized

BOX 7.1

Access to Medicines—A Bundle of Rights Approach to Intellectual Property

The consequences of the COVID-19 (coronavirus) health crisis illustrated a high level of inequality in terms of the state of public health and hospital systems, as well as the numbers of medical staff, beds, prevention tools, and treatments that were available. It has given rise to an unprecedented international response in the provision and development of medical products (medical equipment, diagnostic tests, drugs, and vaccines). Debates have focused on whether there is a need for exclusive intellectual property through patents as a vehicle for innovation or whether intellectual property should be abolished in order to secure access for the greatest number of people.

Certain experiments are exploring different paths by adopting commons-based approaches that operate at two levels (Abecassis et al. 2019). The first level consists of modulating the various attributes of intellectual property in order to put them at the service of access for the most deprived populations. In concrete terms, this means using bundles of rights to think about the rights to be protected and the agreements that must be put in place in this regard between pharmaceutical companies, public health authorities, and international organizations. The second level consists of the mobilization of coalitions of actors (international organizations, public authorities, pharmaceutical companies, funders, doctors, producers, patients) that aim to find affordable and manageable treatments in the social, economic, logistic, and climatic conditions of African countries.

This is the case of the Drugs for Neglected Diseases Initiative (DNDi). Because they mainly affect poor populations, so-called neglected tropical diseases are overlooked by pharmaceutical companies as a result of a lack of market demand and return on investment. Since 2003, the DNDi has been setting up collaborative research platforms in countries affected by these diseases in order to develop accessible medical solutions for the populations concerned. To do this, the foundation negotiates with pharmaceutical companies for access to some of their resources, including molecules that can serve as the basis for the development of new treatments. Various situations arise depending on whether a patent has been filed on the molecule or whether the laboratory is interested in the molecule for future developments. The laboratory holding the rights can, for example, relinquish its rights to all the applications resulting from the research or retain rights to just some of them. The motivation of laboratories to cede part of their rights can be multiple, ranging from the benefits derived from a corporate social responsibility strategy to the shifting of risk to the DNDi concerning molecules on which they are not ready to make any investments. The DNDi therefore proposes an original and creative conception of intellectual property. Its differentiated allocation makes it possible to implement a range of legal solutions based on bundles of rights designed to develop new treatments and to promote the widest possible access to them among disadvantaged populations (Coriat, Legroux, and Leyronas 2020). For example, in November 2018, the European Medicines Agency issued a favorable opinion for the registration of fexinidazole, a new drug to combat sleeping sickness (or human African trypanosomiasis), which had been the result of a partnership between the DNDi, the French pharmaceutical company Sanofi, and experts from endemic countries (see chapter 1).

Source of Inspiration 2—Shifting from Top-Down Observation to an Embedded Approach

Funders rely on concepts and principles that are intended to be universal (Hugon 2011). This attitude manifests itself in the perpetuation of dominant economic and social models, whose promotion is justified by the need to guarantee universal rights and principles. The Sustainable Development Goals are a major expression of this (Mélonio, Naudet, and Rioux 2022). These models, which are employed in a normative manner (Rist 2007), are the subject of much criticism, particularly in the work of development anthropology, which seeks to identify particular aspects of the institutions that are unique to different societies and to take into account the interpretations and meanings of activities, and which favors the qualitative approach. Even when organizations are interested in the local level, this reliance on universalism leads them to favor processes of expansion (increase in activity) or duplication (replication of the model) with a view toward "scaling up." This inevitably introduces a distance between funders and actors, which is seen as guaranteeing a certain objectivity and axiological neutrality (Fontaine 2022). However, this distance becomes a challenge when the funders are part of the game of power, have their own values and objectives, and are subject to multiple constraints (Rottenburg 2009).

On the contrary, commons that are being developed in Sub-Saharan Africa are experimenting with a relationship to territory based on proximity and diversity (Fontaine 2022). Proximity is a key factor because commons are appropriately situated and are built on the commitment of stakeholders to an explicit and context-sensitive purpose (Aubert and Botta 2022). They are based on an understanding of institutional diversity and are organized across multiple spatial scales with horizontal modes of dissemination (see chapter 6).

A commons-based approach may consist of the following (box 7.2):

- Rejecting any position that creates distance and adopting the perspective of an embedded actor by bringing the objectives and constraints of the funders into the discussion with actors
- Basing projects on the principles of codesign and subsidiarity, by adopting a facilitating, even intermediary position, including in the area of monitoring and evaluation
- Encouraging actors to express the desires of the collective, guiding activity in a polycentric way by creating spaces for dialogue before and during projects
- Supporting the deployment of commons at different scales by creating the conditions for their dissemination through processes of mutual inspiration (dissemination and sharing of knowledge and know-how) and cooperation, as well as by facilitating their inclusion in public policy dialogues

BOX 7.2

A Commons-Based Approach to Energy Access Issues in Sub-Saharan Africa

Despite sustained international efforts, there are still 840 million people in the world who do not have access to electricity and 2.7 billion people who cook using traditional biomass. Sub-Saharan Africa accounts for 70 percent of the global deficit. Public, private, and civil society actors are developing solutions for access to electricity (grid extensions, decentralized systems) that bring into play the principles of a commons-based approach, either in theory or in practice. This approach is reflected at several levels (Baudé, Leyronas, and Gasc 2020).

The commons-based approach to energy access issues is above all based on the degree to which the principle of subsidiarity is applied. A wide range of user engagement modalities is possible: identification of sites, selection of delegates, monitoring of service operation, interfaces between delegates and users, collecting suggestions and identifying new services to be developed, conflict resolution, and referral to external authorities in case of problems.

The commons-based approach also results in specific institutional and contractual forms of collective action. In its most accomplished form, this may involve the establishment of a collective committee of users who delegate the provision of the service and the maintenance of the facilities to a local operator (as in the cooperative model developed in Burkina Faso [see Baudé, Leyronas, and Gasc 2020]). Other approaches allow users to exercise varying degrees of control over infrastructure management. This management can be entrusted to a local energy provider (this is the model of the decentralized multiservice energy platforms, or light cafes, supported by Electriciens sans frontières in rural Madagascar) or to a delocalized service company (as in the scheme adopted by the French association GRET in the context of the Rhyviere project to develop mini-hydroelectric networks in rural municipalities in Madagascar).

In each case, the commons-based approach opens up spaces for reflection in the face of the many challenges identified in rural electrification projects: ownership of the projects by the local community, which is a key condition for success; proper maintenance of the installations; limiting fraud and unpaid bills as well as preventing and managing conflicts; and, finally, investment in other social spaces through the development of relevant initiatives that respond to the needs of the inhabitants of the territories (health, education, or access to water). In this way, it leads actors to think about the transition from projects aimed at technical achievements (with the objective of bringing electricity to a given area) to initiatives that have an impact on a wide range of dimensions of sustainable development.

Source of Inspiration 3—Changing a Results-Based Culture into One Supporting the Process

The activities of funders are based on what Santos (2016) refers to as the "monoculture of linear time," that is, a relationship to a causal understanding of time according to which history only has one meaning and one direction. This representation has two consequences. The first consequence is that it presupposes that certain countries are ahead of time, along with the types of knowledge, institutions, and forms of sociability that they control. According to this temporal logic, anything that is asymmetrical vis-à-vis that which is considered "forward" is seen as "backward." The second consequence is that it leads to a mechanical apprehension of change in the sense that value is only appreciated at the end of a predetermined process. This representation of time is manifest, for example, in the logic of "projects," which is the preferred mode of intervention for the majority of funders in Sub-Saharan Africa. A project is based on a characterization of the initial situation, the projection of a final outcome (motivated by its importance), the implementation of the means necessary to achieve this final outcome (whose effectiveness and efficiency are measured), and the use of tools to justify the action a priori or a posteriori with regard to its effect, or even its potential or estimated impact and its expected or observed sustainability.[3]

The types of commons in Sub-Saharan Africa are, on the other hand, undergoing constant mutation. They do not have a predefined goal but build a path via deliberation on their objectives and means, depending on their environment (Chanteau and Labrousse 2013). They also take place over long periods of time. Finally, they produce not only "results" but also, and more important, a social process through the "commoning" of collective action.

A commons-based approach may take the form of the following (box 7.3):

- Moving from a quantitative and "managerialist" approach based on achievements to a process-based approach, one that is necessary for transversality

- Recognizing the value of processes of "commoning" (organizational innovations, the empowerment of individuals, the transformation of narratives, developing methodologies, sharing knowledge), beyond material achievements

- Accompanying "commoning" by relying on specific actors (facilitators, discourse mediators, holders of commons) and ad hoc tools (tools for analysis, for grasping the issues at stake, for understanding motivations, for facilitation and coordination)

Support for "Commoning"—Approaches and Tools That Are Already in Use

The Centre de coopération internationale en recherche agronomique pour le développement (CIRAD) (Agricultural Research Center for International Development) is developing game-based methods and tools to support the participation of users with divergent interests and heterogeneous capacity in adaptive resource co-management. The game allows for the manipulation of possibilities in a protected situation and the ability to act on parameters with the hope of achieving results (Rouchier 2018). In an "engaged research" approach, CIRAD encourages the co-construction of the game and simulation medium by the participating individuals (Bousquet, Antona, and Daré 2022; d'Aquino 2016; Le Page et al. 2022). A game session is a simulation in which each person has autonomy in making decisions. In this sense, it is an example of "commoning" (Aubert and Botta 2022).

CIRAD has also developed a methodological guide for use by Agence française de développement (AFD) staff and their local partners (Aubert et al. 2019). This guide suggests operational tools and support methods for integrating the commons-based approach into the preparation, monitoring, and evaluation of development projects financed by the AFD and involving land and natural resource management issues. The guide shows that, even if it does not immediately seem like the most satisfactory way to operationalize commons, the project approach used by funders can be mobilized as a starting point. It outlines concrete procedures in methodological information sheets that can be used at different stages of the project being funded. The commons-based approach is built on the following steps: making an inventory of the ecological and social alliances present in the project's zone of influence and assessing whether it is advisable to involve the people who sustain them (the "holders of commons") in the project, providing methodological support to one or more holders of commons in order to involve them in the co-construction of a territorial project at the scale of the communities they lead and alongside the project team, providing support to the holders of commons in order to specify the actions to be considered, and collectively specifying the conditions for implementation and laying the foundations for a system of monitoring and evaluation by and for the stakeholders in commons.

GRET, a French nongovernmental organization for international solidarity, has been examining its role as a facilitator for processes leading to the emergence of commons since 2019.[a] It has set up a space for operational experimentation with a commons-based approach with the support of AFD funding. This approach is deployed in natural resource, service, and territorial management projects in the Democratic Republic of Congo, the Republic of Congo, Haiti, the Lao People's Democratic Republic, Madagascar, Mauritania, and Senegal. It aims to support local actors in the construction of shared governance methods throughout the process, but also to promote collective learning and to foster a new level of expertise for GRET agents so that they can make the necessary changes to their approach in order to offer this support.

a. https://gret.org/en/taking-a-commons-based-approach-methods-of-action-for-the-benefit-of-all/.

- Limiting ex ante and ex post impact assessment processes and the use of predetermined aggregate targets and indicators by questioning our understanding of the very notion of "success"[4]

- Providing actors in commons with the possibility of analyzing and adapting their objectives and actions *in itinere*, by setting up monitoring and evaluation systems designed, supplied, and used by these actors

- Accepting things not being finished, mistakes, and even failures by making it possible for actors in commons to experiment so they can figure out the institutional arrangements that they feel are best adapted to the resource systems that they manage and to the territories in which they are rooted

Source of Inspiration 4—Switching from Expert Knowledge to Pluralist Knowledge

Funders mobilize knowledge that favors macro-analyses, quantitative approaches, cross-sectional comparisons, and the use of external expertise and scientific knowledge (Naudet 2021). In Sub-Saharan Africa, this relationship to knowledge is something that is imposed upon people and tends to render other sources of knowledge invisible (Santos 2016).

In the commons that take place in Sub-Saharan Africa, knowledge is distributed locally instead. Commons are nourished by the "ability of different forms of knowledge to coexist, with the understanding that they are equal in dignity" (Fontaine 2022). These are social forms of knowledge (e.g., ancestral, folk, and spiritual knowledge), which produce the diversity necessary to learn from experience (Ostrom and Basurto 2011) and engage in transformative processes (Bousquet et al. 2022).

A commons-based approach could involve the following (box 7.4):

- Questioning our epistemological position, by recognizing the diversity of forms of knowledge and types of otherness, along with their modes of construction and their modes of legitimization

- Designing devices, methods, and tools that allow us to share as well as receive multiple kinds of knowledge and experience, in addition to that which is offered by specialized expertise

Mobilizing Multiple Forms of Knowledge—The "Learning Territories" Approach

The "learning territories" approach is based on the idea that transforming the way people learn is a lever for the transformation of society as a whole (Andriantsimahavandy et al. 2020). It promotes the co-construction of knowledge by using innovative pedagogical approaches involving public officials, specialists (consultants or researchers), and actors in commons (see chapter 4). It entails creating the conditions for changing individual attitudes and breaking down silos; accompanying stakeholders in broadening their interpretations of an issue and creating new ways of thinking; anticipating the systemic impact of political decisions in the short and long run; rapidly producing shared knowledge and adapted, context-sensitive solutions; and, finally, reinventing modes of collaboration and project implementation in the service of a collectively defined goal. It requires a participatory and committed attitude from stakeholders at every level: first, to encourage them to revise their ways of thinking about the world and how they project their own local practices and, second, to ensure that they can find their proper role and mode of expression.

The "learning territories" approach therefore makes it possible to create the conditions for the emergence of "commoning." It is simultaneously part of an institutional process (source of inspiration 1), a process of constructing a collective imaginary (source of inspiration 2), and one of sharing multiple types of knowledge (source of inspiration 4).

Since 2021, the AFD Campus[a] has been experimenting with the deployment of the "learning territories" approach. This approach has been tested, for example, in Mauritius with a view to co-constructing a platform for dialogue between public policy and citizens on biodiversity issues. It has been initiated at a territorial scale in Senegal, in the Kédougou region, with the aim of identifying knowledge, know-how, and interpersonal skills, but also the things that are vital and shared and that which needs to be regenerated, improved, and supported. It also seeks to create a continuous and instructive dialogue both with and among local actors. This should lead to the co-construction of solutions that are appropriate to the local challenges of accelerating transitions and of boosting their territories.

a. https://www.afd.fr/fr/campus-afd.

Conclusion

We are well aware that the changes in interpretations and attitudes that we have outlined here are difficult for both funders and public actors. The present strategic and operational frameworks within which their efforts are carried out do not lend themselves to this process. In view of the ecological and social crises that the continent is facing, the commons-based approach appears to offer several new opportunities. Its plasticity opens up the field of possibilities for reflection and experimentation beyond the traditional divisions between the market and the state, the public and the private, individual interest and collective commitment, "bottom-up" and "top-down" approaches, and the local and the universal. It is true that at present, it remains in an experimental stage and that work must continue, involving all stakeholders and all forms of expertise (people involved in commons, the research community, affected populations, and political and social forces). However, African commons, both in the practices they employ and in the values they embody, are now more than ever a source of inspiration for facing the challenges of collective action raised by the complex issues (whether local or global) that we are all confronted with.

Notes

1. Figures from World Bank: Net official development assistance received (constant 2020 US$) - Sub-Saharan Africa.
2. A "development project" is characterized by a set of activities that meet predefined objectives; the resources made available, particularly in terms of financing; and the components that combine technical achievements (infrastructure, for example) and forms of support (human, technical, and financial resources) to ensure the proper implementation of the project and the sustainability of the funded projects.
3. *Relevance* refers to the appropriateness of the action taken with regard to the objectives and issues decided upon at the outset. *Effectiveness* refers to a comparison made between the expected achievements and objectives of the project and what is concretely achieved. *Efficiency* examines the relationship between the means implemented and their costs, on the one hand, and the results obtained, on the other. *Impact* refers to the long-term outcomes (or expected outcomes), whether these are positive or negative, primary or secondary, that can be reasonably attributed either in part or in whole to the project. These can be attributed either directly or indirectly (direct and indirect outcomes) to the project and can be intentional or unintentional in nature (expected and unexpected outcomes). *Sustainability* is defined as the longevity of the benefits resulting from a development project after the work itself has ended.
4. Ostrom (2011) identifies six ways of gauging the performance of a particular institutional arrangement, noting that no one dogma should prevail and that those ways can be defined, chosen, and selected in each situation by the actors themselves. *Efficiency* consists in producing more from the same amount of resources. *Equivalence* consists in observing the ratio between the costs and benefits of participation in the institution. *Redistributional equity* judges performance according to the satisfaction of everyone's needs and may come into conflict with the efficiency criterion. *Accountability* is a question of decision-makers taking into account the preferences and choices of community members. *Conformance* consists in ensuring that the rules are consistent with the values of local actors. For Ostrom, *sustainability* refers to the ability to cope with unforeseen events and changes in the context or condition of the resource.

References

Abecassis, Philippe, Jean-François Alesandrini, Benjamin Coriat, Nathalie Coutinet, and Stéphanie Leyronas. 2019. "DNDi, a Distinctive Illustration of Commons in the Area of Public Health." AFD Research Papers 93. https://dndi.org/wp-content /uploads/2019/02/CommonsAreaPublicHealth_AFDResearchPaper_2019.pdf.

Alao, Abiodun. 2019. *A New Narrative for Africa: Voice and Agency.* London: Routledge. https://doi.org/10.4324/9780429277313.

Andrews, Nathan. 2009. "Foreign Aid and Development in Africa: What the Literature Says and What the Reality Is." *Journal of African Studies and Development* 1 (1): 8–15.

Andriantsimahavandy, Sylvia, Raphaël Besson, Laëtitia Manach, and Stéphane Natkin. 2020. "Comprendre la dynamique des écosystèmes apprenants en Afrique." https://www.afd.fr /fr/ressources/comprendre-la-dynamique-des-ecosystemes-apprenants-en-afrique.

Aubert, Sigrid, Martine Antona, François Bousquet, Camilla Toulmin, and Patrick d'Aquino, Technical Committee on "Land Tenure and Development." 2017. "Opportunités et défis d'une approche par les communs de la terre et des ressources qu'elle porte." https://www.foncier-developpement.fr/wp-content/uploads/Approche -par-les-communs-de-la-terre2.pdf.

Aubert, Sigrid, Patrick d'Aquino, François Bousquet, Martine Antona, and Camilla Toulmin, eds. 2019. *L'approche par les communs de la terre et des ressources qu'elle porte: Illustration par six études de cas.* Paris: AFD and MEAE. https://www.foncier -developpement.fr/wp-content/uploads/CTFD-Regards-sur-le-Foncier-6-Approche -par-les-communs.pdf.

Aubert, Sigrid, and Aurélie Botta, eds. 2022. *Les communs: Un autre récit pour la coopération territoriale.* Versailles: Éditions Quæ.

Baudé, Stéphane, Stéphanie Leyronas, and Jérémy Gasc. 2020. "Renouveler les approches de l'accès à l'énergie. Propositions de mobilisation des communs pour favoriser et encadrer la subsidiarité." AFD Policy Paper No. 5, 1–32. https://www.afd.fr/fr /ressources/renouveler-les-approches-de-lacces-lenergie.

Bousquet, François, Martine Antona, and William Daré. 2022. "Analyser et s'engager." In *Les communs: Un autre récit pour la coopération territoriale,* edited by Sigrid Aubert and Aurélie Botta, 161–81. Versailles: Éditions Quæ.

Bousquet, François, Tara Quinn, Frédérique Jankowski, Raphaël Mathevet, Olivier Barreteau, and Sandrine Dhenain. 2022. *Attachements et changement dans un monde en transformation.* Versailles: Éditions Quæ. http://publications.cirad.fr/une_notice .php?dk=601831.

Chanteau, Jean-Pierre, and Agnès Labrousse. 2013. "L'institutionnalisme méthodologique d'Elinor Ostrom: Quelques enjeux et controverses." *Revue de la régulation. Capitalisme, institutions, pouvoirs* 14. https://doi.org/10.4000/regulation.10555.

Cooke, Bill, and Uma Kothari. 2001. *Participation: The New Tyranny?* London: Zed Books.

Coriat, Benjamin, Nadège Legroux, and Stéphanie Leyronas. 2020. "Innover pour permettre l'accès à des produits thérapeutiques de première nécessité." AFD Policy Brief No. 2, 1–2. https://www.afd.fr/fr/ressources/innover-pour-permettre-lacces-des -produits-therapeutiques-de-premiere-necessite.

d'Aquino, Patrick. 2016. "TerriStories, un jeu au service de l'invention collective dans les politiques publiques." *Revue internationale animation, territoires et pratiques socioculturelles* 10: 71–80. https://doi.org/10.55765/atps.i10.579.

Dar, Sadhvi, and Bill Cooke. 2013. *The New Development Management: Critiquing the Dual Modernization.* London: Zed Books.

Darbon, Dominique. 2014. "Politiques publiques sectorielles dans les États et sociétés fragiles et science politique." In *Une action publique éclatée? Production et institutionnalisation de l'action publique dans les secteurs de l'eau potable et du foncier (APPI). Burkina Faso, Niger, Bénin*, edited by Héloïse Valette, Catherine Baron, François Enten, Philippe Lavigne Delville, and Alicia Tsitsikalis, 121–26. Nogent sur Marne: GRET.

Delay, Etienne, Sigrid Aubert, and Aurélie Botta, Technical Committee on "Land Tenure and Development." 2020. "Defining and Implementing a Land-Based Commons Approach." https://www.foncier-developpement.fr/wp-content/uploads/2020_Briefing-note_Delay-Aubert-Botta-VF.pdf.

Devarajan, Shantayan, David R. Dollar, and Torgny Holmgren. 2002. "Aid and Reform in Africa." https://doi.org/10.1596/0-8213-4669-5.

DiMaggio, Paul J., and Walter W. Powell. 2000. "The Iron Cage Revisited Institutional Isomorphism and Collective Rationality in Organizational Fields." In *Economics Meets Sociology in Strategic Management*, edited by Joel A. C. Baum and Frank Dobbin, 143–66. Bingley: Emerald Group Publishing Limited. https://doi.org/10.1016/S0742-3322(00)17011-1.

Ferguson, James. 2006. "The Anti-Politics Machine." In *The Anthropology of the State: A Reader*, edited by Aradhana Sharma and Akhil Gupta, 270–86. Oxford: Blackwell Publishing.

Fontaine, Geneviève. 2021. "Les communs de capabilités: Des questions à se poser pour mettre en France efficacement une approche radicale et transformative de la transition." https://hal.archives-ouvertes.fr/hal-03139617.

Fontaine, Geneviève. 2022. "Du social au commun: Des conditions favorables au changement de paradigme." In *Du social au commun: Un changement de paradigme. Regards croisés en droit, économie et philosophie*, edited by Celine Jouin, Muriel Gilardone, and Marie Rota, 2–26. Nancy: Institut de Recherches sur l'Évolution de la Nation et de l'État. https://hal.archives-ouvertes.fr/hal-03815717.

Gulrajani, Nilima. 2011. "Transcending the Great Foreign Aid Debate: Managerialism, Radicalism, and the Search for Aid Effectiveness." *Third World Quarterly* 32 (2): 199–216.

Hugon, Philippe. 2011. "Les sciences sociales africanistes à l'épreuve des projets de développement." *Cahiers d'études africaines* 202–3: 331–52. https://doi.org/10.4000/etudesafricaines.16662.

Kumar, Nalini. 2003. *Community-Driven Development: Lessons from the Sahel—An Analytical Review.* Washington, DC: World Bank. https://documents1.worldbank.org/curated/en/757811468006644217/pdf/11130278070Sahel.pdf.

Lavigne Delville, Philippe. 2011. "Vers une socio-anthropologie des interventions de développement comme action publique." PhD dissertation, Lumière University Lyon 2.

Lavigne Delville, Philippe, and Aghali Abdoulkader. 2010. "A cheval donné, on ne regarde pas les dents: Les mécanismes et les impacts de l'aide vus par des praticiens nigériens." *Etudes et travaux* 83: 1–114. http://www.lasdel.net/images/etudes_et _travaux/Les_mecanismes_de_l_aide.pdf.

Le Page, Christophe, William Daré, Martine Antona, and Sigrid Aubert. 2022. "Se confronter à la cogestion adaptative." In *Les communs: Un autre récit pour la coopération territoriale*, edited by Sigrid Aubert and Aurélie Botta, 183–205. Versailles: Éditions Quæ.

Lévi-Strauss, Claude. 2021. *Wild Thought: A New Translation of 'La Pensée sauvage.'* Chicago: University of Chicago Press.

Leyronas, Stéphanie. Forthcoming. "Déconstruire la vision occidentalo-centriste du développement par une approche par les communs." In *Horizons et défis du Commun: Institution et transmission d'une dynamique sociale émergente*, edited by Hervé Brédif, Danièle Bourcier, Gilles Hériard-Dubreuil, Sylvain Lavelle, and Emmanuel Picavet.

Mansuri, Ghazala, and Vijayendra Rao. 2013. *Localizing Development: Does Participation Work?* Washington, DC: World Bank. https://doi.org/10.1596/978-0-8213-8256-1.

Mbembe, Achille. 2021. "Les nouvelles relations Afrique-France: Relever ensemble les défis de demain." https://www.vie-publique.fr/rapport/281834-nouvelles-relations-afrique -france-relever-ensemble-les-defis-de-demain.

Mélonio, Thomas, Jean-David Naudet, and Rémy Rioux. 2022. "Official Development Assistance at the Age of Consequences." AFD Policy Paper No. 11, 1–43. https://www .afd.fr/sites/afd/files/2022-10-05-32-30/pp11-official-development-assistance-age-of -consequences-melonio-naudet-rioux%20BATWeb.pdf.

Mosse, David. 2004. *Cultivating Development: An Ethnography of Aid Policy and Practice.* London: Pluto Press.

Moyo, Dambisa, and Niall Ferguson. 2010. *Dead Aid: Why Aid Is Not Working and How There Is a Better Way for Africa.* New York: Farrar, Straus, and Giroux.

Naudet, Jean-David. 1999. "Les programmes d'appui à la petite entreprise en Afrique de la coopération suisse: De la démarche projet à la démarche d'accompagnement." Dialogues, Proposals, Stories for Global Citizenship Blog, February 1999. http:// base.d-p-h.info/en/fiches/premierdph/fiche-premierdph-4983.html.

Naudet, Jean-David. 2021. "Sahel: Are Donors Out of Touch with on-the-Ground Knowledge?" ID4D. https://ideas4development.org/en/donors-funds-on-the -ground/.

Ngozi Adichie, Chimamanda, TED Talks. 2013. "The Danger of a Single Story." https:// www.ted.com/talks/chimamanda_ngozi_adichie_the_danger_of_a_single_story.

Nubukpo, Kako. 2022. *Une solution pour l'Afrique: Du néoprotectionnisme aux biens communs.* Paris: Odile Jacob.

OECD (Organisation for Economic Co-operation and Development). 2022. *Geographical Distribution of Financial Flows to Developing Countries 2022: Disbursements, Commitments, Country Indicators.* Paris: OECD Publishing. https://www.oecd.org /dac/geographical-distribution-of-financial-flows-to-developing-countries-20743149 .htm.

Olivier de Sardan, Jean-Pierre. 2021. *La revanche des contextes. Des mésaventures de l'ingénierie sociale en Afrique et au-delà.* Paris: Karthala. https://www.academia .edu/47765745/La_revanche_des_contextes_Des_m%C3%A9saventures_de_l_ing%C3% A9nierie_sociale_en_Afrique_et_au_del%C3%A0.

Olivier de Sardan, Jean-Pierre. 2022. "La délivrance des biens d'intérêt général en Afrique. Pratiques palliatives, réformes de l'Etat et communs." Papiers de Recherche AFD 264, Paris. https://www.afd.fr/fr/ressources/la-delivrance-des-biens -dinteret-general-en-afrique-pratiques-palliatives-reformes-de-letat-et-communs.

Orsi, Fabienne. 2014. "Réhabiliter la propriété comme bundle of rights: Des origines à Elinor Ostrom, et au-delà?" Revue internationale de droit économique 3: 371–85.

Ostrom, Elinor. 2011. "Background on the Institutional Analysis and Development Framework." Policy Studies Journal 39: 7–27. https://doi.org/10.1111/j.1541 -0072.2010.00394.x.

Ostrom, Elinor, and Xavier Basurto. 2011. "Crafting Analytical Tools to Study Institutional Change." Journal of Institutional Economics 7 (3): 317–43.

Perrin, Geneviève. 2019. "Les communs de capabilités: Une analyse des pôles territoriaux de coopération économique à partir du croisement des approches d'Ostrom et de Sen." PhD dissertation, University Paris-Est. https://tel.archives-ouvertes.fr/tel-02513416.

Rist, Gilbert. 2007. "Development as a Buzzword." Development in Practice 17 (4–5): 485–91. https://doi.org/10.1080/09614520701469328.

Rottenburg, Richard. 2009. Far-Fetched Facts: A Parable of Development Aid. Cambridge, MA: MIT Press.

Rouchier, Juliette, IGDPE. 2018. "Les Serious Games et l'éducation au bien commun: L'exemple du jeu PollutionSolutions." https://www.economie.gouv.fr/igpde-editions -publications/larticle_n2#jeux,%20jeux%20s%C3%A9rieux,%20serious%20games.

Santos, Boaventura de Sousa. 2016. Epistemologies of the South: Justice against Epistemicide. Abingdon and New York: Routledge.

Sarr, Felwine. 2019. Afrotopia. Minneapolis: University of Minnesota Press.

Trosa, Sylvie. 2017. "L'intérêt général: Une réalité introuvable?" Gestion & Finances Publiques 3: 82–7. https://doi.org/10.3166/gfp.2017.00053.

Weber, Max. 2019. Economy and Society. Cambridge, MA: Harvard University Press.

Wiredu, Kwasi, ed. 2004. A Companion to African Philosophy. Oxford: Blackwell Publishing.

World Bank. 2017. World Development Report 2017: Governance and the Law. Washington, DC: World Bank. https://www.worldbank.org/en/publication/wdr2017.

Xifaras, Mikhaïl. 2004. La propriété. Etude de philosophie du droit. Paris: Presses Universitaires de France.

The Commons: Choosing Solidarity and Looking Ahead

Tanella Boni, philosopher, essayist, poet, and novelist, Côte d'Ivoire

> *"Bolo fila le be nyongon ko."*
> *"One hand washes the other."*
> —Translated from Dyula, Côte d'Ivoire

The commons-based approach adopted within these pages introduces the reader to experiences and practices based on solidarity, sharing, and equal access to natural and intangible resources. It also addresses how the knowledge and skills that political decisions often neglect or exclude can be passed on.

What lies behind the word *commons* (often used in the plural form)? Ostrom's initial work led to the notion of commons being understood in terms of the management of renewable resources. That interpretation, alongside her later work, provides some context for the theoretical framework of the research contained within this book. However, applying the principle of commons to African practices in many different locations and countries is a significant undertaking. The results of the research presented in this book are surprising. Not only do they highlight the commonplace but vital practices that tend to go unnoticed because they have always been part of the way of life in some places, but they also reveal some innovative, experimental, and successful practices. A number of issues are addressed. Land ownership, housing, energy, and other important facets of daily life are analyzed in the place where they are actually happening.

Africa is a land of contrasts with an abundance of such experiences, but they are not widely known. In that context, are commons not examples of solidarity in action, self-governance, self-management, and sharing? In these ever-shifting societies where, from the past to the present day, identities are forever being reconstructed, **African men and women have not forgotten what they can create together, just as their parents and ancestors did.** Their participation in the commons movement reminds them of *who* they are (or have become) in the places *where* they are, at the crossroads of several cultures, for example. They know that commons are everyday practices that are transformed by proposing new ways of living together in different kinds of rural and urban spaces. Commons have therefore created a space for themselves within contemporary lifestyles in new, unknown territories where ancient values are no longer deemed appropriate and every commodity and resource can be turned into merchandise.

Solidarity in Action

African men and women do not think about colonialism every day. Often, they even forget about it. However, that era could be considered seminal in terms of how African decision-makers respond to "development aid." It is as if, whenever a problem arises, their only answer is to seek help from funders or the world's governing elite. That said, **viewing Africa through the lens of commons serves as a reminder that some local economic and social practices were a part of how people lived well before they encountered those from far away**—the colonists with their language, their culture, and their objects. Accounts of that unimagined head-on collision certainly still feed the collective imagination today. Scars from the violence that turned African societies upside down and destroyed much of the continent's fauna and flora, sacred objects, works of art, primary forests, and biodiversity live on in people's memories. The borders dividing cultural and linguistic regions add to their sense of anguish. However, although that encounter has left its mark on memories, awakens consciences from one generation to the next, and has brutally transformed how people live and inhabit the continent, all is not lost. A few intangible resources (tales, proverbs, adages, and other oral texts) containing life's maxims are still rooted in the collective imagination.

The Dyula proverb cited at the beginning of this afterword is one such maxim. It is an invitation to act in solidarity at all times. In English, it is rendered as **"one hand washing the other."** What connects this proverb and an academic publication on commons? Initially, one might imagine that these two hands belong to the same person, someone in full possession of their faculties and able to take care of themselves without any outside assistance. I feel that the idea of assistance is important. It is about helping ourselves and not waiting for someone else to do it for us, be it in times of crisis, conflict, or peace. However, the image of those two hands is also a reference to a lifestyle based on a community providing itself with the means to survive. It recalls the kind of subsistence economy practiced on a small scale in rural areas, as well as within neighborhoods in large cities. In this context, the idea of solidarity is not limited to a rudimentary understanding of the subsistence economy. It is less restrictive and more wide-ranging than that. It encompasses health, peace and harmonious relations, prosperity, well-being, and happiness. So, how can we go about achieving happiness together through cooperation? That is indeed the question.

Self-Governance and Self-Management

This book provides a rigorous analysis of "commons," a complex word that crops up from time to time in our conversations. It is about Africa in all its diversity, how Africa is inhabited, and the choices of its communities, alongside the choices of states and public policies. Undoubtedly, the latter can play many roles in "commoning": they can assist commons, support them, unite them, or remain indifferent and even oppose them.

Let us not forget that **commons are also forms of social resistance when public policies are weak or nonexistent.** They want to be seen as local, deliberative, and participatory spaces that operate according to the laws and rules they choose *for* themselves and *by* themselves. That is why **self-governance and responsibility lie at the heart of commons.**

I believe that this Africa is far removed from the mythical version frozen in time whose image continues to travel around the world. This is the Africa that experienced colonization in its various forms, independence, and other more recent episodes. This is the Africa that is still looking for itself today, the Africa of cities and new technologies. This Africa is moving forward, but not in the same way as the politicians awaiting development aid. **This commons-based Africa thinks, moves, proposes, and invents while learning to be accountable for its actions.** Collective responsibility lies at the heart of "commoning."

Commons are participatory spaces. This means that everyone accepts responsibility for their own actions, discovers their own purpose, and follows their own aspirations. However, they also respect the horizontal bonds they share with the kindred spirits who are involved in the same exercise or struggle, in order to **achieve big things on a small scale together.**

Other forms of commons tackling global challenges such as climate change and threats to the future of humanity are also possible. Again, local stakeholders play their own autonomous role alongside politicians and funders. **It seems to me that commons seek to start from a local perspective and carve out their own role, even making their own contributions to resolving global problems.**

Property and Commons

Commons help demonstrate how autonomous decision-making works and how participatory spaces operate. In this book, life within commons is analyzed from several complementary points of view. Each one provides a different perspective to better understand the rationale at work within these experiences, be they based on protecting renewable resources; managing urban environments, community ventures, or cooperatives; or providing knowledge and skills to a larger number of people, particularly online.

Empirical research is used to **challenge the notion of property** as conceived within the capitalist system. The latter holds that profitability is fundamental because "property" is owned by individuals, belongs to them, and can yield a profit for them according to their own desires. It is not something to be shared. Meanwhile, in a commons-based approach, everything is shared, from land ownership to intellectual property. Nothing is held back from the co-contributors and co-dwellers.

For example, the question of how a large number of people in Africa could receive vaccines made elsewhere became an issue during the pandemic. What should be done? **How can one go about democratizing both the things that ought to be democratized and the resources that can be too?** How can the inflexible notion of "intellectual property" be made to evolve? Are we ready to view "property" differently? To no longer see it as an attribute benefiting an individual and its rights holders or a private company and its shareholders? Commons seem to be a promising and necessary approach based on the principle of sharing and providing for the many, whatever patents need to be taken into account.

This reassessment of intellectual property could affect many areas. Free and creative knowledge can be used in the field of education and continuous learning, for example, which is advantageous to all. What is, and what will be, Africa's role in producing the kind of content that can be shared on a large scale? **Africa must play a role in creating and sharing academic, cultural, and educational content in different ways.** With its diverse and rich supply of knowledge and skills, it cannot continue simply acting as a consumer in all respects.

Commons: Somewhere between Rural Life and City Life

Diverse and complex situations are never static, so commons should be considered through the lens of their history and evolution, located somewhere between rural life and city life. **Although they take inspiration from some community experiences inherited from the past, commons resolutely look to the future.** That is why the **reality of life within commons is unique,** although it needs to be understood from several points of view.

Although history lies at the heart of narratives about commons, one of the chief political experiences affecting the imagination of Africans is the idea of always feeling in "transition," awaiting a better tomorrow. African countries seem to be running after a "development" train they are trying to catch. At the moment, some believe they are "emerging." According to the rhetoric of the good life relayed by the media that uses indicators for "measuring" development, a country possessing the means to solve its citizens' fundamental problems is said to be "developed" or "emerging," depending on which group of countries it is classified alongside. The present participle "developing"—emphasizing that this development or emergence is still in progress—demonstrates the extent to which this race remains incomplete. Numerous African countries therefore do not seem to have achieved all their aspirations. They are trying to reach a particular standard by any means possible, including international aid, even while the issue of debt hangs heavily over their fragile ability to repay, like a sword of Damocles.

Meanwhile, individuals act responsibly and organize themselves into groups or cooperatives to look after their own material and moral interests. Sometimes, this involves entire communities. In their local area, they provide themselves with the means to manage how they live and protect their natural and intangible resources. The role of commons is to **find new forms of solidarity beyond state borders.** There are some pitfalls to be avoided, such as withdrawing into one's own community to the detriment of all the others who must also share in collective experiences and resources.

Humans, like other living things, resist the violence that surrounds them through an awareness of their own vulnerability. The colonial period unsettled the collective imagination. It shaped generations endeavoring to discover who they were: men and women beset by doubts over their abilities and their responsibilities. Independence also contributed to compounding the gap between humans and the natural world thanks to some major infrastructure projects. Hopes have been broken, but they continue to be rebuilt in participatory and deliberative spaces, leaving their mark on daily life. Commons certainly cannot escape the distant influence of the colonial experience that has become part of the collective imagination, but they prioritize their autonomy while states continue to wait for international assistance. **They have therefore understood life's most important ingredient for current and future generations.**

The African Commons at Global Crossroads

Thomas Mélonio, Economist, Executive Director of Innovation, Strategy, and Research at the Agence française de développement (AFD)

Kako Nubukpo, Economist, Commissioner responsible for Agriculture, Water Resources, and the Environment at the Commission of the Union économique et monétaire ouest-africaine (UEMOA) (West African Economic and Monetary Union)

> *Given the severity of the [climate] threat, simply waiting for resolution of these issues at a global level, without trying out policies at multiple scales because they lack a global scale, is not a reasonable stance.*

—Ostrom (2009, 28)

Our current state of geopolitical fragmentation is making international cooperation more difficult, just when it is so necessary to protect global health, reduce climate change, and protect biodiversity. Recent history has shown to what extent states can turn inward when faced with urgent social issues. And yet, if we tackle the future from the perspective of a series of crises managed one after the other, a short-term outlook will systematically defeat any long-term one. The national view will defeat the international one. Privatization will overwhelm public goods. We will therefore imperil our chances of initiating the collective, multiscale, and multilevel action currently required to address the challenges facing us and to protect our global common goods.

In terms of health, the closure of borders and attempts to procure the best vaccines during the COVID-19 (coronavirus) pandemic demonstrated the prevalence of such national and regional interests. Some called for health products to be made common goods. However, although vaccine research, manufacturing, and marketing relied heavily on public money, in practice, health

products have remained the exclusive property of the pharmaceutical laboratories that hold the intellectual property rights and are subject to market regulations. The wealthiest states sought to mitigate market failures by supporting
international mechanisms such as the ACT-A and COVAX initiatives to reduce
unequal access to vaccines. However, they could not prevent these inequalities
altogether. To make global health a common good, new research and development models for medicines and health care products (and for vaccines, first
and foremost) must be considered, connecting innovation and access to as
many people as possible. Collective initiatives already exist and deserve our
attention—consider, for example, the ANTICOV consortium coordinated by
the Drugs for Neglected Diseases Initiative (DNDi). This consortium consists
of nearly 30 global research and development organizations. They are collaborating on one of the largest multicountry trials involving mild and moder-
ate cases of COVID-19. ANTICOV is therefore helping to rectify the lack of
clinical research carried out in Africa, Asia, and Latin America during the
pandemic.

In terms of the climate, the scientific reality of the current imbalance is
beyond doubt. However, in 2022, we observed an overwhelming return of fossil fuel subsidies in reaction to the invasion of Ukraine and higher oil prices.
This is another example of social and economic crises disrupting attempts
to construct coherent and effective international action and endangering
our ability to achieve the Paris Agreement goals. The UN Climate Change
Conference (UNFCCC COP 27), held in Sharm el-Sheikh, the Arab Republic
of Egypt, in October 2022, did not report any clear progress in terms of reducing anticipated carbon emissions. However, it did recall the urgency of immediate massive mobilization in the form of multiple communities. Within the
framework of her work on commons, Elinor Ostrom had already proposed
the notion of "polycentric governance" as a version of collective mobilization.
She was paving the way for entirely independent collective action on a variety
of scales to counteract the shortfalls of centrally defined policies and structur-
ally insufficient state resources.

Finally, in politics, we are witnessing increased criticism of nations, societies, and democratic practices, as well as the temptation of a form of illiberalism
making its presence felt across the world. However, at the same time, collective
modes of governance, operating at different scales, are engaging more effectively
with citizen participation, democratic decision-making mechanisms based on
deliberation, diversified methods for delivering public goods and services, and
"bottom-up" approaches.

Proposals such as withdrawing some goods from the market, polycentric governance, new forms of democracy, and methods for delivering public services should be discussed and, where necessary, critiqued. At any rate,
these forms of governance are too often ignored but deserve to be included in

international debates, if only to serve as sources of inspiration. Global governance may currently appear to be under severe pressure, but it would be hasty and inappropriate to conclude that this will always be the case. Nor would it be justifiable to become resigned to such a state of affairs. It is our belief that this kind of defeatist attitude does nothing to guarantee a better future for humanity or our planet.

African commons, operating at their own level, are paving the way for new perspectives and innovative thinking. They demonstrate that it is possible to inhabit the world differently, simultaneously protecting human and nonhuman communities and ecosystems. In that sense, this book should inspire us collectively to commit to doing what is necessary to reduce the risk of our global common goods being gradually destroyed. We believe that this goal is both necessary and realistic.

This book introduces the reader to a number of situations where commons can demonstrate their effectiveness—for example, management of land and natural resources against a background of growing demographic and security tensions. Land commons are a testament to what we might call the "intelligence of diversity" (diverse methods of access and use, as well as diverse authorities providing regulation). This is also true of urban commons whose structure takes the form of hybrid social and cultural places and technological innovation. These are spaces where social, educational, and environmental functions converge.

Mention should also be made of the quite remarkable potential of commons within the digital sector. Initial evidence of its potential can already be seen across the continent: digital archives sharing African knowledge, platforms for shared testimony following periods of violence, freely available educational material, and many other examples. The digital sector is particularly interesting because it reinvents the usual commons categories. First, it is not limited to a specific geographical location to the same extent so there can be a separation between contributors and users, on the one hand, and creation of original commons, on the other. Second, sharing digital common goods is very inexpensive so they have the potential to have a more significant impact through the circulation of methods for teaching a language, mathematics, or knowledge in general. Finally, within global digital commons (such as Wikipedia and OpenStreetMap), many communities form on the basis of specific resources— for example, Wikipedia communities focusing on a country or an African language, or groups contributing to the creation of major geographical databases in Sub-Saharan Africa.

The commons described in this book are home to innovative and inspiring experiences that make us question our traditional categories (public/private, private interests/public interest, state/market). Furthermore, they go beyond local/universal boundaries. They remind us that many African common goods serve humanity as a whole. For example, the Congo Basin rainforest is the planet's second green lung after the Amazon, not only in terms of its size but also in respect of its ability to regulate the climate and the biodiversity to which it is home.

These commons-based organizations are being set up against a background of both failing states and failing markets. If we took them into account, we could expect them to be substantially developed across the continent. It is our belief that extensive and long-term social development in Africa based on commons principles is entirely feasible and would be a step toward rapid growth of the social economy. What singular political project for Africa could be underpinned by the development of commons? What kind of alliance could be developed between community groups and African states that protects commons while preventing states from discharging all their responsibilities and duties onto them? We believe in this revamped development narrative for Africa. This book marks a first step along that path for its readers (researchers, decision-makers, funders, and civil society stakeholders).

Beyond their own continent, African commons also encourage us to consider the international policies and mechanisms to be implemented to protect our global common goods by making us face up to the responsibilities, vulnerabilities, and adverse effects involved. Indeed, for the first time, this very issue, what António Guterres called a "Climate Solidarity Pact," was placed on the agenda of the official climate negotiations at COP 27. Our most pressing challenge is to decide how the financial rules should be changed to develop collective international finance capable of protecting our global common goods.

Reference

Ostrom, Elinor. 2009. "A Polycentric Approach for Coping with Climate Change." SSRN. https://dx.doi.org/10.2139/ssrn.1934353.